Managing
the
Presidency

TRANSFORMING AMERICAN POLITICS SERIES
Lawrence C. Dodd, Series Editor

Dramatic changes in political institutions and behavior over the past two decades have underscored the dynamic nature of American politics, confronting political scientists with a new and pressing intellectual agenda.

Transforming American Politics is dedicated to documenting these changes, reinterpreting conventional wisdoms, tracing historical patterns of change, and asserting new theories to clarify the direction of contemporary politics.

TITLES IN THIS SERIES

Managing the Presidency: The Eisenhower Legacy—From Kennedy to Reagan, Phillip G. Henderson

Remaking American Politics, edited by Richard A. Harris and Sidney M. Milkis

Democracies in Crisis: Public Policy Responses to the Great Depression, Kim Quaile Hill

The Congress, the President, and Public Policy: A Critical Analysis, Michael Mezey

Managing
the
Presidency

THE EISENHOWER LEGACY—
FROM KENNEDY TO REAGAN

Phillip G. Henderson

Westview Press
BOULDER & LONDON

Transforming American Politics

Copyright © 1988 by Westview Press, Inc.

Published in 1988 in the United States of America by Westview Press, Inc.; Frederick A. Praeger, Publisher; 5500 Central Avenue, Boulder, Colorado 80301

Library of Congress Cataloging-in-Publication Data
Henderson, Phillip G.
  Managing the presidency.
  (Transforming American politics)
  Bibliography: p.
  Includes index.
1. Presidents—United States—Staff. 2. United
States—Executive departments—Management. 3. United
States—Politics and government—1953–1961. 4. United
States—Politics and government—1981–   . 5. Iran-
Contra Affair, 1985–   . I. Title. II. Series.
JK518.H43 1988   353.03'1   87-31716
ISBN 0-8133-0606-X

Printed and bound in the United States of America

The paper used in this publication meets the requirements of the American National
Standard for Permanence of Paper for Printed Library Materials Z39.48-1984.

10   9   8   7   6   5   4   3   2   1

TO
my wife, Mary Lou,
my father, Paul Glen Henderson, Sr.,
and the memory of
my mother, Beatrice "Dolly" Henderson
(January 15, 1920, to March 27, 1987)

Contents

Preface

My interest in the organization and management of the Presidency was kindled nearly a decade ago in my first seminar as a graduate student in political science at the University of Michigan. Under Professor George Grassmuck's able guidance, the seminar served as a useful sounding board for many of the ideas discussed in this book.

Research for the book began in earnest when I visited the Eisenhower Library in Abilene, Kansas, during the summer of 1981. The recently declassified materials of the Ann Whitman File of the Eisenhower Library confirmed my expectation that an entire book on Eisenhower's management of the Presidency was well warranted. But I decided early on that the Eisenhower legacy could not be treated in a vacuum. Indeed, the richness of Eisenhower's contributions to the organization and management of the Presidency can best be understood if one views them in the context of how his successors have fared as administrators. Hence, substantial portions of this study are devoted to appraisals of the approaches of Eisenhower's successors in managing the Presidency.

The recent Iran-Contra debacle of the Reagan administration warrants special attention in this study because of the stark contrast it provides with the orderly and methodical advisory and decision-making processes of the Eisenhower years. Whereas Eisenhower's Presidency offers remarkably fresh insights on how to improve the organization and management of the Presidency, the recent experience of the Reagan administration is rich in lessons on what to avoid in presidential policymaking. In this book I shall discuss both the successes and the failures of presidential management on the premise that much can be learned from both.

In completing this book I received wise counsel and assistance from several individuals. The staff of the Eisenhower Library was exceptionally helpful throughout my extended research visit in 1981. I was impressed with the high level of professionalism and unfailing courtesy of the entire staff. In particular, I wish to thank archivists David Haight and Rob Soubers, who pointed me to many useful collections of documents concerning Eisenhower's use of the Cabinet, National Security Council, and White House staff.

I am indebted to several individuals at the University of Michigan for their helpful insights and advice. George Grassmuck was instrumental in sparking my interest in the topic of presidential management; he also provided expert guidance on all but one of the chapters of the book. Harold Jacobson stimulated my thinking on several of the major issues addressed in this study regarding the organization and conduct of American foreign policy. I gratefully acknowledge Gerald Linderman's thoughtful and perceptive comments on the manuscript. His perspective as an historian and his meticulous comments helped refine and improve the final product in many ways. His kind encouragement throughout the course of the project and his expert advice are greatly appreciated. Jack Schroeder has had a major influence on my writing since my days as an undergraduate student in his courses on American government. More than any other person he shaped my interest in political science. His comments on the manuscript were typically incisive and useful.

In addition, I wish to thank Dr. R. Gordon Hoxie, the Director of the Center for the Study of the Presidency, for granting me the permission to use material from an essay that I contributed to his volume, *The Presidency and National Security Policy* (copyright 1984, by the Center for the Study of the Presidency in New York). Dr. Hoxie has made a major contribution to revisionist scholarship on the Eisenhower Presidency and to the literature on White House organization. His expansive knowledge of the Presidency has been very helpful, as has his support of my work.

I also wish to thank two members of the Eisenhower administration, General Andrew Goodpaster and Bradley Patterson, for graciously granting illuminating interviews on the Eisenhower Presidency. Their insights form an important part of this work.

My thanks also go to Dennis Muniak, Lou Cantori, John Streby, Jim Miclot, and Ray Taras for commenting on various chapters in the manuscript. All provided insights that served to strengthen the final product.

Finally, I would like to note that my wife, Mary Lou, was truly an inspiration throughout this project. She listened patiently to my ideas, provided meaningful comments on many portions of the work, shared in the burden of typing the text, and quietly tolerated my weekend writing and my soap opera–like addiction to the televised Iran-Contra hearings. For all of this, I am very grateful.

For errors of omission, accuracy, interpretation, or content, the buck stops with me.

Phillip G. Henderson

Introduction

MANAGEMENT AND MISMANAGEMENT OF THE MODERN PRESIDENCY

The Iran-Contra affair has called into question more than just the structure of decision-making processes in the Reagan administration. It has brought to the fore the larger question of how to manage the Presidency—a question of ever-growing complexity in the postwar era. Not since the Bay of Pigs fiasco of the Kennedy years has so much attention been focused on the need for well organized and highly disciplined advisory and decision-making processes in the conduct of foreign policy. The Tower Commission, after an exhaustive investigation, concluded that the Reagan administration's decision to sell arms to Iran and the ensuing National Security Council staff support of the Contras of Nicaragua illustrate "the perils of policy pursued outside the constraints of orderly process." In testimony before Congress, former National Security Advisor Robert McFarlane added: "In the six months since the Iran-Contra controversy erupted, many people have come to believe there is something wrong with the way this country makes foreign policy. They probably don't know how wrong."

In light of these revelations of a foreign policy-making process in disarray, the administrative contributions of Dwight D. Eisenhower's Presidency assume striking contemporary relevance. Indeed, Eisenhower, more than any other postwar President, valued organization as a cornerstone of effective policy-making and as a bulwark against chaos, confusion, and failure. The development of staff and Cabinet secretariats, the revitalization of the National Security Council through such supporting mechanisms as the Planning Board and Operations Coordinating Board, and the creation of the positions of White House Chief of Staff and Assistant to the President for National Security Affairs exemplify Eisenhower's efforts to enhance policy-making processes through improved governmental machinery.

Eisenhower's formal advisory institutions, and the philosophy of administration upon which they were predicated, are vitally important

1

in explaining the President's formidable—but, until recently, greatly underrated—skills as Chief Executive. Yet, the administrative contributions of the Eisenhower years remain largely unappreciated by scholars and public servants alike. Indeed, some of Eisenhower's successors have entered the Presidency seemingly oblivious to the advantages that accrue from the use of a well organized and well administered White House system.

This book is written to foster a fuller appreciation of Eisenhower's important legacy in organizing and managing the institution of the Presidency. Through the incorporation of insights on the Kennedy, Nixon, Carter, and Reagan administrations, the book offers prescriptive implications that go far beyond Eisenhower's Presidency. Substantial portions of the book are devoted to an examination of the problematic state of affairs engendered by the post-Eisenhower trend toward White House centralization of policy-making processes and the corresponding decline of the Cabinet and National Security Council as advisory and administrative forums in the past quarter-century.

In the name of flexibility, many of the canons of sound presidential administration have given way to the stylistic preferences and proclivities of those who occupy the Oval Office. John F. Kennedy, for example, had no use for formal organization and frequent meetings of advisory bodies of the type utilized by Eisenhower. He decided to dispense with both, thus precipitating the Bay of Pigs disaster early in his administration. Richard Nixon, despite his promise to return to the Eisenhower era practice of Cabinet government, allowed his White House staff and Cabinet to become competing entities, with adverse consequences for both. Jimmy Carter tried, unsuccessfully, to be his own Chief of Staff. The breakdown of formal organization in the second term of the Reagan administration unquestionably contributed to the policy-making environment in which the Iran-Contra debacle occurred. These and other events will be discussed at length in the pages that follow. As will be shown, the post-Eisenhower experience is replete with examples of the pitfalls that can arise from faulty organization and mismanagement of policy-making processes.

Although the office of the Presidency will continue to be shaped by each new occupant, the time has come for Presidents to recognize that formal techniques of organization and management offer distinct advantages over haphazard and loosely structured policy-making. Many principles of presidential administration are inherently sound and deserve far more emphasis than they receive. The Eisenhower Presidency, more than any other, is rich with organizational and administrative precedents worthy of emulation by future Presidents. Indeed, many of the problems that continually plague modern Presidencies would likely be averted, or at least mitigated, through the adoption of administrative principles similar to those that characterized Eisenhower's approach to leadership.

In order to build a case for emulation of Eisenhower's administrative contributions, however, we must first set the record straight on some important misconceptions that linger on, with regard to both Eisenhower's effectiveness as a political leader and the manner in which his key advisory and administrative bodies functioned. Hence, much of our early discussion will be devoted to reinforcing and advancing revisionist scholarship on Eisenhower's Presidency. Drawing on minutes from the debates of the National Security Council and Cabinet, internal White House memoranda, oral history interviews, and other documents from the Eisenhower Library (many of which are cited herein for the first time), new insights will be offered regarding Eisenhower's important legacy in the development of the institutional Presidency.

1

Changing Perspectives on the Eisenhower Presidency

At a three-day conference on Dwight David Eisenhower held at Hofstra University in March 1984, scholars, journalists, and statesmen portrayed the former President as a skillful, politically astute, and effective leader. Such assessments provide a striking contrast to the perceptions of Eisenhower that prevailed in the academic community during the 1950s and 1960s. Although public regard for Eisenhower was extremely high during this period, the assessments of scholars and journalists were frequently far less flattering. Eisenhower averaged a remarkably high 64 percent Gallup poll approval rating over the eight years of his Presidency. His support dipped below 50 percent for only two months out of this eight-year period.[1] Indeed, he holds the distinction of being the only President in the postwar era who had broader popularity upon leaving office than upon entering.[2] Yet, although Eisenhower's popularity in public opinion polls remained high, his standing among historians was appreciably lower. In the famous Schlesinger poll of American historians, published in 1962, Eisenhower was rated twentieth out of the thirty-one Presidents who were evaluated. Only one President, Andrew Johnson, stood between Eisenhower and the "below average" category. Chester Arthur, Martin Van Buren, Benjamin Harrison, and Herbert Hoover were among the Presidents who were held in higher regard than Eisenhower by historians.[3]

As late as the mid-1970s, accounts of Eisenhower's Presidency were generally lacking in archival documentation. Compounding the problem created by the paucity of primary sources, scholarship on the Presidency was laden with what political scientist Thomas Cronin refers to as "inflated and unrealistic" expectations regarding the Presidency.[4] Many of the scholars of the New Deal and post–New Deal generations used the crisis-dominated Roosevelt Presidency as a standard by which to judge succeeding Presidents without acknowledging the growth in constraints—congressional, bureaucratic, and otherwise—that limit the President's authority in the domestic realm.

Many of Eisenhower's critics attacked him not so much for what he had done, but for what he had failed to do. William Shannon, for example, referred to the Eisenhower Presidency as "the great postponement."[5] Historian Eric Goldman wrote that the Eisenhower years were possibly "the dullest and dreariest in all our history."[6]

Several writers found it useful to draw comparisons between Eisenhower and so-called weak or passive Presidents to illustrate more forcefully their perceptions of Eisenhower's shortcomings. Marquis Childs, for example, asserted that Eisenhower bore a striking resemblance to the President who had served one hundred years before him, James Buchanan. In Childs' view, Buchanan was a "weak" President who came into office at a time of supreme crisis, only to evade and procrastinate. "It was not that President Buchanan did anything bad," Childs observed; "he simply did nothing." Viewing Eisenhower with similar disdain, Childs concluded his book with the warning that Eisenhower's successor "will have to reassert the authority that has been permitted to decline."[7]

In 1953, Wilfred E. Binkley suggested in an article for the *New Republic* that Eisenhower shared with fellow West Pointer, Ulysses S. Grant, a naiveté about government and politics.

> Eisenhower needs to learn, learn fast, very fast, the perplexing art of politics. He is unquestionably bedeviled by some of the same handicaps as Grant. Both entered the Presidency inexperienced in the most essential of all Presidential qualifications, the skill of the politician. . . . Both Grant and Eisenhower started out unfamiliar with some of the most fundamental usages by which government operates.[8]

Perhaps the most noteworthy of the Eisenhower analogies is the one drawn by James David Barber in his classic study, *Presidential Character*. In Barber's view, there are striking parallels between Eisenhower and Calvin Coolidge that explain why neither man was well suited for the Presidency.

> What Coolidge and Eisenhower shared was a political character and, to a degree, similar views of the world. . . . Both shared with other passive-negative people in politics a propensity for withdrawal, for moving away from conflict and detail. Their stance toward political life was one of irritated resignation. . . . Beneath the surface, they seem to be saying that they should not have to initiate, that problems should come to them rather than they to the problems.[9]

According to Barber, the political weakness of a passive-negative President is his "inability to produce," although he "may contribute by preventing. . . . Typically, the passive-negative character presides over drift and confusion, partially concealed by the apparent orderliness of the formalities." In all these respects, Barber asserts, "Eisenhower fits the character of the passive-negative type."[10]

Even though widespread perceptions of the President as an indecisive, passive, and ineffective leader prevailed throughout most of the 1950s and 1960s, there were occasional glimpses of a different Eisenhower. Historian Vincent De Santis, in reviewing accounts written during the 1950s and beyond, notes that *New York Times* reporter Arthur Krock was among those who offered a different view of Eisenhower. As early as 1957, Krock concluded that Eisenhower was "remarkably well informed in a vast field of governmental operations" and was not a "lazy or a reluctant President."[11]

In 1960, Richard Rovere argued that if there were cause for criticism of Eisenhower, it should be directed not against his ability as an executive but against the decisions themselves. Rovere's observation was significant for its implicit recognition that many critics had blurred their own normative judgments of administration policies with assessments of Eisenhower's skill as President.[12]

In 1967, Murray Kempton authored a pioneering revisionist appraisal of Eisenhower for *Esquire* magazine. Eisenhower, Kempton wrote, was "the great tortoise upon whose back the world sat for eight years. We laughed at him; we talked wistfully about moving; and all the while we never knew the cunning beneath the shell."[13] In anecdotal fashion, Kempton offered the first glimpse of Eisenhower as a shrewd and calculating President. When things were at their stickiest in the Formosa Strait crisis, Kempton revealed, Eisenhower was told by his Press Secretary, James Hagerty, not to answer any questions at his press conference concerning the possibility of using tactical nuclear weapons in the event of a general war in Asia. "Don't worry, Jim," the President responded; "if that question comes up, I'll just confuse them."[14]

Several years before Kempton's article appeared, Richard Nixon provided similar insights in his book *Six Crises*. Eisenhower, Nixon observed, "was a far more complex and devious man than most people realized, and in the best sense of those words."[15]

In 1969, Garry Wills argued that Eisenhower was "a political genius."[16] Two years later, William O'Neill portrayed him as "a man of drive, intelligence, ambition and ruthlessness."[17] The theme that Eisenhower was a politically shrewd President was elaborated on by Robert L. Branyan in 1972.[18] Historian Vincent De Santis, upon reviewing the revisionist trend in literature on Eisenhower, concluded that the former President was a more discerning, skillful, and forceful politician in office than was generally acknowledged.[19]

The work of early revisionist writers suffered, however, from the same fundamental weakness of many highly critical accounts of Eisenhower's Presidency. Simply put, their conclusions were often based on conjecture rather than on solid documentary evidence. Noting the paucity of materials available on which to base assessments, Richard Neustadt prefaced his appraisal of Eisenhower in his 1960 edition of *Presidential Power* with a cautionary note concerning the tentativeness of his own conclusions:

> One cannot assess Eisenhower's motives with the same assurance one can bring to F.D.R.'s. Roosevelt had an entourage of diarists and note-takers; most of them have published what they wrote. . . . He, himself, was a prodigious correspondent and a most revealing talker to the press. And he has fascinated the historians. . . . Eisenhower, on the other hand, is only to be known, as yet, by what he has said publicly and by what men around him will say privately. Appraisal on the basis of such sources calls for caution. It may turn out that he was not the man they make him seem.[20]

As it turns out, Neustadt's caution was warranted. The negative inferences that he proceeded to make with regard to Eisenhower's leadership ability are now beginning to crumble under the close scrutiny of archives that are remarkably rich in the type of holdings that Neustadt cited as our key to understanding Franklin Roosevelt. We find that the Eisenhower administration, like Roosevelt's, was rich with diarists—including the President himself, who kept a daily record of his activities, including reflections on personalities and events. Others who kept diaries included the President's personal secretary, Ann Whitman; his Press Secretary, James Hagerty; and a member of his congressional liaison staff, Jack Z. Anderson.

We now know that Eisenhower, like Roosevelt, was a prolific writer whose correspondence is highly revealing of his own political philosophy. In addition to their access to personal correspondence and diary entries, scholars now have at their disposal a wealth of declassified materials from White House files that document, in detail, the operations of the Eisenhower administration in a far more complete fashion than was possible even a decade ago. From these materials, the theories of revisionists such as Kempton, which were necessarily speculative a decade ago, are now being substantiated.

A pioneer in this form of documented, or "substantive," revisionism is political scientist Fred Greenstein of Princeton. Using documentation from a variety of White House sources, including Eisenhower's personal diaries, Greenstein has made a major contribution with his reassessment of Eisenhower as an activist President. From careful examination of these materials, Greenstein concludes that "Eisenhower was politically astute and informed, actively engaged in putting his personal stamp on public policy, and applied a carefully thought-out conception of leadership to the conduct of his Presidency."[21]

Not surprisingly, other scholars who have made extensive use of archival materials take on a distinctively revisionist tone in their writing. Gary Reichard, in a systematic study of Eisenhower's relationship with Congress during his first two years in office, provides evidence of the President's effective leadership in legislative affairs. Through analysis of congressional roll-call votes and legislative leadership conferences, along with Eisenhower's own written and spoken words, Reichard concludes that Eisenhower "had a keen sense of his role as party leader" and exercised this leadership effectively.[22]

In a 1977 case study of the development of Eisenhower's "New Look" policy, Douglas Kinnard finds that "contrary to the conventional portrayal of Eisenhower as a passive President, he was, at least in matters of strategic policy-making, very strong indeed."[23] Blanche Cook reaches a similar conclusion in her recent study of foreign economic policy during the Eisenhower years. Relying heavily on recently declassified documents at the Eisenhower Library in Abilene, Kansas, Cook argues that "Eisenhower was the most undervalued and misunderstood statesman of the twentieth century."[24]

How might we explain the vast disparity between the relatively contemporary revisionist appraisals of Eisenhower and the highly critical works of earlier years? Historian Stephen Ambrose attributes the rise of favorable assessments in part to the relative failure of Eisenhower's successors. After the Vietnam War and Watergate, Ambrose writes, "it is no wonder that there is an Eisenhower revival going on."[25] Another possible explanation for the current Eisenhower boom, Ambrose suggests, "is nostalgia for the 1950s—a decade of peace with prosperity, a 1.5 percent annual inflation rate, self-sufficiency in oil and other precious goods, balanced budgets, and domestic tranquility."[26]

These observations offer a partial explanation, but a more cogent argument is that the academic community now has at its disposal a much broader and more revealing array of first-hand materials on which to form concrete appraisals of Eisenhower's Presidency. "Eisenhower revisionism" is the natural outgrowth of the utilization of these materials.[27] To paraphrase Richard Neustadt, Eisenhower was not the President that earlier accounts made him seem.

Although recent scholarship has significantly reshaped our understanding of Eisenhower's Presidency, the study of "how Eisenhower managed his leadership" has, in Fred Greenstein's words, "only just begun." Indeed, as Greenstein suggests:

> It behooves Americans who are concerned about the future of their institutions to continue to dig and learn more about this unexpectedly fascinating Presidency. In doing so we are sure to gain insight into the potential for successful leadership in a complex society with a political system that often seems unmanageable and poses truly formidable obstacles to achieving intelligent direction.[28]

Consistent with Greenstein's observation, the central objective of this book is to demonstrate the contemporary relevance of Eisenhower's major contributions to the art of presidential management. A major premise, which shall be discussed throughout this book, is that the manner in which Presidents organize and manage the policy-making machinery of the Presidency has profound impact in shaping their ability to make good decisions. Comparisons with post-Eisenhower Presidencies shall be used to demonstrate that Eisenhower's well developed philosophy of management, as well as his many organizational innovations as President, offered clear advantages over the deinstitutionalized and compartmentalized approach to leadership adopted by some of his successors. Eisenhower's contributions to the development of the Presidency were profound and remain critically important to our understanding of executive branch leadership. The content of subsequent chapters of this book is aimed at clarifying and reinforcing this central theme.

NOTES

1. This summary of Gallup results is offered by Fred Greenstein and Robert Wright in *Public Opinion*, December-January, 1981, p. 51.
2. Stephen Ambrose, "The Ike Age," *New Republic*, May 9, 1981, p. 26.
3. The Schlesinger poll is cited in Thomas A. Bailey, *Presidential Greatness* (New York: Appleton-Century-Crofts, 1966), pp. 24–35.
4. See Thomas Cronin, "The Textbook Presidency and Political Science," in Stanley Bach and George T. Sulzner (eds.), *Perspectives on the Presidency* (Lexington, Mass.: D. C. Heath and Company, 1974), pp. 54–74.
5. Shannon, quoted in Vincent De Santis, "Eisenhower Revisionism," *Review of Politics*, vol. 38, April 1976, p. 191.
6. Goldman, quoted in Blanche W. Cook, *The Declassified Eisenhower* (New York: Doubleday and Company, 1981), Preface, p. v.
7. Richard Strout, review of *Eisenhower: Captive Hero*, by Marquis Childs, *New Republic*, September 5, 1958, p. 21.

8. Wilfred E. Binkley, "West Pointers in the White House," *New Republic,* March 9, 1953, pp. 15–17.

9. James David Barber, *The Presidential Character: Predicting Performance in the White House* (Englewood Cliffs, N.J.: Prentice-Hall, 1972), p. 172.

10. Ibid., p. 160.

11. Krock, quoted in De Santis, "Eisenhower Revisionism," p. 193.

12. Rovere, quoted in De Santis, "Eisenhower Revisionism," p. 193.

13. Murray Kempton, "The Underestimation of Dwight D. Eisenhower," *Esquire,* September 1967, p. 156.

14. Ibid., p. 108.

15. Richard M. Nixon, *Six Crises* (New York: Doubleday and Company, 1962), p. 161.

16. Garry Wills, *Nixon Agonistes: The Crisis of the Self-Made Man* (Boston: Houghton Mifflin, 1970), quoted in De Santis, "Eisenhower Revisionism," p. 198.

17. O'Neill, quoted in De Santis, "Eisenhower Revisionism," p. 199.

18. De Santis, "Eisenhower Revisionism," p. 199.

19. Ibid., p. 201.

20. Richard Neustadt, *Presidential Power: The Politics of Leadership* (New York: John Wiley and Sons, 1960), p. 163.

21. Fred I. Greenstein, "Eisenhower as an Activist President: A Look at New Evidence," *Political Science Quarterly,* vol. 94, Winter, 1979-1980, p. 577. This article was instrumental in sparking my own lengthy research visit to the Eisenhower Library during the summer of 1981. Greenstein's seminal volume, *The Hidden-Hand Presidency: Eisenhower as Leader* (New York: Basic Books, 1982), appeared less than a year after I had begun sifting through my own rather extensive collection of documents from the Eisenhower Library. *The Hidden-Hand Presidency* is clearly among the most impressive and enlightened accounts of Eisenhower's Presidency, or any other Presidency for that matter, written to date.

22. Gary Reichard, *The Reaffirmation of Republicanism: Eisenhower and the Eighty-Third Congress* (Knoxville: University of Tennessee Press, 1975), Preface, p. ix.

23. Douglas Kinnard, *President Eisenhower and Strategy Management: A Study in Defense Politics* (Lexington: University Press of Kentucky, 1977), Preface, p. x.

24. Cook, *The Declassified Eisenhower,* Preface, p. v.

25. Ambrose, "The Ike Age," p. 26.

26. Ibid., pp. 25–27.

27. Although Stephen Ambrose takes on the role of a scholarly devil's advocate in his aforementioned article for the *New Republic,* his brilliant biography *Eisenhower: The President* (New York: Simon and Schuster, 1984) makes a compelling case, through meticulous use of newly declassified documents from the Eisenhower Library, for the argument that new archival materials, more than any other factor, are responsible for the growth of Eisenhower revisionism.

28. Greenstein, *The Hidden-Hand Presidency: Eisenhower as Leader,* p. 248.

2

Eisenhower as Chief Executive

DEVELOPMENT OF THE
INSTITUTIONAL PRESIDENCY

When President Franklin Roosevelt appointed Louis Brownlow to direct the Committee on Administrative Management in 1936, his principal objective was to search for methods to assist the Chief Executive in the increasingly complex task of managing the federal government. The Brownlow Committee began its report by stating the obvious: "The President needs help. His immediate staff assistance is entirely inadequate."[1] In accordance with Roosevelt's wishes, the Committee sought to develop proposals that would ultimately provide the President "with simple but effective machinery which will enable him to exercise managerial direction and control appropriate to the burden of responsibility imposed upon him by the Constitution."[2]

A major outgrowth of the Brownlow Committee's report was the establishment in 1939 of the Presidential institution known as the Executive Office of the President. In appraising the impact of the Executive Office, Clinton Rossiter wrote: "It converts the Presidency into an instrument of twentieth-century government; it gives the incumbent a sporting chance to stand the strain and fulfill his Constitutional mandate as a one-man branch of a three-part government."[3]

The White House Office and Bureau of the Budget (created in 1921) provided a firm foundation for the new Executive Office complex. Over time, other Executive Office units such as the Council of Economic Advisors (created in 1946) and the National Security Council (created in 1947) have become indispensable components of the modern Presidency. Together, the organs of the Executive Office help "facilitate the integration of the whole executive establishment with the Presidential program."[4]

The growth of importance of presidential staff support has led one observer to conclude that presidential leadership today is not so much the work of an individual as it is the work of an organization.

Staff agencies and individual staff members are today so completely involved in the actions of the Chief Executive that only an analysis of the total structure will afford an adequate description of leadership.[5]

To deal effectively with the multiplicity of demands placed upon them, modern Presidents must fully utilize Executive Office agencies and members of the Cabinet in the formulation and execution of executive programs. The President must also assemble a competent White House staff to assist in preparing for speeches and press conferences, scheduling appearances, coordinating activities between the White House and executive departments, and maintaining a good working relationship with Congress.

As organizations and procedures designed to assist the President are emulated by successive administrations, a process of institutionalization unfolds. A simple test for institutionalization, as set forth by political scientist Richard Neustadt, rests with determining whether an organizational or procedural innovation survives a change of administration from one party to another.[6] Applying this yardstick, we find that Eisenhower's administration takes on central importance in the evolution of the Presidency in that it is the first Republican administration in the modern era to continue and to refine the innovations of previous Democratic administrations. Furthermore, the administration laid the foundation for the adoption of several of its own innovations by succeeding Presidents from both parties.

Eisenhower inherited and retained such basic staff offices as Press Secretary, Appointments Secretary, and a Special Counsel's Office—all of which had been created during Roosevelt's administration. The process of legislative clearance that had developed in the Bureau of the Budget during Truman's administration was carried over into the Eisenhower administration in a similar fashion. Furthermore, two organizations within the Executive Office—the Council of Economic Advisors and the National Security Council, which had gotten off to a shaky start in the Truman years—were given additional staff support and upgraded in importance early in Eisenhower's administration. The actions taken to bolster these organizations helped ensure their survival (i.e., their "institutionalization") in future administrations.

The lineage of many of Eisenhower's own innovations is less readily discernible, however. Nor do some of his innovations fit neatly into Neustadt's definition of institutionalization, despite their important impact on the institution of the Presidency during their existence. The Office of Science and Technology, for example, was created by Eisenhower and given "institutional" status under Kennedy, only to be abolished by Nixon and later revived by an act of Congress under Carter. The

Eisenhower-inspired Council on Foreign Economic Policy was abolished by Kennedy, but it reappeared in function, if not in title, under Gerald Ford's expanded Economic Policy Board. Similarly, the concept of a Cabinet secretariat, first implemented by Eisenhower, was abolished by Kennedy but reappeared in Ford's administration. More recently, Edwin Meese refined and modified the concept of the Cabinet secretary in the Reagan administration.

Another important administrative innovation of the Eisenhower era, the utilization of a White House Chief of Staff, has become a significant element in White House operations, despite temporary efforts to dispense with the position in the Ford and Carter administrations. Likewise, the position of Assistant to the President for National Security Affairs has become ingrained in the modern Presidency, although the complexion of the position has changed dramatically from the one envisioned by Eisenhower when he created the office.

The haphazard pattern evidenced in the development of some of the aforementioned innovations reflects the propensity of some Presidents to enter the Oval Office *tabula rasa*. All too often, Presidents seem to lack "institutional memory" or even an interest in what their predecessors have done to enhance decision-making and advisory processes in the White House. Hence, although some aspects of White House organization and operations eventually become institutionalized, the overall complexion of White House organization continues to vary dramatically depending on the philosophy of management (or lack of philosophy) that each President brings with him to office.

Generally speaking, it seems that Republican Presidents have favored a formalistic approach to White House management with an emphasis on systematic organization and procedures. Democrats, on the other hand, have tended to place more emphasis on a highly personalized and informal approach. There are, of course, notable exceptions. Truman, for example, established an orderly administrative approach in response to the "organized chaos" of the Roosevelt years. Gerald Ford, on the other hand, initially adopted a fairly informal approach to some aspects of White House management in order to disassociate his administration from the "palace guard" stigma attached to his predecessor.

The leadership styles of Roosevelt and Eisenhower reveal a particularly marked contrast in presidential administration. Roosevelt's administrative style, which was quite fluid, emphasized ad hoc advisory processes rather than a formal, hierarchical system. Roosevelt surrounded himself with generalists who were seldom given fixed assignments. He sought advisors of divergent opinions and often pitted them against one another. Although Roosevelt's system lent itself to diversity and a broad base of information for decision-making, the excessive competition it engendered often had negative effects. Overlapping effort led to frequent duplication and at times created infighting among members of the staff. The system also placed excessive demands on Roosevelt's time.[7]

Comparatively speaking, Eisenhower's formalistic style of administration was far removed from Roosevelt's personalized approach. As Edward H. Hobbs notes, the Presidency was "converted into a systematic, businesslike administrative organization."[8] Eisenhower insisted upon a well ordered system with precise staff work. As one writer put it: "Instead of brilliant improvisation, he believes in good organization, thorough staff work, and an orderly play of many minds upon every issue before it is resolved."[9]

Eisenhower came into office with definite ideas of what could be done to improve the administration of the Presidency. "For years," he wrote,

> I had been in frequent contact in the executive office of the White House, and I had certain ideas about the system, or lack of system under which it operated. With my training in problems involving organization it was inconceivable to me that the work of the White House could not be better systemized than had been the case in the years I observed it.[10]

In defending his reliance on a formally organized White House staff system, Eisenhower added:

> Organization cannot make a genius out of an incompetent; even less can it, of itself, make the decisions which are required to trigger the necessary action. On the other hand, disorganization can scarcely fail to result in inefficiency and can easily lead to disaster. Organization makes more efficient the gathering and analysis of facts, and the arranging of the findings of experts in logical fashion. Therefore organization helps the responsible individual make the necessary decision, and helps assure that it is satisfactorily carried out.[11]

Some Washington observers became alarmed by the growth of administrative machinery in the Eisenhower White House and looked back nostalgically to the "disorderly but very human days of Franklin D. Roosevelt."[12] Eisenhower, in his search for efficient staff support, was accused of constructing a colossus around him.[13] He was perplexed that these critics seemed oblivious to the benefits that could be obtained through the use of sound administrative machinery. "I have been astonished," he wrote, "to read some contentions which seem to suggest that smooth organization guarantees that nothing is happening, whereas ferment and disorder indicate progress."[14]

DEMYTHOLOGIZING THE MILITARY ANALOGY

In line with Eisenhower's commitment to organization as a necessary ingredient of effective leadership, several important administrative innovations were introduced early in the President's first term of office. Many of these innovations were the direct result of recommendations set forth in the Hoover Commission's "Report on the General Management of the Executive Branch," published in 1949.[15] The Commission, chaired by former President Herbert Hoover, was highly critical of the haphazard organization of the executive branch and the lack of clearcut lines of authority. The Commission concluded that "the exercise of authority is impossible without a clear line of command from top to bottom, and a return line of responsibility and accountability from bottom to top."[16] Consistent with its objective of more structured lines of authority, the Hoover Commission called for the expansion of the White House staff and the creation of a staff secretary, along with a new foreign policy position of Special Assistant to the President for National Security Affairs. The Eisenhower administration was quick to adopt each of these recommendations in addition to several others presented by the Hoover Commission.

The appearance of a well ordered staff system led many Washington observers to conclude erroneously that the new administrative machinery had its origins in concepts rooted in Eisenhower's extensive military experience. In an article appearing in the July 1953 issue of *Fortune*, for example, Charles Murphy wrote:

> There has unmistakably descended upon the White House a formality, an orderliness, and a quietude reminiscent of SHAEF and SHAPE [Supreme Headquarters Allied Expeditionary Force and Supreme Headquarters Allied Powers Europe, respectively]. Moreover, the President in his approach to the machinery of government employs much the same methods that he perfected as the Supreme Commander of highly variegated forces.[17]

In his observations, Murphy merely reiterated the widely held belief that the organization and operations of the Eisenhower White House had been consciously adopted along the lines of a military model—with analogous functions and procedures. Murphy suggested, for example, that the Assistant to the President, Sherman Adams, had "turned himself into a civilian counterpart of 'Beedle' Smith and Al Gruenther, Ike's able military Chiefs of Staff."[18]

Even today, the military analogy continues to receive uncritical acceptance among writers. In an article appearing shortly after Ronald Reagan's electoral victory in 1980, columnist Max Lerner suggested that

Eisenhower used a "line-and-staff" model for his Presidency—"like [that of] an army. . . . The trouble with the army model is that a government is not an army, with fixed lines of authority over life-and-death situations."

Accounts depicting an omnipresent military influence on White House organization misrepresent the true character of Eisenhower's approach to governance. Indeed, the very people who were most conscious of the distinction between military and governmental organization in the Eisenhower administration were those who had served extensively in the military. One such individual, Andrew Goodpaster, held the rank of Colonel in the Army before serving as Staff Secretary to the President. In December 1954, Goodpaster sent a memorandum to Sherman Adams in which he urged that in seeking to improve the functions of the White House staff, an effort should be made not to lean "too heavily on the analogy of the White House setup with a military or departmental staff." "There are important differences," Goodpaster cautioned,

> which influence the proper role and functions of a White House secretariat— e.g., department heads and White House staff members do not fall into simple pigeon-holes analogous to subordinate commanders, or special assistants, but mix and merge such roles. To attempt to impress a "model" secretariat function or staff pattern on our operations in these circumstances would probably result in more harm than good, and I suggest we will do best to take up a series of rather specific and pointed questions of procedure.[19]

The creation of a staff secretariat early in the administration and the designation of Sherman Adams as the "Assistant to the President" presented popular targets for military analogies among writers. Yet, although Eisenhower had served as Army Chief of Staff and had worked extensively with the General Staff system, the staff secretariat and White House Chief of Staff (as Adams' position was called) were strictly nonmilitary in origin.

Suggestions for a White House Chief of Staff date all the way back to 1920, when C. E. McGuire discussed the idea in an article appearing in the *Harvard Graduate's Magazine*.[20] Seven of the nine major executive reorganization studies appearing prior to 1937 included the addition of a central administrative official, or "Chief of Staff," who would be the principal assistant to the President.[21]

As with the Chief of Staff position, the historical antecedents for the Cabinet and staff secretariats were governmental rather than military in character. As Bradley Patterson, assistant to the secretary of the Cabinet in the Eisenhower administration, puts it: "The idea of a secretariat, whether staff secretariat or Cabinet secretariat, is emphatically

not a military idea."[22] Eisenhower was familiar with the Cabinet secretariat from his experience during World War II in England, where he
had observed it while serving as Supreme Commander. He "knew exactly
what a Cabinet secretary could do and could not do, what its limitations
were, from seeing the British arrangements."[23]

Because Eisenhower was favorably impressed by the orderly func-
tioning brought about by the Cabinet secretary in England, he asked
Carter Burgess to put together a memorandum on how a secretariat
might work in his administration. Then, at a Cabinet meeting in August
1954, the President asked Burgess to explain how the plan for a Cabinet
secretariat would strengthen staff work between the White House and
executive departments. After Burgess finished his presentation, Eisenhower addressed the Cabinet, saying:

> I have always wanted to put in such a project, but when we first came
> in, I thought it would look too military in complexion. We have lived in
> this long enough . . . and I think we should put it into effect.[24]

Patterson recalled that shortly after the news of the creation of the
Cabinet secretariat was released to the press, the *Washington Daily News*
came out with a headline reading "Eisenhower Setting Up White House
Like a Military Staff." Patterson expressed disbelief that the secretariat
concept, which had been pioneered in Great Britain and in the U.S.
State Department, long before the Pentagon had adopted it, could be
so widely misunderstood.

Not surprisingly, the military analogy carried over into appraisals of
Eisenhower's leadership style as well. Richard Neustadt, for example,
in his seminal study, *Presidential Power*, suggests that Eisenhower brought
with him to the Presidency the perspective of a military commander,
naively expecting that the principles of leadership he had learned as a
career army officer would readily transfer to executive branch management. Harry Truman, we are told, anticipated the essence of the problem
that Eisenhower would face in his role as a political leader when he
said: "He'll sit here, and he'll say, 'Do this! Do that!' and nothing will
happen. Poor Ike—it won't be a bit like the army."[25] "As late as 1958,"
Neustadt asserts, Eisenhower "had not quite got over 'shocked surprise'
that orders did not carry themselves out."[26] The message is clear:
Eisenhower did not understand the important distinction between command authority and political persuasion. And by definition, Neustadt
suggests, "presidential power is the power to persuade."[27]

There is more than a touch of irony in Neustadt's assessment, for
Eisenhower held a profoundly "Neustadtian" conception of presidential
power long before the author's ideas appeared in print. In a letter to

William Phillips dated June 5, 1953, for example, Eisenhower wrote: "I think it is fair to say that . . . only a leadership that is based on honesty of purpose, calmness and *inexhaustible patience in conference and persuasion* . . . can, in the long run, win out" (emphasis added).[28]

Eisenhower elaborated on his philosophy of leadership at a presidential press conference on November 14, 1956, when he said:

> Leadership is a word and a concept that has been more argued than almost any other I know. I am not one of the desk-pounding type that likes to stick out his jaw and look like he is bossing the show. I would far rather get behind and, recognizing the frailties and the requirements of human nature, I would rather try to persuade a man to go along— because once I have persuaded him, he will stick. If I scare him, he will stay just as long as he is scared, and then he is gone.[29]

Several years later, when Eisenhower was asked whether there was any carryover from his experiences, training, and decision-making in the military to the kind of problems that he had to solve as President, he had this to say:

> Well, there's a great carryover in this way, that I did not abandon methods of getting the information on which I had to make decisions. I'd get the facts and the views from people around me, particularly when they had some expertise in one particular facet of a problem. That was all done.
>
> Now what I had to do then when I made my own decisions was different. In the army you gave orders, but in politics how was I to get the decision implemented? . . . You have to make a decision not only that you believe right, but a plan for selling it. This puts a different side on the thing. And this was particularly true in my case because I had a hostile Congress, I mean politically hostile. . . .
>
> I had to use methods of persuasion, almost cajolery, rather than those of command. . . .
>
> I had to use a lot more salesmanship in political administration than I did in other places. I had some of that, of course, with the Allies, but by and large, that was simple. This other was much tougher, because you just could not use similar methods.[30]

Eisenhower's unstinting efforts at salesmanship and persuasion are exemplified by the administration's annual battle to secure congressional support for the Mutual Security Program. Eisenhower believed that the Program was vital to the security interests of the nation, and he worked tirelessly in its behalf. This topic, along with Eisenhower's general philosophy of leadership vis-à-vis the Congress, will be explored in detail in Chapter 3. For now, let it suffice to note that the art of political persuasion had been ingrained in Eisenhower's thought and practice long before he entered the White House.

EISENHOWER AS POLITICIAN

It is somewhat perplexing that historians and political scientists have only recently begun to develop an appreciation for Eisenhower's unassuming style of leadership as President in light of his tremendous success during World War II in shaping the direction of the war effort with such strong-willed personalities as Bernard Montgomery and George Patton.[31] The complexities of Eisenhower's war-time leadership are nicely summarized by Blanche Cook in *The Declassified Eisenhower:*

> Eisenhower's military strategy depended on his ability to secure the trust of both Churchill and Stalin, negotiate with all the bitterly contending French factions, coordinate the frequently opposing political and military interests within his own command, and convince all the delicate personalities of the international anti-Fascist forces that he was sensitive to their specific and personal needs.[32]

Franklin Roosevelt apparently recognized Eisenhower's talents long before others appreciated them. In selecting Eisenhower to serve as Supreme Allied Commander, Roosevelt told his son James that although he thought Marshall the wisest of the generals, "Eisenhower is the best politician among the military men. He is a natural leader who can convince men to follow him."[33]

Although Roosevelt recognized Eisenhower's skill as a politician, most scholars did not. The image of Eisenhower as a President devoid of direct interest in politics pervaded the literature on the Presidency for more than two decades. James David Barber, author of one of the most widely cited books on the Presidency in the 1970s, seemed to represent the general thinking of scholars when he suggested that Eisenhower's "stance toward political life was one of irritated resignation."[34] Indeed, Barber added, the President was "repelled by politics."[35] Such notions were undoubtedly fueled in part by Eisenhower's own attempts to distance himself publicly from traditional images of politics and politicians. As presidential aide Robert Murphy notes, Eisenhower

> had that ability to dissimulate that I've seen on so many occasions, putting on that bland exterior and saying, "Well, I'm just a simple soldier, I don't know anything about politics." If he said that once, I've heard it a dozen times, and he did have good political instincts and a certain knowledge

that was very helpful to him. . . . But this was very useful as a sort of pose. . . . Lots of people believed that he was a nice simple man. But Eisenhower had a very definite shrewdness and purpose in it all.[36]

Andrew Goodpaster, on a similar note, suggests that Eisenhower intentionally gave the appearance of being above politics. He wanted to "disguise politics" so that he would have a "freer hand" in exerting influence over political affairs while avoiding the stigma of being a politician.[37]

New evidence indicates that Eisenhower was not only politically adept but also had an avid interest in politics and could be quite attentive to political detail. An example of Eisenhower's concern for the political ramifications of his decisions is found in a letter that he wrote to Lucius Clay on December 18, 1958. In recalling his decision to appoint Douglas McKay as Secretary of Interior, the President wrote:

One of the controlling factors in the selection of McKay involved the matter of geography. It had become customary that the Secretary of the Interior should be appointed from an area west of the Mississippi (Ickes was an exception). Moreover, it was a delicate matter to pick the particular state from which the man should come, one reason being the perennial struggle over water rights between California on the one hand and several of the upper river states on the other.

At the time the Hell's Canyon controversy was a bitter one and we felt that about the only states that we could consider were first Oregon or Nebraska, and secondly, the state of Washington or possibly the Dakotas. Since we wanted a man who had a record of political and business accomplishment, we fixed on ex-Governor McKay.[38]

Another revealing glimpse of Eisenhower the politician is provided by Press Secretary James Hagerty in his diary entry for the evening of December 20, 1954. On that occasion, the President held a stag dinner at the White House with some nineteen guests, including the Vice President and several members of the Cabinet and White House staff. According to Hagerty, the President set the tone of the dinner at the outset by remarking that he wanted to devote the evening's discussions "entirely to politics."[39]

The ensuing discussions included, among other items, remarks about the political strength of the Republican party in the state of New York. Lucius Clay argued that it was immediately necessary to set up an organization to replace that of Governor Dewey. Then, Hagerty records,

[t]he President, displaying a great deal more knowledge of the New York situation than anyone had ever expected, said that as he saw it, Javits

was the highest ranking elected Republican state official but that he was quite aware that Javits would have to work in Albany with Speaker Oswald Heckt of the Assembly and Senator Walter Mahoney. However, he thought that Javits, as the highest elected official, should be the head man and that Heckt and Mahoney, or at least one of them, should be talked into working closely with Javits.[40]

Eisenhower expressed a similar interest in state politics in a letter to his friend Meade Alcorn, in which he wrote:

The mention of Wisconsin above recalls to my mind the coming election in New Jersey. It seems clear that in Wisconsin the organization did not work together—in fact it seems doubtful that there was any work whatsoever at the level where it counts most, namely the precinct level. I wonder if we are doing all we can to help the Jersey Republicans organize fully and effectively on the precinct, county, district and State levels. I believe that hard work now will save a lot of grief later. For example, I believe that the State organization should know the name of every precinct captain and his address. There should be available lists of all the block and apartment house workers that serve under the precinct captain. In fact, I believe that every precinct captain—maybe every precinct *worker* in the State—should get a letter signed by you telling that individual how important he or she is to the whole Republican Party and thanking them for the work that they do.

We cannot leave these things to chance. Experience and common sense alike dictate a thorough and full organization of all the strength we can bring to bear.[41]

The fact that a President of the United States had a lively interest in politics and in the political ramifications of decisions would ordinarily be so obvious as to scarcely deserve mention in a book on presidential management. But the pervasive image of Eisenhower as an apolitical officeholder renders our attempt to build a case for emulation of Eisenhower's administrative system less convincing, unless it can first be demonstrated that Eisenhower was a credible political leader. Hence, in our discussions of Eisenhower's organizational apparatus in the pages that follow, we shall not lose sight of Eisenhower's skill as a politician and leader. Although his military experience undoubtedly sensitized him to the demands and methods of managing large organizations, it is not accurate to think of Eisenhower as a military leader who could not make the transition to effective leadership in government because of an alleged distaste for politics. Rather, he was a superb politician whose political instincts served him well in both military and governmental settings.

THE ROLE OF THE WHITE HOUSE STAFF

Eisenhower's White House staff was responsible for coordinating the activities of the executive branch, for following through on the President's initiatives to see that they were faithfully executed, and for keeping the President fully informed on major policy developments. It was up to the staff to identify problems, state facts, sift alternatives, and make recommendations.[42] Final decisions on important matters were reserved for the President alone to make.

In addition to the Cabinet and staff secretariats, the White House staff included a congressional liaison office, an executive branch liaison office, and an office of public and press relations. Among other activities, these units worked together to provide support for the development of speeches and appearances by the President and the Cabinet, to fill appointments in the executive branch, and, most important, to coordinate policy-making and implementation with the executive departments.

To direct the White House staff, Eisenhower named former New Hampshire Governor Sherman Adams as White House Chief of Staff. Adams' task, Eisenhower wrote,

> was to coordinate all of these sections and their operations, to make certain that every person in them understood the purport and the details of each directive issued, and to keep me informed of appropriate developments on a daily basis. He did not lay down rigid rules to restrict the staff members in their access to me; they worked flexibly, with a voluntary cooperation based on mutual friendship and respect.[43]

Throughout Eisenhower's Presidency and beyond, Washington observers were inclined to exaggerate Adams' authority as Chief of Staff. In 1960, political scientist Louis Koenig wrote:

> For the better part of President Eisenhower's two terms, Adams exercised more power than any other presidential assistant in modern times. He made decisions and performed acts which Presidents, since the establishment of the Republic, have been given to doing themselves. Indeed, it is demonstrable that his power and impact upon the national destiny have exceeded that of not a few Presidents of the United States.[44]

Sidney Hyman, a Washington journalist, described Adams as the "de facto Vice President of the United States."[45] Some Washington observers were said to have joked irreverently: "What if Adams should die and Eisenhower should become President?"[46] Such pronouncements, Koenig asserted, were "indicative of the fact that Sherman Adams was the instrument by which Dwight D. Eisenhower accomplished one of the most thoroughgoing withdrawals from the duties of the Presidency in the history of the office."[47]

In his memoir of the Eisenhower years, presidential speechwriter Emmet John Hughes offers a more enlightened depiction of Adams' role: "Notwithstanding descriptions of him through the years as an eminence grise, he scarcely ever sought to work as a policy-maker. He interceded even in the planning of presidential speeches only occasionally and superficially."[48]

In reality, Adams' role was primarily that of a coordinator and facilitator of domestic affairs, not unlike the role undertaken by the President's Special Assistant for National Security Affairs on foreign policy matters. As Hughes suggests, Adams was not involved in policy-making, nor did he hold reign over members of the Cabinet. More typically, Adams served as an envoy, organizer, and troubleshooter. Fred Greenstein provides us with a cogent example of the President's informed, and rather specific, instructions to Adams in the form of a teletype dated September 25, 1954.

> This morning you and I talked briefly about the program for starting up expenditures to stimulate industrial activity. You stated you would soon see [Labor] Secretary Mitchell. Please ask him to show you the memorandum he wrote me under the date of September 16, which came to my attention this morning. I should very much like to push in the direction he advocates.[49]

The teletype of September 25 scarcely conveys the image of a President readily acquiescing to an agenda set by his staff. Rather, in this case at least, Adams was given explicit instructions by the President to push forward on Labor Secretary Mitchell's initiatives. In the same teletype, Eisenhower informed Adams that he had been "urging the Defense Department to do the major portion of its buying now and not wait until the last half of the fiscal year." Noting that "this does not seem to be happening," Eisenhower instructed Adams "to get this going and be sure to notify everybody of my personal anxiety."[50]

Popular notions notwithstanding, Sherman Adams did not have the ability to restrict the access of most top administration officials who wished to see the President. Included on the list of individuals who had direct access to the President, unencumbered by Adams, were the Cabinet secretaries from the ten departments, the directors of the Bureau of the Budget, the Council of Economic Advisors, and the Office of Defense Mobilization, the Special Assistant for National Security Affairs, and the staff secretary, among others.[51] The staff secretary provided a particularly noteworthy check on the Chief of Staff's capacity to screen important information, in that all proposals dealing with major problems were staffed out by the staff secretary for clearance with all relevant officials before the proposals were forwarded to the President.

The Hoover Commission, in its proposals for the creation of the office of staff secretary, noted that the person filling this position "would not himself be an advisor to the President on any issue or policy nor would he review in supervisory capacity the substance of any recommendation made to the President by any part of the staff."[52] In accordance with the Hoover Commission's recommendations, the Eisenhower staff secretariat was small, flexible, and low-profile. It served as a nerve center of information available to the President and his top aides. The secretariat was initially headed by Brigadier General Paul T. Carroll. He was succeeded in 1954 by Andrew J. Goodpaster, an army officer with a Ph.D. in international relations from Princeton University. Goodpaster was assisted by Arthur Minnich, a former history professor. William Hopkins, the executive clerk of the White House, also assisted the secretariat in its operations.

Arthur Minnich described the task of the staff secretariat as ensuring "that those who had some capacity for contributing to the solution of a problem had a chance to get cut in on it."[53] The staff secretary and his assistants were responsible for the coordination of all White House activities. The most important coordinating function was that of controlling the flow of correspondence in and out of the White House.

Most documents received by the President had a one-page synopsis on top. The "covering brief," as it was called, was a document drawn up by the staff secretariat to provide a brief summary of the problem at hand, the recommended course of action, a discussion of implementation, and the necessary lateral clearance and concurrences. Consequently, Eisenhower received not only the original proposal, but also comments by all White House aides and department officials who had an interest in the issue.

Although Eisenhower was much maligned over his so-called one-page rule, he was not the first President to require an abbreviated cover memo. Franklin Roosevelt once offered justification for the one-page idea in a conversation with Louis Brownlow:

> I learned a trick from Wilson. He once told me: "If you want your memoranda read, put it on one page." So I, when I came here, issued a similar decree, if you want to call it that. But even at that I am now forced to handle, so the oldsters around tell me, approximately a hundred times as many papers as any of my predecessors.[54]

Faced with a paperwork load even larger than Roosevelt's, the staff secretariat became, in Minnich's words, a "clearing-house" of ideas and information.

> Without having a monopoly on handling all papers that came through the White House, we managed to move a great many of the papers, with help from the established lines of receiving mail, sorting it, screening it, getting some of the barest routine out of the way, and then selectively, through three or four steps, bringing up to the surface at our level those things—in excess quantity, I must say—that seemed to need top-level attention. If there was any fault, it was for screening too loosely rather than screening too tightly.[55]

Closely complementing the work of the staff secretariat in the White House was the office of Executive Branch Liaison, directed by Stanley Rumbough. Among other activities, this office coordinated all speeches by anyone considered to have a policy-making role in the administration. The liaison office disseminated one-page "fact sheets" twice a week to the President, members of the Cabinet, and the White House staff. The fact sheets contained succinct summaries of controversial issues and highlights of administration objectives and accomplishments. The liaison office also coordinated radio and television appearances for administration spokespersons and kept a cross-indexed file of all the President's public speeches and statements. One of the objectives of the liaison office was to avoid inaccurate or conflicting statements by administration spokespersons.

Another important organizational innovation of the Eisenhower White House was the formal establishment of a congressional liaison office. To complement the work of the liaison staff, Eisenhower introduced the practice of holding weekly congressional leadership meetings in the White House—a practice that became the cornerstone of his legislative leadership. These meetings allowed Eisenhower to lobby on behalf of his legislative program and to keep abreast of recent developments in Congress.

When Eisenhower's legislative liaison team was assembled, the top criterion was experience with Congress. Wilton (Jerry) Persons, who served as director of the liaison staff, had worked for fifteen years in congressional liaison for the Army. Persons' assistants—Edward McCabe, Bryce Harlow, Jerry Morgan, and Jack Z. Anderson—all had considerable knowledge of Congress and its members. Anderson was himself a former member of Congress. Harlow had been with Persons in the congressional liaison office of the War Department. Morgan had served as Legislative Counsel for the House of Representatives. McCabe had been Chief Clerk of the House Labor Committee. The staff had a combined total of more than seventy-five years of experience with Congress.[56]

The congressional liaison staff met at least once a day to discuss strategy. On all major legislation, members of the staff made personal contact with legislators to inform them of the President's position and to provide information in support of the administration's stand. On Tuesday morning, the President and his liaison staff hosted the Republican leaders of Congress at the White House. (On occasion, the meetings were expanded to include members of both parties, particularly when the President wished to discuss major foreign or defense policy developments.) As in the Cabinet and National Security Council meetings, the White House staff prepared a formal agenda for the legislative leadership meeting. A large board was used to display pending legislation—with particular attention devoted to anticipated problems or trouble spots. Every major Eisenhower proposal was discussed with congressional leaders before it went to the Hill. The legislative leadership meetings were one means of winning the support of the Republican members of Congress by allowing direct participation in executive branch initiatives. In light of the Democratic control of Congress during the last six years of the Eisenhower administration, the President made a point of supplementing his legislative leadership meetings with informal get-togethers with Senate Majority Leader Lyndon Johnson and Speaker of the House Sam Rayburn.

In his memoirs, Eisenhower described the legislative leadership meetings as the most effective mechanism for developing coordination with Congress.[57] "Together," Steven Wayne notes, "Eisenhower and his liaison staff succeeded in formalizing institutional relationships with Congress and thereby established a Presidential presence on Capitol Hill."[58]

Despite the many organizational innovations of the Eisenhower years, there was considerable flexibility in the assignments and working relationships among the members of the White House staff. Wilton Persons, for example, while directing the office of congressional liaison, was also a deputy assistant to Sherman Adams. With his broad experience, Persons had no problem moving into the Chief of Staff position after Adams left the White House. Bryce Harlow, though initially concerned with legislative liaison activities, was drawn into speech-writing activities for the President on many occasions. Similarly, Gerald Morgan made a smooth transition from congressional relations to serve as Special Counsel to the President. Maxwell Rabb, Eisenhower's first Cabinet secretary, also served as liaison with the Jewish community. And Andrew Goodpaster, who served as Eisenhower's second staff secretary, was also responsible for day-to-day liaison on national security affairs.

Another versatile member of the Eisenhower staff was the President's press secretary, James Hagerty. In his regular activities, Hagerty met twice a day with members of the press to keep them informed of White House activities. He attended all Cabinet and National Security Council (NSC) meetings, and took the place of Sherman Adams as chairman of the White House staff meetings prior to the President's Wednesday morning press conferences. Hagerty was more than a press aide to the President. He shared with Adams the role of White House troubleshooter and, to a greater extent than Adams, was called upon to act as an occasional advisor to the President.

THE USE OF DELEGATION
AND THE MYTH OF ABDICATION

One of the principal functions of Eisenhower's advisory and administrative apparatus was to allow the President to use his time effectively. As one White House aide put it, if the President "is distracted from the big choices by the torrent of petty details, the big choices will not get made."[59] Eisenhower entrusted his Cabinet and White House staff with considerable authority for administrative matters while retaining direct control over all major policy decisions. The President explained his philosophy of delegation in a letter to Henry Luce written on August 8, 1960.

> The government of the United States has become too big, too complex, and too pervasive in its influence on all our lives for one individual to pretend to direct the details of its important and critical programming. Competent assistants are mandatory; without them the executive branch would bog down. To command the loyalties and dedication and best efforts of capable and outstanding individuals requires patience, understanding, a readiness to delegate, and an acceptance of responsibility for any honest errors—real or apparent—those associates and subordinates might make. . . . Principal subordinates must have confidence that they and their positions are widely respected, and the chief must do his part in assuring that this is so.[60]

An incident that took place soon after Eisenhower was elected in 1952 illustrates the President's willingness to deflect criticism from high-ranking members of the administration in order to protect their reputation. Prior to the 1952 election, the American Ambassador to Great Britain, Walter Gifford, informed Eisenhower that he planned to retire from his post soon after the new administration took office. With this information in hand, Eisenhower decided on a replacement for Gifford's post. A confidential decision was made shortly after the election to offer the appointment to Winthrop Aldrich, but news of the appointment was leaked. With the story already in the newspapers, Secretary of State designate John Foster Dulles decided to make a prompt public announcement of the fact that the administration intended to nominate Aldrich to the post as soon as it took office in January. The announcement was made hastily, without formal consultation with the British government regarding the acceptability of Aldrich as a replacement for Gifford's position. Eisenhower revealed in his personal diary that British Prime Minister Anthony Eden was understandably upset that the customary consultation had not taken place. In order to placate the British government, Eisenhower noted in his diary that he would advise Anthony Eden "to lay the blame for this whole unfortunate occurrence squarely on me." He went on to explain that Eden

> will have the logical explanation that my lack of formal experience in the political world was the reason for the blunder. Actually, I was the one who cautioned against anything like this happening, but manifestly I can take the blame without hurting anything or anybody; whereas if the Secretary of State would have to shoulder it, his position would be badly damaged.[61]

Eisenhower's behind-the-scenes activities in this episode illustrate what Fred Greenstein refers to as "hidden-hand leadership."[62] At times, this type of leadership left the appearance of excessive delegation, if not abdication, of the President's constitutional authority. Until recently, the prevailing view among scholars was that Eisenhower delegated such tremendous authority to John Foster Dulles that the Secretary of State overshadowed the Cabinet and, more critically, the President himself. Marquis Childs asserts, for example, that "no President in history delegated so much of his constitutional authority over the conduct of foreign policy."[63] And Roscoe Drummond and Gaston Coblentz conclude that "no Secretary of State in American history ever operated under such a prodigious mandate of authority as Eisenhower gave to Dulles."[64]

As might be expected, those who served Eisenhower hold a markedly different view of Eisenhower's relationship with Dulles, but, despite the subjective nature of their judgments, one that is more compatible with the archival record. Taking exception to the notion that Eisenhower delegated extraordinary authority to Dulles, the President's brother and trusted advisor, Milton, has asserted that "nothing can be further from the truth."[65] Presidential advisor Arthur Larson adds that "the main direction and tone of American foreign policy" was Eisenhower's, as "were the first line decisions."[66] Eisenhower offered his own assessment of his relationship with Dulles in 1968, stating:

> Of all the men in my Cabinet there was no one whom I respected more than Secretary of State John Foster Dulles. I depended greatly on his wisdom. Yet Foster made no important move without consulting the President. I reviewed in advance all his major pronouncements and speeches, and when he was abroad he was constantly in touch by cable and telephone. If we did not see eye to eye—and these instances are rare—it was, of course, my opinion that prevailed; this is the way it has to be. The persistent statement that I turned foreign policy over to Dulles is—to use a more civilized word than it deserves—incorrect.[67]

The records of the administration confirm that Eisenhower's relationship with Dulles was marked by close interaction between a well-informed President and a trusted advisor. Presidential Press Secretary James Hagerty's diary entry for November 30, 1954, documents one such instance of the type of collaboration described by Eisenhower. Hagerty recorded that he asked Eisenhower what he should say if he were asked at his morning press briefing whether the President approved of an important foreign policy statement delivered by Dulles on the previous day. Eisenhower responded that Hagerty should say that the President "had not only approved the speech, but that the Secretary and he had consulted in advance on it, as they always do, and that the final consultation on the speech had occurred yesterday."[68]

When, on occasion, Dulles and Eisenhower disagreed, it is clear that the President prevailed. Eisenhower's personal secretary, Ann Whitman, recorded one such incident in her own diary entry for May 14, 1955. In this entry, Whitman noted that the Secretary of State wanted to delay the four-power summit in Geneva scheduled for July 1955. Eisenhower flatly rejected the idea on the grounds that if the meeting were not held as soon as possible, expectations of what might be accomplished at the conference would likely exceed the possible outcomes.[69] Hence, the summit was held in July as originally scheduled.

Eisenhower's ability to entrust subordinates such as Dulles with important responsibilities led some scholars to erroneously conclude that he was a "passive" President—reluctant to make decisions on his own. Richard Tanner Johnson, for example, wrote that "Eisenhower usually acquiesced in the face of opposing counsel."[70] As on other issues of contention, however, administration insiders offer a sharply different perspective. Robert Bowie, who served as Director of the Policy Planning Staff and as the State Department's representative on the National

Security Council Planning Board until 1957, had this to say about Eisenhower's decision-making style:

> It seems to me that there is quite a false impression which has been partly fostered by the press or by critics about his [Eisenhower's] attitude toward making decisions. In my observation, on the issues of foreign policy . . . I did not see any evidence of this hesitancy to make decisions or reluctance to face the issues or unwillingness to resolve them. On the contrary, after a discussion, he would generally sum up where he came out. . . . This was recorded as the record of action taken.[71]

Wilton Persons, who replaced Sherman Adams as White House Chief of Staff in 1958, suggests that misperceptions with regard to Eisenhower's decision-making style stem from the President's own lack of concern for appearances.

> I think the news people who were writing got his method of operation mixed up with the question of a decision. For example, on numerous occasions he would talk a matter out with one of his Cabinet members and make the decision, and then the Cabinet member would say, "all right, Mr. President, when I go outside, I'm going to be hit by the reporters. How do you want the publicity on this to be handled? Would you like to call them in now or would you like me to handle it?" And the President would say, "Go ahead, you can handle it." Some people jumped to the conclusion that the individual who handled the publicity end of it had made the decision. For example, every now and then they would write that Mr. Dulles was running foreign policy. . . . The President leaned on him very heavily for advice and so forth, but I think Mr. Dulles if he were here would be the first man to say he wasn't running foreign policy, that the President was running it. But you cannot straighten out a thing like that once it gets going.[72]

In 1968, Eisenhower responded to criticism regarding his decision-making style:

> Some writers have said that I conducted the Presidency largely through staff decisions. This, of course, is nonsense. Naturally, I consulted constantly with my staff, and I valued their opinions. But staff work doesn't mean that you take a vote of your subordinates and then abide by that majority opinion. On important matters, in the end, you alone must decide. As a military leader I had learned this hard lesson. Many times during my two terms, my decisions ran contrary to the majority opinion of my advisers.[73]

DELEGATION IN CONTEMPORARY CONTEXT:
THE EXPERIENCE OF JIMMY CARTER

Eisenhower apparently recognized from his pre–White House experience that an executive must learn to entrust subordinates with the details of operations while retaining ultimate authority and responsibility for important decisions. In explaining his philosophy of delegation, he wrote:

> Any Chief Executive who tries to do everything himself, as some Presidents have, is in trouble. He will work himself into a state of exhaustion and frustration, and drive everyone around him half crazy. Franklin Pierce, for example, was so preoccupied with patronage decisions and other petty matters that he never was able really `- -` President.[74]

Whereas Eisenhower has been criticized for "excessive" delegation by such writers as James David Barber,[75] at least one recent President, Jimmy Carter, would undoubtedly have benefited from the ability to delegate authority as skillfully. President Carter, as others have noted, seemed to have an obsession with the details of his job. James Fallows, White House speechwriter for President Carter during his first two years in office, observed that Carter "showed in practice that he was still the detail-man used to running his own warehouse, the perfectionist accustomed to thinking that to do a job right you must do it yourself."[76] According to Fallows, Carter

> would leave for a weekend at Camp David laden with thick briefing books, would pore over budget tables to check the arithmetic, and, during his first six months in office, would personally review all requests to use the White House tennis court.[77]

Harrison Wellford, the head of Carter's reorganization team, boasted that the memos sent to Carter "sometimes came back with more comments than original text."[78] In admiration of the President, Wellford wrote,

> I don't know how long he can keep this up but he has a passion for getting involved in the details of a lot of these decisions—even decisions that less hard-working Presidents probably felt could have been handled below the oval office.[79]

What appeared to be virtuous behavior to Wellford at the time of these comments was later perceived by more dispassionate observers as a grave weakness in Carter's performance as Chief Executive. In one assessment of the Carter years, veteran White House correspondent Hugh Sidey concluded that Carter was gripped by "the tyranny of the trivial."[80]

Exacerbating the problems created by such attention to detail was Carter's insistence upon acting as his own Chief of Staff. Early in his administration Carter made it clear that he did not want a Chief of Staff in the Sherman Adams mold. Carter, James Fallows wrote,

> did not scramble to hire someone with a talent that Powell, Eizenstat, Jordan or Rafshoon did not happen to possess. None of them would have made a good Chief of Staff, so that function simply did not enter into the organization chart. Carter would do it himself. . . . By the end of the first year, this system had become more or less workable; everyone had learned whom to call to get a telegram sent, which Congressman to notify when news of a home-town project was released. . . . But a year was wasted as we blindly groped for answers and did for ourselves what a staff coordinator could have done.[81]

Carter's predecessor, Gerald R. Ford, also dispensed with the position of Chief of Staff early in his administration—largely because of the stigma associated with the highly centralized staff system headed by H. R. Haldeman in the Nixon years. Robert Hartmann, an advisor to the President, described Ford's early staff arrangements as somewhat analogous to "the Knights of the Round Table, where all are equal."[82] The informality of this staff system created problems for the President, however. As Hartmann put it, "Ford's Knights were riding off in all directions."[83] After a few weeks under this arrangement, Ford appointed Donald Rumsfeld in September 1974 to serve as staff "coordinator." Rumsfeld moved quickly to put an end to the free-form structure that had prevailed, reinstituting, with some modifications, the Chief of Staff system of earlier years.

Carter, like Ford before him, opted for a "spokes of the wheel" approach to White House administration, giving nine main aides equal access to him and another two dozen people access through memos.[84] After two years, however, Carter followed Ford's earlier example by designating Hamilton Jordan as White House Chief of Staff. It was not until the final year of Carter's administration, when Jack Watson replaced Jordan as Chief of Staff, that the White House became fully systematic in its organization and procedures. In his memoirs, Carter's National Security Advisor, Zbigniew Brzezinski, describes the change in White House organization that took place after the appointment of Watson:

> It started being more like a joint staff. Until then it was a series of separate entities. I suspect [the reason for the change] was more Watson's man-

agement skills, but I think the President recognized the need for a more integrated staff, and so did the key principals, Wexler, Cutler, Powell, and Eizenstat. This helped pull things together to a greater extent than was the case during the first two years or so.[85]

CONCLUSION

The relatively unstructured staff arrangements that prevailed early in the Ford and Carter administrations draw attention to a problem endemic to the modern Presidency. Despite the development of more extensive transition efforts, Presidents have typically experienced extended "learning periods" during which administrative techniques are developed through trial and error. Eisenhower's Presidency represents a notable exception to the haphazard approach to White House management utilized by some of his predecessors and successors. Thorough staff work, active participation by departmental representatives in policy formulation and implementation, and continuous coordination of executive branch activities were hallmarks of the Eisenhower years.

Eisenhower well understood the disinclination among most people to focus on the organizational and administrative aspects of government. In his memoirs he discussed the problem of inattention to governmental organization and defended his reliance on it. "To the public," he wrote,

> there is nothing intriguing about government structure, operations, and systems of policy formation and execution. To the young the word "organization" has little meaning. Because hero worship is natural to them, they think not of organization but of leaders . . . as individuals of much mental agility, personal magnetism, moral and physical courage—in short, of genius. . . . What does he need with organization? . . . To the adult mind "organization" seems to summon visions of rigidity and machine-like operation, with an inescapable deadly routine and stodginess in human affairs. Yet it is not the enemy of imagination or of any other attractive human characteristic. Its purpose is to simplify, clarify, expedite, and coordinate; it is a bulwark against chaos, confusion, delay, and failure.[86]

Eisenhower's appreciation for the virtues of organization found expression in his administration's multifaceted efforts to modernize the office of the Presidency. His revitalization of the Cabinet and National Security Council as advisory forums, and his careful development of institutional mechanisms to promote methodical coordination and consultation among top advisors, reflected his commitment to the use of organization as a cornerstone of effective leadership.

Unfortunately, the Eisenhower legacy has been lost on some students of the Presidency and misunderstood by others. Contrary to traditional scholarship, Eisenhower's administrative system did not undermine the President's personal authority. Rather, the system complemented and bolstered the President's greatly underrated skills as a politician and leader. Eisenhower delegated authority without abdicating constitutional responsibility. He drew extensively on his staff while carefully guarding against staff dominance. The prevailing wisdom of scholars and journalists of his era notwithstanding, Eisenhower did not try to turn the White House into a military-style staff system within the executive branch. His public and private statements reveal a highly sophisticated understanding of the pronounced differences between military leadership and public administration. The President's administrative style reflected a refined but greatly underrated sensitivity to the political dimensions of executive branch leadership. Indeed, Eisenhower's approach to management and his many organizational innovations are richly illustrative of the ways in which advisory and decision-making processes can best serve the needs of modern Presidents.

In subsequent chapters we shall focus on the interplay between Eisenhower's impressive skills as Chief Executive and the carefully developed policy-making machinery of his Presidency. By confronting misleading notions from the past with newly available archival evidence, we can now develop a far better understanding of Eisenhower's lasting contributions to executive branch management.

NOTES

1. Louis Brownlow, Charles E. Merriam, and Luther Gulick, *Report of the President's Committee on Administrative Management* (Washington, D.C.: U.S. Government Printing Office, 1937), p. 5.

2. Louis Brownlow, *A Passion for Anonymity: The Autobiography of Louis Brownlow*, vol. 2 (Chicago: University of Chicago Press, 1958), p. 337.

3. Clinton Rossiter, "The Constitutional Significance of the Executive Office of the President," *American Political Science Review*, vol. 43, 1949, p. 1206.

4. Lester G. Seligman, "Developments in the Presidency and the Conception of Political Leadership," *American Sociological Review*, vol. 20, 1955, p. 708.

5. Ibid., p. 710.

6. Richard E. Neustadt, "Staffing the Presidency: Premature Notes on the New Administration," *Political Science Quarterly*, vol. 93, Spring 1978, p. 2.

7. For a discussion of Roosevelt's management style, see Stephen Hess, *Organizing the Presidency* (Washington, D.C.: Brookings Institution, 1976), Chapter 2; Richard Tanner Johnson, *Managing the White House* (New York: Harper and Row, 1974), Chapter 2; and Arthur Schlesinger, Jr., "Franklin Roosevelt's Approach to Managing the Executive Branch," in Richard J. Stillman, ed., *Public Administration: Concepts and Cases*, 2nd ed. (Boston: Houghton Mifflin, 1980), pp. 266–274.

8. Edward H. Hobbs, "The President and Administration—Eisenhower," *Public Administration Review*, vol. 18, 1958, p. 307.

9. Merlo J. Pusey, *Eisenhower, the President* (New York: Macmillan, 1956), p. 87, quoted in Hobbs, "The President and Administration—Eisenhower," p. 307.

10. Dwight D. Eisenhower, *The White House Years: Mandate for Change* (Garden City, N.Y.: Doubleday and Company, 1963), p. 87. Hereinafter cited as *Mandate*.

11. Eisenhower, *Mandate*, p. 114.

12. Hobbs, "The President and Administration—Eisenhower," pp. 307–308.

13. Ibid., p. 308.

14. Eisenhower, *Mandate*, p. 114.

15. U.S. Congress, "Report on the General Management of the Executive Branch," *Commission on the Organization of the Executive Branch of the Government*, 83rd Congress, 1st Session, 1949.

16. Ibid., pp. ix–x, 1.

17. Charles J. Murphy, "Eisenhower's White House," *Fortune*, July 1953, p. 75.

18. Ibid., p. 76.

19. Memorandum, Andrew Goodpaster to Sherman Adams, December 30, 1954, Folder: Organization (8), White House Office: Office of the Staff Secretary, White House Subseries, Box 4, Eisenhower Library.

20. C. E. McGuire, "A Program of Administrative Reform at Washington," *Harvard Graduate's Magazine*, vol. 28, 1920, pp. 580–581, cited in Edward H. Hobbs, "An Historical Review of Plans for Presidential Staffing," *Law and Contemporary Problems*, vol. 21, Autumn 1956, p. 675.

21. Hobbs, "An Historical Review of Plans for Presidential Staffing," p. 675.

22. Bradley H. Patterson, Jr., interviewed by Paul L. Hopper, September 19, 1968, Oral History Interview #225, p. 7, Eisenhower Library.

23. Ibid., p. 3.

24. James C. Hagerty diary, August 13, 1954, Diary Entries Box 1, Eisenhower Library.

25. Richard E. Neustadt, *Presidential Power: The Politics of Leadership* (New York: John Wiley and Sons, 1976 edition), p. 77.

26. Ibid., p. 231.

27. Ibid., p. 78.

28. Dwight D. Eisenhower to William Phillips, June 5, 1953, Folder: Phillips, William, Papers of Dwight D. Eisenhower as President of the United States, 1953–1961, Ann Whitman File, Letter Series, Box 25, Eisenhower Library.

29. R. Gordon Hoxie, "Eisenhower and Presidential Leadership," *Presidential Studies Quarterly*, vol. 13, no. 4, Fall 1983, p. 605.

30. Dwight D. Eisenhower, Columbia Oral History Interview, Interviewed by Ed Edwin, July 20, 1967, pp. 106–107, Eisenhower Library.

31. Hoxie, "Eisenhower and Presidential Leadership," p. 605.

32. Blanche W. Cook, *The Declassified Eisenhower* (New York: Doubleday, 1981), p. 64.

33. Ibid.

34. James David Barber, *The Presidential Character: Predicting Performance in the White House* (Englewood Cliffs, N.J.: Prentice-Hall, 1972, paperback edition), p. 172.

35. Ibid., p. 163.

36. Robert Murphy, Oral History Interview #224, p. 14, Eisenhower Library.

37. General Andrew Goodpaster, interviewed by Phillip G. Henderson, Institute for Defense Analyses, October 7, 1983.

38. Dwight D. Eisenhower to General Lucius D. Clay, letter of December 18, 1958, Folder: DDE Dictation, December 1958, Papers of Dwight D. Eisenhower as President of the United States, Ann Whitman File, Dwight D. Eisenhower Diary Series, Box 37, Eisenhower Library.

39. James C. Hagerty Diary, December 20, 1954, Diary Entries Box 1, Eisenhower Library.

40. Ibid.

41. Dwight D. Eisenhower to Meade Alcorn, letter of August 30, 1957, Folder: DDE Diary 7-1-57 to 8-31-57, Papers of Dwight D. Eisenhower as President of the United States, Ann Whitman File, Dwight D. Eisenhower Diary Series, Box 25, Eisenhower Library.

42. Steven Wayne, *The Legislative Presidency* (New York: Harper and Row, 1978), p. 36.

43. Eisenhower, *Mandate*, p. 116.

44. Louis W. Koenig, *The Invisible Presidency* (New York: Rinehart and Company, 1960), p. 338.

45. Ibid.

46. Ibid., p. 339.

47. Ibid.

48. Emmet John Hughes, *The Ordeal of Power: A Political Memoir of the Eisenhower Years* (New York: Atheneum, 1963), p. 64.

49. Fred I. Greenstein, *The Hidden-Hand Presidency: Eisenhower as Leader* (New York: Basic Books, 1982), p. 144.

50. Ibid.

51. Ibid., p. 146.

52. Bradley H. Patterson, "An Overview of the White House," in Kenneth W. Thompson, ed., *Portraits of American Presidents Volume III: The Eisenhower Presidency* (Lanham, Md.: University Press of America, 1984), p. 121.

53. Arthur L. Minnich, Oral History Interview, p. 13, Eisenhower Library.

54. Arthur Schlesinger, Jr., "Roosevelt as Chief Administrator," in Richard J. Stillman, *Public Administration: Concepts and Cases* (Boston: Houghton Mifflin, 1980), p. 267.

55. Minnich, Oral History Interview, p. 11, Eisenhower Library.

56. Wilton B. Persons, Oral History Interview, p. 27, Eisenhower Library.

57. Eisenhower, *Mandate*, p. 194.

58. Wayne, *The Legislative Presidency*, p. 145.

59. James Fallows, "The Passionless Presidency: The Trouble with Jimmy Carter's Administration," *Atlantic*, May 1979, p. 38.

60. Dwight D. Eisenhower to Harry Luce, August 8, 1960, Folder: Luce Harry (1), Papers of Dwight D. Eisenhower as President of the United States, 1953–1961, Ann Whitman File, Letter Series, Box 5, Eisenhower Library.

61. Eisenhower, quoted in Robert H. Ferrell, ed., *The Eisenhower Diaries* (New York: W. W. Norton, 1981), pp. 230–232.

62. Greenstein, *The Hidden-Hand Presidency: Eisenhower as Leader*. See especially pp. 58–65.

63. Childs, quoted in George Dangerfield, "Eisenhower: the Image Fades," *Nation*, vol. 187, September 20, 1958, p. 156.

64. Roscoe Drummond and Gaston Coblentz, *Duel at the Brink* (Garden City, N.Y.: Doubleday, 1960), p. 12.

65. Milton Eisenhower, quoted in Herbert S. Parmet, *Eisenhower and the American Crusades* (New York: Macmillan, 1972), p. 185.

66. Arthur Larson, *Eisenhower: The President Nobody Knew* (New York: Charles Scribner's, 1968), p. 74.

67. Dwight D. Eisenhower, "Some Thoughts on the Presidency," *Reader's Digest*, November 1968, pp. 54–55.

68. James C. Hagerty, diary entry of November 30, 1954, Folder: November 29–30, 1954, Box 1, Eisenhower Library.

69. Diary entry of May 14, 1955, Dwight D. Eisenhower Papers as President of the United States, 1953–1961, Ann Whitman File, Whitman Diary Series, Box 5, Eisenhower Library.

70. Richard Tanner Johnson, *Managing the White House* (New York: Harper and Row, 1974), p. 111.

71. Robert Bowie, Oral History Interview #102, August 10, 1967, p. 6, Eisenhower Library.

72. Wilton Persons, interviewed by John Luter, Oral History Interview #334, Eisenhower Library.

73. Eisenhower, "Some Thoughts on the Presidency," p. 54.

74. Ibid.

75. James David Barber, *The Presidential Character: Predicting Performance in the White House*, 2nd ed. (Englewood Cliffs, N.J.: Prentice-Hall, 1977), p. 163.

76. Fallows, "The Passionless Presidency," p. 38.

77. Ibid.

78. Harrison Wellford, "Staffing the Presidency: An Insider's Comments," *Political Science Quarterly*, vol. 93, Spring 1978, p. 11.

79. Ibid.

80. Hugh Sidey, "Assessing a Presidency," *Time*, August 18, 1960, p. 14.

81. Fallows, "The Passionless Presidency," p. 39.

82. Hartmann, quoted in Juan Cameron, "The Management Problem in Ford's White House," *Fortune*, July 1975, p. 77.

83. Ibid.

84. Fallows, "The Passionless Presidency," p. 38.

85. Brzezinski, quoted in John Kessel, *Presidential Parties* (Homewood, Ill.: Dorsey Press, 1984), p. 62.

86. Dwight David Eisenhower, *Waging Peace, 1956–1961* (Garden City, N.Y.: Doubleday, 1965), p. 630.

3

Eisenhower as
Domestic Political Leader

RELATIONS WITH CONGRESS
AND THE CABINET

In 1963, Emmet Hughes wrote that "there may have been no aspect of Eisenhower's Presidency misunderstood so widely" as his relationship with Congress. The caricature of Eisenhower was that of a President

> too lazy to lead. . . . He lacked both the interest and the ingenuity to work with Congressional leaders. Or, He really was intimidated by the arch-conservatives with the loudest voices in his party. Or, He was a helpless amateur ringed by professionals far more tough and determined. Or, He simply was slack of spirit and tired in body.[1]

"All such images," wrote Hughes, "were oddly, but profoundly, false. Far from reflecting either acquiescence or abdication, the conduct of Eisenhower's Congressional relations bespoke a most deliberate intent."[2]

Although Eisenhower relied heavily on the Cabinet and on his White House legislative liaison staff to foster a good working relationship with the members of Congress, his personal involvement in legislative affairs was extensive and profound. Throughout his Presidency he made skillful use of Cabinet meetings, legislative leaders' meetings, and private diplomacy to inform, persuade, and mobilize support for his legislative program.

From the very start, Eisenhower pursued good relations with the legislature. During his first weeks in office, he invited every member of Congress—more than 500 in all—to a series of luncheons at the White House. Wisely, biographer Peter Lyon suggests, Eisenhower's courtship with Congress was bipartisan in nature. He would have to call on the Democrats no less than fifty-eight times to support the administration, "their votes providing the margin of victory when Republican defections or absences imperiled" the chances of success.[3]

In the early months of his administration, Eisenhower discussed his philosophy of leadership at length in his correspondence with friends. A letter to William Phillips is particularly revealing of that philosophy. "Clearly," the President wrote,

> there are different ways to try to be a leader. In my view, a fair, decent, and reasonable dealing with men, a reasonable recognition that views may diverge, a constant seeking for a high and strong ground on which to work together, is the best way to lead our country in the difficult times ahead of us. A living democracy needs diversity to keep it strong. For survival, it also needs to have the diversities brought together in a common purpose, so fair, so reasonable, and so appealing that all can rally to it.
>
> I deplore and deprecate the table-pounding, name-calling methods that columnists so much love. This is not because of any failure to love a good fight; it merely represents my belief that such methods are normally futile. Speaking from a more distinctly personal point of view, the present situation is, I think, without recent precedent in that the particular legislators who are most often opposing Administration views are of the *majority* party. People like to think of Mr. Roosevelt as a leader; in the situation where his own party was delighted to hear a daily excoriation of the opposite political party, his methods were adequate to his time and to the situation. As of today, every measure that we deem essential to the progress and welfare of America normally requires Democratic support in varying degrees. I think it is fair to say that, in this situation, only a leadership that is based on honesty of purpose, calmness and inexhaustible patience in conference and persuasion, and refusal to be diverted from basic principles, can, in the long run, win out. . . . I simply must be permitted to follow my own methods, because to adopt someone else's would be so unnatural as to create the conviction that I was acting falsely.[4]

Eisenhower understood legislative politics far better than surface appearances would suggest—so well, in fact, that he was not beyond issuing instructions to his subordinates—even mild reprimands to members of the Cabinet—when relations with Congress seemed strained. Such was the case in a letter that Eisenhower drafted to his Secretary of Agriculture, Ezra Taft Benson, in 1958. The text of Eisenhower's letter demonstrates his political astuteness, not just in stating his desire to avoid extremes in his legislative program but also in his suggestion that Benson develop a more flexible approach in dealing with congressional leaders. As Eisenhower put it:

> In your efforts to improve Federal programs affecting agriculture I have always supported you enthusiastically; I shall continue to do so. But in

what follows I shall attempt to give you some of my thinking about the legislative procedures through which we hope to secure an improvement in those and other necessary laws. I think my text could well be the old German aphorism, "Never lose the good in seeking too long for the best," or as some say it, "The best is always the enemy of the good."

I was impressed by the apparent attitude of some of the leaders at the [legislative leadership] meeting Tuesday. They, while announcing their continuing approval of the flexible price support system, believe that *we*, the members of the Administration, are now guilty of *inflexibility.*[5]

In his next paragraph, Eisenhower was careful to note that Republicans in Congress were divided over several issues, not just the Farm Program. Eisenhower finished setting the stage for his reprimand of Benson by noting "that never in any one year have we gotten exactly what we wanted." Then, diplomatically but forcefully, Eisenhower made his point:

All I want to say here is that I believe it is *not* good Congressional politics to fail to listen seriously to the recommendations of our own Congressional leaders. Charlie Halleck, Les Arends, Joe Martin and Bill Hill from the House, as well as Bill Knowland, Everett Dirksen and others from the Senate, will find it difficult to keep their cohorts solidly together in critical moments unless we are ready to make what they consider are some necessary concessions from time to time.[6]

Eisenhower undoubtedly had in mind Secretary Benson's reputation as a stubborn ideologue when he tailored the final paragraphs of his letter:

Sometimes in the workings of a democratic society, it is not sufficient merely to be completely right. We recall that Aristides lost the most important election of his life because the Athenian people were tired of hearing him called "The Just."

As of this moment, I can see no way in which you can logically take action that our best Congressional friends would consider as an amelioration of their legislative difficulties. But I do believe that in future planning we should avoid advanced positions of inflexibility. We must have some room for maneuver, or we shall suffer for it.[7]

Eisenhower's efforts to coach members of the Cabinet on their relations with Congress were not uncommon. At an early Cabinet meeting, the President urged all members to be silent in the face of hostile sniping from Congress. He was confident that everything would simmer down so long as "no rancors were tossed on the fire."[8]

Although Eisenhower practiced what he had preached to his Cabinet in public, his private views were far less restrained. His frustration over popular support for Senator John W. Bricker's proposed constitutional amendment to limit the treaty-making authority and his disdain for Senator Joseph McCarthy are sharply revealed in the President's personal diary entry for April 1, 1953.

Senator Bricker wants to amend the Constitution to limit the power of the President in making international agreements. Likewise, he wants to limit the position of an approved treaty as "the supreme law of the land." By and large I think the logic of the case is all against Senator Bricker, but he has gotten almost psychopathic on the subject, and a great many lawyers have taken his side of the case. This fact does not impress me very much. Lawyers are trained to take either side of any case and make the most intelligent and impassioned defense of their adopted viewpoint. This tends to create a practice of submerging conviction in favor of plausible argument. . . .

In any event, such lawyers as John W. Davis, General Mitchell, Foster Dulles, and Herbert Brownell are of the opinion that the effect of the amendment would be to damage the United States materially in its efforts to lead the world in support of the free way of life. These are not only able lawyers; they are also experienced in government. This is important.

Senator McCarthy is, of course, so anxious for the headlines that he is prepared to go to any extremes in order to secure some mention of his name in the public press. His actions create trouble on the Hill with members of the party; they irritate, frustrate, and infuriate members of the Executive Department. I really believe that nothing will be so effective in combatting his particular kind of troublemaking as to ignore him. This he cannot stand.[9]

Despite his private misgivings about some members of Congress, Eisenhower continually sought to promote a leadership based on moderation and cooperation. Emmet Hughes tells us of an incident, early in Eisenhower's first term, in which the President lectured a member of the White House staff about the problem of recalcitrant members of Congress. "Now look," Eisenhower said,

I happen to know a little about leadership. I've had to work with a lot of nations, for that matter, at odds with each other. And I tell you this: you do not lead by hitting people over the head. Any damn fool can do that, but it's usually called "assault"—not "leadership." . . . I'll tell you what leadership is. It's *persuasion*—and *conciliation*—and *education*—and patience. It's long, slow, tough work. That's the only kind of leadership I know—or believe in—or will practice.[10]

At times, Eisenhower was conciliatory to a fault in his dealings with Congress. The President spent months trying to avoid what he glumly called "a head-on collision over the Bricker Amendment."[11] At one point he privately proposed the establishment of a study group called the "Bricker Commission" in the hope that "all Bricker wants is something big in public with his name on it."[12] Frustrated by his unsuccessful efforts to placate Bricker without sacrificing either the President's constitutional prerogatives or the constitutional sanctity of treaties, Eisenhower exclaimed at his Cabinet meeting of April 3, 1953:

> I'm so sick of this I could scream. The whole damn thing is senseless and plain damaging to the prestige of the United States. We talk about the French not being able to govern themselves—and we sit here wrestling with a Bricker Amendment.[13]

Yet, as Emmet Hughes suggests, Eisenhower's impulse to conciliate could not be suppressed. The fact that sixty-two Senators had cosponsored the Bricker Amendment did not make matters easier for the President. Despite grave reservations, Eisenhower gave the appearance of being willing to search for compromise wording that would dilute the amendment. But Eisenhower's impulse to conciliate did not, in this case, produce satisfactory results. His personal efforts to work out a compromise over the wording of the amendment created a public impression of ambiguity regarding Eisenhower's stand, whereas privately there was no doubt of his opposition to the amendment.

Secretary of State Dulles brought the issue to a head at the Cabinet meeting of July 17, 1953, when he said point-blank: "We just have to make up our minds and stop being fuzzy about this."[14] Eisenhower responded, "I haven't been fuzzy about this. There is nothing fuzzy in what I told Bricker. I said we'd go just so far and no further." Dulles retorted: "I know sir, but you haven't told anybody else."

In time, Eisenhower would begin to doubt the wisdom of his earlier flexibility. Hence, on January 25, 1954, the President addressed Congress in unmistakable terms. In a letter to Senate Majority Leader William Knowland, the President wrote that he was "unalterably opposed to the Bricker Amendment."[15] His rationale was forcefully stated:

> Adoption of the amendment in its present form by the Senate would be notice to our friends as well as our enemies abroad that our country intends to withdraw from its leadership in world affairs. The inevitable reaction would be of major proportion. It would impair our hopes and plans for peace and for the successful achievement of the important international matters now under discussion.[16]

Before the final vote, Eisenhower put his legislative liaison staff to work contacting every last Senator, thereby making clear the fact that the administration was opposed not only to the Bricker Amendment but to any substitute amendments as well. Ultimately, the Bricker Amendment and its substitutes were defeated in the Senate, but only by the narrowest of margins. Yet, although Eisenhower's philosophy of conciliation may not have served him well in the Bricker case, it certainly benefited him greatly on many other issues of the day. The greatest dividends of this approach may well have come in the arena of inter-national affairs. Eisenhower the war-time commander was now in a position as a civilian leader to wage peace.

Frequently, Eisenhower used his Cabinet and legislative leadership meetings to allay anxieties in the supercharged atmosphere of Cold War relations between the United States and the Soviet Union. At the height of tensions over Berlin in 1959, for example, Eisenhower briefed members of his Cabinet on his view of the problem. The Cabinet minutes reveal that the President began his discussion

> by reminding the Cabinet that Berlin is merely an incident in a continuing series and that the adequacy of our defenses should not be measured in terms of the existence of the Berlin problem. . . .
>
> The President stated that in this particular instance there was unusual difficulty, that the Russians had the advantage of pressing the issue by doing nothing instead of engaging in some overt action; hence the United States had to be very careful to avoid doing anything that could be regarded as aggression.[17]

In a similar briefing with members of Congress, Eisenhower reiterated his belief that the United States should not overreact to current tensions. Bryce Harlow, the President's assistant for congressional liaison, provides us with an insightful account of the President's remarks in his mem-orandum for the record of the meeting on March 10:

> The President stressed that we should not now go to any sort of extreme military action, such as partial mobilization. He said that we do not want to, and should not, look upon this situation as "a Berlin crisis"; instead, he said, we can anticipate two or three decades of tension, with the Soviets attempting to get us off balance and so upset that we will act unwisely. In order to keep our allies together, . . . we must hew to a positive position and follow it through no matter whether the strain at any particular moment happens to be acute in Berlin or elsewhere in the world.[18]

Later in the meeting, the record shows:

[Congressman John] McCormack said that the Democrats agree with the President's firm stand on Berlin but do not believe that America is strong enough militarily. The Congressman said, however, that the President is in far better shape on this issue than Macmillan is in Britain; here the opposition wants to increase our strength, whereas in Britain Communist and Labor Party spokesmen are on the side of weakness.

The President commented that the easiest thing in the world is to confuse strength with bad deportment. He said we must conduct ourselves so that the world can believe we are conciliatory—that we must always emphasize strength and yet always hold out the hand of friendship if only the Soviets will receive it. Otherwise the world is liable to run away from us in this situation, with the result that we would become fortress America.[19]

The Berlin crisis showed Eisenhower at his best—as "a master diplomat, statesman, and politician. . . . His most basic strategy was to simply deny that there was a crisis. His most basic tool was patience."[20] Eisenhower's leadership was characterized by his willingness to be conciliatory and his steadfastness in mollifying congressional leaders in the face of demands for more action.[21] "More than any other individual," writes historian Stephen Ambrose, "the man who held the Berlin crisis in check was Dwight Eisenhower."[22]

EISENHOWER'S LEADERSHIP: THE CASE OF MUTUAL SECURITY

Eisenhower's support of the Mutual Security Program provides one of the best examples of Eisenhower's leadership, precisely because it was an area in which the President's personal convictions were strong.[23] As historian Herbert Parmet notes, gaining support for even a modest Mutual Security Program meant challenging head-on the cherished beliefs and predispositions of Congressmen and key constituent groups.

His administration's initial burden was to convince skeptical conservatives that money and supplies shipped overseas could not only enhance the economies of non-Communist nations but would have significant long-term benefits to the United States. . . .

The issue illustrated Eisenhower's dilemma as party leader. Conservative GOP Congressmen, especially from the Midwest and the Far West, plus their Democratic allies from Dixie, were bent on economizing with little regard for the President's desires. Some businessmen worried that the money would be used to socialize foreign economies.[24]

Eisenhower recognized that efforts to build support for the Mutual Security Program had to begin at the grass-roots level, where opposition was strongest. White House files for the year 1958 indicate that the President's extensive lobbying efforts on behalf of the Mutual Security Program began with the very group that had expressed the most vocal opposition—the business community.

On January 27, 1958, Eisenhower gave a luncheon in the State Dining Room of the White House for businessmen invited from all parts of the nation. After speeches by economic advisors Eric Johnston and Clarence Randall, as well as the Vice President, Eisenhower addressed the group. In a memorandum for the record, presidential aide Bryce Harlow recorded the President's remarks:

> He said that he had asked, as President, some businessmen to help in such programs as this and had found in them exactly the same instinctive reaction against foreign assistance as the uninformed had. Then, however, he mentioned George Humphrey, saying that when Humphrey first entered the Cabinet he was strongly opposed to foreign assistance but, being a man who saw a great virtue in facts, soon conceded, after learning the facts, that these programs had to be done. . . .
>
> He said that when Eric Johnston told of the Senator who knows these programs are needed but opposes them for political reasons, he almost wanted to put his napkin over his face. He said he couldn't understand how any man of responsibility could do such a thing—but if this is the situation in America, then we must build a public sentiment that will assure backing for such people to support the program. This, he said, should be the responsibility of all businessmen and every American. He said we cannot have prosperity without security and that we must have friends abroad with whom to trade. He said he could not overemphasize his feeling of deep conviction on this matter and while he thought no one at the table needed convincing, yet he thought they should get their friends to proselyte their friends and bring about in the country a renaissance of conviction and determination to carry through these programs.[25]

In the weeks and months that followed, Eisenhower held breakfasts, luncheons, and White House evening sessions to meet with both Democrats and Republicans, appealing to their patriotism and sense of duty.[26] In his meetings with congressional leaders, Eisenhower pleaded and persuaded, but never threatened or ordered. "Always he was the advisor," writes Herbert Parmet, "not the boss."[27]

Eisenhower's letter to Senate Majority Leader Lyndon Johnson on August 1, 1958, reflected the President's appreciation of the virtues of political persuasion over methods of command.

I am deeply sensitive to the fact that the Congress is a coordinate branch of the government and can and must work its own will in regard to this matter; but I would be remiss in my duty should I fail to point out the utter gravity of this situation as it appears to me.[28]

In reviewing the impact of Eisenhower's constant lobbying of Congress to forge support for the Mutual Security Program, Emmet Hughes perceptively commented:

An Everett Dirksen, unflattered and uncourted, would never have committed the political act of tearing up years of speeches in opposition—to lead the fight for Mutual Security legislation. And there were quite a few Republican Congressmen who occasionally marveled a little at their own audacity in rebelling against their own voting records. Any one of them might have made the humorful phone call that came to the White House, from a Midwesterner in their group, one early summer afternoon: "Hello, put me through to Persons. This is internationalist [George] Allen speaking—*brand new* internationalist. . . . I just voted for Mutual Security for the first time in my life."[29]

Eisenhower's extensive efforts in 1958 helped ensure funding for the Mutual Security Program, but not at the level that the administration had hoped for. Funds were cut by some $1 billion, nearly one-fourth of the total requested. Much of the opposition to the program continued to come from within the President's own party. Plainly and simply, the Mutual Security Program—or the "foreign aid giveaway program," as it was called by some—was not popular with the folks back home in the districts.

Yet Eisenhower was not completely dismayed with the cuts in his budget. Instead, he was even more intent on redoubling his efforts for the following year's budget. Hence, in 1959, and again in 1960, the administration set out to generate support for foreign aid legislation in Congress. In 1960, the administration had the advantage of drawing upon the resources of a private organization called the "Committee to Strengthen the Frontiers of Freedom." The committee, which was created at the initiative of the White House, consisted of prominent Republicans and Democrats who supported the President's Mutual Security Program. Among those called upon for assistance were James B. Conant, Leonard Firestone, John Gardner, Averell Harriman, Grayson Kirk, Henry Luce, Dean Rusk, William Vanderbilt, and Henry Wriston.[30]

In May 1960, Eisenhower activated the "very considerable letter-writing powers" of this group on behalf of the Mutual Security Program. The mobilization of this committee complemented the intense lobbying of the administration. Secretary of Defense Thomas Gates, for example, contacted 130 personal friends, mostly business leaders, and his efforts precipitated an estimated 1,200 letters in support of Mutual Security.[31] The Chamber of Commerce, the AFL-CIO, and major veterans' groups also assisted the administration. As a result of this massive lobbying effort, the Mutual Security appropriations cut was held to only 9 percent, the lowest in Eisenhower's eight years—this, despite the fact that Eisenhower had requested a billion dollars more than during the previous three years.[32]

Four years later, in June 1964, President Lyndon Johnson called on Eisenhower for help in enlisting Republican support for the Mutual Security appropriation. Eisenhower, according to Stephen Ambrose, was both amused and irritated.

> He called Michigan Congressman Jerry Ford on the telephone and said, "I can remember LBJ whimpering and crying that Senator George was defeated because of his support for Mutual Security and he was afraid he would be too when I asked his support."[33]

Nevertheless, Eisenhower was quick to oblige Johnson. He would not let die on the vine a program that he had struggled so hard to build.

EISENHOWER AND CABINET GOVERNMENT

In his classic study on the Cabinet, Richard Fenno perceptively noted that Presidents who employ a haphazard, nonhierarchical, or highly personalized method of delegation are less likely to accord Cabinet members special emphasis. If, on the other hand, a President delegates regularly through the chain of command, greater reliance on the Cabinet will likely be accorded. In Fenno's view, Franklin Roosevelt epitomized the haphazard approach to delegation.

> He sought always to preserve his discretionary "freedom of action." He accomplished this by delegating responsibility and authority in small, vague, and sometimes conflicting fragments, to a point where only he could contribute consistency and direction. "Nothing whatever counted in the entire administration," said Henry Wallace, "except what went on inside FDR's head." The result was an essentially unpatterned technique of administration. It resulted in fuzzy lines of responsibility, no clear chain of command, overlapping jurisdictions, a great deal of personal squabbling, and a lack of precision and regularity. It was, in short a "fantastically complex administrative mechanism," so labelled by Henry Stimson who protested vigorously over its sometime sterilizing effect on Cabinet officers.[34]

Eisenhower's approach to leadership was strikingly different from Roosevelt's. In his utilization of the Cabinet, Eisenhower was eager, Fenno noted, to

> pass problems around for discussion among his advisors, listen carefully to their debates, and use them as a sounding board for his own ideas. He is apt, in other words, to do his thinking in the presence of others, in a group meeting. Most important of all, he frequently if not usually makes his final decision on the spot. When he wants to act, he wants to make certain that his decision is clear, understood by all and concurred in by all, conditions which are best secured in a meeting rather than afterward.[35]

Eisenhower used Cabinet meetings as an opportunity to voice his views regarding what he wanted accomplished in order to rally the departments together behind him. His aim, in the view of one participant, was to minimize the centrifugal forces pulling the members of the Cabinet away from the President by fostering a concept of teamwork. As Bradley Patterson, assistant to the Cabinet secretary under Eisenhower, put it:

> Cabinet members are beset from every side by Congressional pressures, by the pressures of special constituencies, by the pressures of their bureaucracies, by the pressures of the press, by the pressures of foreign nations, heaven knows what other sources—all of these pressures tending to grind special axes and sort of turn their heads away from the President who put them in office, and to whom they're responsible. And it actually takes some special effort to remind them that they are the President's men. . . . The President needs to take all the occasions he can to remind them of what his views are. So the Cabinet meeting is the time when he does that.[36]

Eisenhower was particularly effective in using the Cabinet as a forum for bringing the departments into line with his expectations regarding the federal budget. Of special importance to the President were the annual budget forecast meetings held in June. The President used these meetings to bring projected budget requests into line with the forecast for the economy and projected revenues. He also used them to inform Cabinet members of the areas he regarded as priorities. After hearing Eisenhower's talks at these meetings, one participant concluded that "all the staffs and executive officers in the world can't substitute for that kind of lecture."[37]

Eisenhower believed that frequent meetings of the Cabinet offered many advantages, not the least of which was to provide presidential direction in policy development and administration. Consequently, the Cabinet met a total of 227 times during Eisenhower's Presidency. The President presided over 205 of these meetings, with Vice President Nixon chairing the rest.[38]

In an oral history interview with Columbia University, Eisenhower had this to say about his use of the Cabinet:

> One of the big purposes that I wanted to achieve was to make sure that everybody was informed on the workings of the administration, so that no matter whether you were before Congress, making a speech, or anywhere, we would not be working at opposite ends of the spectrum.[39]

To ensure effective coordination and to invigorate the Cabinet as an advisory body, Eisenhower enthusiastically supported the creation of the first Cabinet secretariat in American history. On October 19, 1954, Eisenhower appointed Maxwell Rabb, a Harvard-trained lawyer who had served as an administrative aide for Senators Henry Cabot Lodge and Sinclair Weeks, to serve as secretary of the Cabinet. Rabb was assisted in his work by Bradley Patterson, Jr., a career civil servant.

In setting up the Cabinet secretariat, the White House borrowed heavily from the executive secretariat developed in the State Department by General George Marshall in 1946 and 1947. Bradley Patterson, who had served as a member of the State Department secretariat prior to his appointment as assistant to the Cabinet secretary, notes that there were clear parallels between the two organizations.

> I think State's experience which set the groundwork stemmed largely from the modesty of that secretariat: the fact that it did not in any way try to second-guess in a policy sense the line officers. In other words, they created and maintained a reputation of career professionalism, anonymous professionalism. We in no way tried to get out and interpose ourselves between the line officers of State and Mr. Marshall and Mr. Acheson. So through the experience in the State Department we proved that you could have a secretariat which was modest and behind the scenes, professional, quiet and anonymous. If we had not been able to do that, I think the White House, even in the Eisenhower time, would not have been so receptive [to a Cabinet secretariat].[40]

Under Rabb's leadership, the Cabinet secretariat prepared the agenda for Cabinet meetings and screened formal presentations to the Cabinet. After thorough study and preparation, the Cabinet secretariat distributed information papers and drafts of Cabinet papers to members of the Cabinet and their assistants. Each Cabinet member was expected to study these papers in advance of the Cabinet meeting and to come to the meeting ready to advise the President. The secretariat also maintained records of Cabinet actions and minutes of meetings. A post-meeting statement was prepared, given to the President for his approval, and then circulated to the departments so as to give members of the Cabinet a clear idea of what was expected of their departments in implementing policy.

The Cabinet secretariat was an important catalyst in the development and presentation of agenda items for the Cabinet. During a fourteen-month period from December 5, 1958, to February 26, 1960, a total of 36 Cabinet meetings took place at which 119 matters were placed before the Cabinet. Of these 119 items, 69 were initiated by the Cabinet secretariat, 15 were proposed by the President, 16 came from Executive Office agencies, 14 originated with the departments, 4 originated with the White House staff, and 1 came from the Vice President.[41] Bradley Patterson characterized the agenda-setting function of the Cabinet secretariat under Eisenhower in the following way:

> Now this put us . . . in a position of being like a radar set, looking around the whole spectrum of the executive branch and picking up in a sensitive way indications of things that were happening and that were coming toward the President's desk for decision. Or if they weren't coming there, things that ought to be, so that people wouldn't duck them or try to do it unilaterally.[42]

One method of carrying out the agenda-setting task was to attend all Cabinet committee meetings regularly. Eisenhower had appointed several Cabinet committees on such topics as energy resources, water resources, communications, and other policy areas to study problems in depth. The Cabinet secretary or his assistant attended each of these meetings to make sure that when reports were ready for consideration by the President they would come before the Cabinet and not become bottled up in committee.

Another source for agenda-setting within the Cabinet came from close monitoring of newspapers. When a story in a major newspaper mentioned a conflict developing between departments over an issue, a Cabinet agenda item was prepared. Getting controversial items on the Cabinet agenda was not, however, an easy task. The Cabinet secretary, according to Patterson,

> had to dig, wheedle, persuade and finesse Cabinet members to bring to the common table what were clearly common matters, but which the department heads, in their century-and-a-half-long tradition, would much prefer to bring privately to the Oval Office. It was only because they

knew that Eisenhower wanted it this way and no other that they reluctantly acceded to the Cabinet secretary's or Sherman Adams' agenda-planning.[43]

The Cabinet secretariat played a valuable role at the implementation stage as well. Typically, formal meetings of the Cabinet were followed by a meeting with the Cabinet secretary and the assistant secretaries of the departments to ensure that they were aware of the decisions that had been made and of the background to those decisions. Whenever possible, the individuals who had made presentations to the Cabinet were asked to give the same presentations to the assistant secretaries.

The implementation stage was further enhanced by the detailed follow-up of the Cabinet secretariat. Every three months or so, the Cabinet secretary prepared a Cabinet Action Status Report to summarize the various assignments given to the departments in the form of weekly Record of Action statements. The Cabinet Action Status Reports were used to report on the degree to which policy implementation had succeeded. Members of the Cabinet and their assistants knew that eventually they would be held accountable for their actions through these reports.

The Cabinet secretariat was instrumental in sparking departmental development of programs worthy of Cabinet-level debate. One such idea, which had its genesis in a newspaper feature article that caught the attention of the Cabinet secretary, was the development of a long-term program to refurbish the National Park system. At the suggestion of the Cabinet secretary, Interior Secretary Douglas McKay drafted and later presented a proposal for a comprehensive Parks program entitled "Mission 66."

At the Cabinet meeting of January 27, 1956, Secretary McKay and the Director of the Park Service used charts, color slides, and a short film to outline the inadequacies of the current Parks system relative to the projected needs of the 1960s. The proposed remedies called for an increase of about 25 percent in Park expenditures to improve the overcrowded facilities in the National Parks. After debate in the Cabinet over the costs of the program, Eisenhower agreed to forward a letter to Congress underscoring the need for action to rectify the inadequacies of the Parks program. The support generated from the Cabinet presentation resulted in a substantial upward revision of the 1957 appropriations for the National Park service.

Under Eisenhower's leadership, the Cabinet served as an important medium of information exchange.[44] Through briefings, formal presentations, and the President's own remarks, the heads of the departments were kept abreast of important developments at home and abroad. Cabinet meetings were particularly important in allowing the President to convey his decisions and the philosophical reasoning behind them. As Bradley Patterson notes, "Cabinet remarks by the Chief Executive carry a strength and an indelibility which the seniormost White House official cannot duplicate."[45] Cabinet meetings thus held a crucial place in Eisenhower's approach to governance. As Emmet Hughes writes:

> They fixed the occasions for exchange of facts and views between a President and department heads who, in the majority, had little other opportunity to see and to hear him. Again and again, the President would seize on some particular matter of legislation or administration as spark for a warm homily on his most personal views—the world need for freer trade, or the practical necessity (and "cheapness") of programs of mutual security, or the need to temper austere "businesslike" administration with signs of serious concern for "the little fellow," or the "unthinkable" dimensions of nuclear warfare. For almost all the persons present, these fervent sermons carried an authority almost scriptural. And they tempered, if they did not alter, some of the Cabinet's own generally more conventional predispositions.
>
> Moreover, . . . they took on added force because of the repeatedly proven range and specificity of the President's knowledge of the matters confronting the various departments. Practically and detailedly, he would comment on technical procurement problems in Defense or aberrations of the parity laws in Agriculture, the economic impact on New York Harbor of the projected St. Lawrence Seaway or the economic plight of Massachusetts' textile industry, the collapse of zinc prices or the worthlessness of Bolivian tin—and on from there to the warmth of his friendship for Harold Macmillan or his tolerance of the idiosyncracies of Charles De Gaulle. To a Charles Wilson or a George Humphrey, not to mention an Arthur Summerfield or a Douglas McKay, such a range of acquaintanceship with things and with people seemed no less than dazzling.[46]

In addition to its role as a medium of information exchange, Eisenhower's Cabinet served as an important sounding board in the formulation of policy. Eisenhower encouraged broad, statesmanlike debate on the important policy questions of the day. Attorney General Herbert Brownell, in discussing the Cabinet, said:

> I didn't make a point of speaking up in the Cabinet meetings about the problems of other departments. . . . But that was not his way of doing things. He appreciated comments that were made on all subjects that came up. I think that's one reason he liked Foster Dulles and George Humphrey. . . . They freely commented on other departments' operations. . . . The Cabinet meetings created a sense of unity in Washington that was almost unprecedented. We felt a loyalty to our colleagues as well as to him.[47]

The vitality of the Cabinet as a forum for debate and decision-making is well illustrated in the minutes to the Cabinet meeting of January 16, 1959.[48] The central agenda item for the Cabinet that day was the question of whether the administration should send before Congress a proposal for a modest program of federal aid to the states for the construction of classroom buildings. Eisenhower's philosophical opposition to the concept of federal aid to education was well known to members of the Cabinet, but it did not inhibit several of those present from candidly stating their belief that some form of an aid to education package was necessary. A verbatim transcript of the meeting on January 16 shows that a lively exchange unfolded among the participants. The President introduced the proposal to the Cabinet, saying:

> Arthur Flemming is considering a bill to service the debt on school construction. . . . I personally believe there has been a trend toward federal dependency and we cannot get away from it. But we must consider what the United States wants and what a few of us still believe. It is a hard decision. I am not thinking, today, about the amount of money, but about the principle of the thing. It still shocks me. . . .
>
> Now, having put you in that much of a halter, and having put that much of a noose around your neck, go ahead, Arthur.

Health, Education, and Welfare Secretary Arthur Flemming then proceeded to propose a modest program authorizing poor school districts to finance the building of classrooms with federal assistance in the form of guaranteed bonds. At the end of Flemming's presentation, the President commented:

> You are saying: if a school district in the United States is incapable of buying all the facilities that that particular district needs, then it becomes the federal government's responsibility; we are going to do this forever.

In the ensuing lengthy discussion, a number of significant points were made. Acting Commerce Secretary Lewis Strauss foresaw a technical difficulty for a local school board to commit itself and its successors over a long period. Treasury Secretary Robert Anderson thought it desirable to maintain the provision (originated by Treasury) for possible repayments by the localities after retirement of the bonds—"especially since the Federal Government already has difficulty marketing securities reasonably and would be encouraging competition in the securities market through this proposal." Agriculture Secretary Ezra Taft Benson feared "there would be no end to such a program," and that it would "jeopardize our fiscal integrity." Benson asserted that "there really are not any poor States any more," and that "the majority of Americans don't really want the Federal Government getting into school construction."

Vice President Nixon then offered an incisive appraisal of the political ramifications of the aid to education proposal.

> All of us have a view as to whether there is a need; I happen to think there is a need in terms of classrooms and that likely there is not going to be a solution without some kind of program. . . .
>
> The ultimate majority of people will say "There is a need." Nothing hits people more directly than their kids in school. We cannot win on this issue by saying "There is no need" or that "The need will soon be met by closing the gap." . . .
>
> We can say: "There is a need and a program should be adopted, but we cannot afford it." This will be indefensible. . . .
>
> From the standpoint of the country, people feel that government should get into this kind of program—and of course people do not distinguish between State and Federal government.
>
> We cannot oppose it on grounds of budget. . . .
>
> We can say that "the States should do it" until we are blue in the face, but from a practical standpoint, we cannot expect states to do all they should do.

Moments later, Ambassador Lodge spoke on behalf of the program. "At the moment the Federal income tax started we prevented the States from getting their hands effectively on this great source of tax money—and at that moment we took on responsibility for this kind of program."

Secretary Benson responded: "The whole thing is a matter of human judgment; it is hard to say that the Federal government can afford this and that the States cannot—with the debt which the Federal government has."

Perhaps the most interesting exchange of the debate then took place between Labor Secretary Mitchell and the President. The transcript records the debate as follows:

> *Secretary Mitchell:* When you talk of need and of the present capability—and I am talking about the need of children for education—we must project that need into the 1960s and 70s. Even if the ratio of school construction continued at the high rate [it is] now, your elementary and secondary school capacity is going to be very short of the school population of the 60s. The gap today, if closed, will be opened again then.
>
> *The President:* Yes—the argument is that we have fallen behind because of the two wars. Many people say that if the States and localities caught

up, they could keep up. But I agree with Neil McElroy—a federal program would dilute State incentive.

Secretary Mitchell: There is another point I want to make: I feel, as Arthur Flemming does, that the Administration would be in a bad position not to have some program. We are dealing with a national resource—our human resources—one of our most important resources, and therefore I do not think we can take the position that the States will have to do this job. Children are a national resource and thus of concern to the Federal government.

The President: Then you are arguing that the Federal government should take over this function—that is clear as a bell.

Secretary Mitchell: No, I am not. The States have an obligation; the States should do this if they can. . . .

The President: Stop right there.

Secretary Mitchell: If the States cannot do it, the Federal government must not close its eyes to this.

Later in the debate, discussion focused on the political logistics of the proposed program. The Postmaster General inquired: "Has our leadership on the Hill been pressing for this?" The President responded: "They are against it." The President then asked how Senator Dirksen stood on the issue. Wilton Persons said: "He is on the fence." The Vice President added that "the leadership will probably be against it, but I do not think this should be controlling." Secretary Flemming agreed, saying: "We have many Republicans who are for it."

Near the end of the debate, the President commented: "I have listened to these arguments on this for several days—in fact I am getting almost weary." Then, in recognition of the persuasiveness of the arguments of Flemming, Nixon, Mitchell, and others, Eisenhower told his Cabinet: "We are going to put up some kind of program." After making his decision to support Flemming's initiative, Eisenhower commented: "We have had a good growl."

The aid to education debate captures the Cabinet at its best—as a forum for a lively and far-reaching exchange of ideas and information. As the debate developed, Eisenhower's questions remained tough, and his outlook seemed skeptical with regard to Federal intervention in an area that he viewed as a province of the states. But by debate's end, the President had been convinced to go forward with a program of aid to the states. As on many issues of the day, Eisenhower demonstrated that he was not inflexible when practical political reasoning challenged his philosophical beliefs.

One of the most impressive aspects of Eisenhower's legacy in the realm of domestic policy rests with his commitment to utilize members of the Cabinet as partners in the development and implementation of policy initiatives. Although the White House staff played an important role in coordinating policy initiatives and facilitating communications with Congress and the executive departments, the staff did not take on a policy-making role. Rather, policy development remained a joint enterprise among the President, the Cabinet, and Congress.

Eisenhower provided energetic and forceful leadership in rallying the departments in pursuit of his most cherished political goals, such as balancing the budget and sustaining the vitality of the mutual security program. But the President also listened carefully to his Cabinet in developing new policies, as with the aid to education program of 1959 and the renovation of the National Park system under the Mission 66 program.

Domestic policy-making has taken on a dramatically different tone throughout much of the post-Eisenhower era. Increasingly, Presidents have allowed expanding White House staffs to take on actual authority in the development and even the operationalization of policy. Correspondingly, the Cabinet as an advisory and administrative body has declined in importance at a time when Presidents, more than ever before, need the expertise and support of the career bureaucracy to carry out their policies. The ensuing discussion will outline the development of this problematic state of affairs in the post-Eisenhower period.

WHITE HOUSE CENTRALIZATION OF POLICY-MAKING: THE DEMISE OF CABINET GOVERNMENT IN THE POST-EISENHOWER ERA

Despite the many benefits that resulted from the President's close consultation with the Cabinet during the Eisenhower years, the role of the Cabinet fell into disfavor during the Presidencies of John F. Kennedy and Lyndon Johnson. From the start, Kennedy relegated the role of the Cabinet to one of secondary importance in his administration. As Kennedy aide Theodore Sorensen suggests:

> No decisions of importance were made at Kennedy's Cabinet meetings and few subjects of importance, particularly in foreign affairs, were ever seriously discussed. . . . There were no high-level debates, or elaborate presentations, or materials circulated in advance.[49]

Throughout the Kennedy and Johnson years, there developed a discernible trend toward greater White House control over policy-making to the exclusion of the Cabinet. Richard Tanner Johnson, in his comparative study of presidential management styles, provides an illuminating portrait of policy processes during this period:

> The always delicate distinction between staff or advisory roles of the White House and operational administrative line responsibilities in the Cabinet departments became overly blurred during the Kennedy and Johnson years. Too many staff tried to do more than they were supposed to be doing and gradually came "to give orders" rather than transmit requests. . . . One danger of this approach, in the words of one top Johnson aide, was that "after awhile he [the President] never even bothered to sit down with most of the Cabinet members even to discuss their major problems and program possibilities. Johnson wound up using some of his staff as both line managers as well as staff and, I think in retrospect, it frequently didn't work out!"[50]

Both Kennedy and Johnson turned increasingly to ad hoc task forces as a "second track" for executive branch policy formulation outside established departmental channels. "In the process," writes Lester Salamon,

> little attention was paid to problems of implementation, to overlap with other programs, to legitimate technical problems, or to the capacity of the operating agencies to understand what was intended and to carry it out.[51]

Richard Nixon sought briefly to restore the Cabinet to the preeminence that it had enjoyed during the Eisenhower years. But as Richard Nathan notes in *The Plot that Failed*, Nixon's strong-willed Cabinet secretaries frequently found themselves at odds with members of an activist-oriented White House staff over the formulation and implementation of domestic policy.[52] Although Nixon had vowed at the onset of his administration that he would not allow the White House staff to run domestic affairs, the trend by the end of his first term was clearly moving in that direction. The Cabinet met less often, whereas the White House staff was called upon more. The Cabinet agenda itself was frequently controlled by the White House staff—a practice that Eisenhower delegated primarily to the Cabinet secretariat.

An important factor influencing the shift in policy-making authority to the White House involved the creation in 1970 of a Domestic Council along the lines of Henry Kissinger's White House–centered National Security Council apparatus. John Ehrlichman, as head of the Domestic Council, developed a "working group" system to centralize policy development in the White House, thereby further diluting the authority of the Cabinet.

Both Housing and Urban Development Secretary George Romney and Interior Secretary Walter Hickel became outspoken in their criticism of the President for consolidating policy-making in the White House. Romney, for example, attacked the administration for drafting revenue sharing proposals secretly, with only the White House staff and personnel from the Office of Management and Budget participating. Similarly, Walter Hickel complained in the fall of 1970 that the President was "isolated—just sitting around listening to his staff."[53] Romney focused attention once again on the problem of limited access to the President when he announced his decision to resign from the Cabinet in August 1972.

By the end of his first term, Nixon appeared to be moving away from a Cabinet of nationally known figures in favor of members with unwavering loyalty. On the day after the 1972 presidential election, the President called on all political appointees to submit their resignations with the understanding that many would be accepted. The trend away from "Cabinet government" in favor of a White House–centered policy-making system became more pronounced over time. With the proliferation of White House staff and the tremendous expansion of White House responsibilities, "it was often impossible," writes Nathan, "to find out who was handling a particular matter, much less to decide which one of several crosscutting decision systems in the White House should be assigned any given issue."[54]

When Gerald Ford took office in August 1974, the administrative innovations of the Eisenhower years found a more receptive audience. Ford became the first President of the post-Eisenhower era to "restore a sense of purpose to the Cabinet as a deliberative, meaningful advisory and administrative body."[55] In his comprehensive study of White House organization under Ford, R. Gordon Hoxie suggests that the President's success in utilizing the Cabinet rested in large part on his willingness to emulate the practice of the Eisenhower years.

> Ford restored the Cabinet secretariat, which Eisenhower had created and Kennedy had eliminated. Ford's conception, like Eisenhower's, was not only to prepare for Cabinet meetings but also to have a follow-up to insure Cabinet decisions were acted upon. Ford made his Cabinet meetings meaningful. By contrast with his predecessor and his successor, there were no basic conflicts between the senior staff and the Cabinet.[56]

Ford's emulation of the Eisenhower system was short-lived, however. Jimmy Carter was quick to revive the practice, which had become so pronounced during the Nixon years, of placing great reliance on White House staff activists in both the domestic and the foreign policy arenas.

Dom Bonafede, White House correspondent for the *National Journal*, observed in April 1978 that Carter's Cabinet secretaries "are keenly aware that all domestic policy issues are filtered through [Stuart] Eizenstat and all foreign policy issues through [Zbigniew] Brzezinski. Inevitably, personality clashes arise."[57]

By the spring of 1978, relations between Cabinet members and the White House staff had become severely strained. Policy disagreements were now more visible and more divisive. Health, Education, and Welfare Secretary Joseph Califano openly opposed the President's proposal for a new Department of Education. Secretary of the Treasury Michael Blumenthal said there would be no tax reforms at the very time that the White House staff was putting together a reform package. The Secretary of Housing and Urban Development was drawing up plans for programs that went beyond the President's budget.[58]

One year later, in July 1979, the President attempted to resolve the tensions between his Cabinet and the White House staff by demanding, as Nixon had done seven years earlier, the resignations of his entire Cabinet. In all, five of the resignations were accepted. Transportation Secretary Brock Adams, who was not among those initially targeted for removal, was asked to leave after he expressed misgivings in public about the responsiveness of the White House staff to Congress and the American people.[59]

Many of Carter's department heads were as surprised as the press and the public by the President's sudden purge of the Cabinet. As political scientist Betty Glad notes:

> Blumenthal told the press that the President cited "incompatibility with my staff" as the only reason for his firing. . . . Califano, often praised by Carter for his performance at HEW, told reporters that Carter thought the very drive and independence that had made him the best HEW head ever had also brought him into collision with the White House. Brock Adams was perhaps the most vocal of those fired. A few weeks after he left the Cabinet he said: "I think one of the problems is . . . there's a difference between campaigning and governing. Governing takes a different kind of person. You can't govern [by] being against government."[60]

Carter's reliance on a loosely structured staff system, as well as his failure to place explicit limits on the role of the White House staff, undoubtedly contributed to the President's abandonment of his earlier commitment to Cabinet government. Rather than strengthen the hand of his Cabinet, Carter turned increasingly to his White House staff for policy-making and operations.

As White House responsibilities grew, so did the size of the White House staff. Carter requested and received congressional authorization to increase the number of senior White House aides from 55 to 100. In contrast, Eisenhower had only 33 principal aides on his White House staff in November 1960. Similarly, Eisenhower's NSC staff functioned quite effectively with a modest staff of 28, of whom only 11 were considered to be professional assistants. The corresponding figures for the Carter years were 98 and 35, respectively. Although Carter's NSC staff was somewhat smaller than the Nixon era staff of nearly 120 (including 40 principal aides), the Carter staff was still more than three times the size of the Eisenhower organization.

Proponents of White House centralization argue that larger, more policy-oriented White House staffs are necessary to coordinate the complex problems that require executive attention. But White House initiatives do not implement themselves. Paradoxically, an executive branch that is given less and less opportunity to participate in the development of policy through interaction with members of Congress, Cabinet spokespersons, and representatives from the White House is called upon to carry out White House–centered policy initiatives more and more. Understandably, the morale and performance levels of career bureaucrats in the executive departments are not as high in periods of centralized White House control over operations as in periods of active departmental input.

More important, perhaps, White House centralization places inordinate demands on Presidents who are unwilling or unable to entrust their Cabinets with a substantial part of the burden of executive branch management. As Stephen Hess notes:

> The centralized Presidency largely depends on the leader's ability to keep lines open to those outside his immediate circle and to resist minutiae. If the President is suspicious of Cabinet members and relies too heavily on overworked assistants, he is apt to lose perspective and even his sense of reality.[61]

Some observers attribute the Watergate catastrophe of Richard Nixon to the centralization of power in the White House staff. George Reedy, Jr., former Press Secretary to Lyndon Johnson, commented as early as April 5, 1970, that Nixon had erred in "enlarging the White House staff. . . . Now you can take it as virtually certain," Reedy warned, that they will "envelop" the President.[62] Gordon Hoxie, in a retrospective assessment written several years later, suggested that the "very growth in size and authority of the Nixon personal staff . . . led to the Watergate tragedy."[63]

Eisenhower recognized far better than some of his successors that the size of a staff can ultimately defeat the purpose of good organization. He made it clear that he did not want White House staff fiefdoms growing all around him. It was also clear to all who served him that Eisenhower would not tolerate the development of a situation in which members of the White House staff sought to interpose themselves between the President and his department heads. Nor would Eisenhower countenance the practice, so common in modern administrations, of allowing members of the White House staff to sit at the Cabinet table during Cabinet meetings. In Eisenhower's time, the White House staff sat quietly against the wall, on the periphery of the Cabinet table—as well they should.[64] They spoke only when called upon by the President, and their comments were limited to those inquiries made by the President— nothing more.

Former Secretary of State Alexander Haig found the blurring of the line between staff and Cabinet officials disquieting in his early days in the Reagan administration. In his memoirs, Haig describes the seating arrangements at the first meetings of the Cabinet:

> On entering the Cabinet room, I saw that [Counselor to the President Edwin] Meese and [Chief of Staff James] Baker were seated at the Cabinet table. This was a startling departure from tradition. . . . [Deputy Chief of Staff Michael] Deaver was seated [against the wall] now—but a meeting or so later, he joined the others. . . .
>
> Sitting at the table, the triumvirate of Meese, Baker and Deaver had the school-boyish habit of scribbling and passing notes among themselves. During the first Cabinet meeting, I wrote on my notepad: "Government by Cabinet or troika?"[65]

The seating arrangements at the first meetings of the Reagan Cabinet in some ways foreshadowed the struggle that unfolded in the early months of the administration over control of policy-making processes in the realm of foreign affairs and defense policy. This topic will be addressed in detail in Chapter 7. First, though, we shall turn our attention to the impressive contributions of Eisenhower's Presidency to the organization and management of foreign and defense policy. As we shall see, the Eisenhower years are rich with prescriptive lessons for avoiding the tensions of the recent past.

NOTES

1. Emmet John Hughes, *The Ordeal of Power: A Political Memoir of the Eisenhower Years* (New York: Atheneum, 1963), p. 123.

2. Ibid.

3. Peter Lyon, *Eisenhower: Portrait of the Hero* (Boston: Little, Brown, 1974), p. 501.

4. Dwight D. Eisenhower to William Phillips, letter of June 5, 1953, Folder: Phillips, William; Ann Whitman File, Letter Series, Box 25, Eisenhower Library.

5. Dwight D. Eisenhower to Ezra Taft Benson, letter of March 20, 1958, Folder: DDE Diary: March 1958; Ann Whitman File, DDE Diary Series, Box 31, Eisenhower Library.

6. Ibid.

7. Ibid.

8. Lyon, *Eisenhower: Portrait of the Hero*, p. 501.

9. Robert H. Ferrell, ed., *The Eisenhower Diaries* (New York: W. W. Norton, 1981), pp. 233–234.

10. Hughes, *The Ordeal of Power*, p. 124.

11. Ibid., p. 143.

12. Ibid.

13. Ibid.

14. Ibid., p. 144.

15. Lyon, *Eisenhower: Portrait of the Hero*, p. 528.

16. Ibid.

17. Minutes of the Cabinet meeting of March 13, 1959, Folder: Cabinet Minutes January 16, 1959—; White House Office, Cabinet Secretariat Records 1953–1960, Box 26, Eisenhower Library.

18. Bryce Harlow, Memorandum for the Record, March 26, 1959, Folder: Conferences-Staff Coverage (5); White House Office: Office of the Staff Secretary, White House Subseries, Box 1, Eisenhower Library.

19. Ibid.

20. Stephen E. Ambrose, *Eisenhower: The President* (New York: Simon and Schuster, 1984), pp. 517–518.

21. Ibid., pp. 511, 517–518.

22. Ibid., p. 517.

23. Herbert S. Parmet, *Eisenhower and the American Crusades* (New York: Macmillan, 1972), pp. 286–287.

24. Ibid., p. 285.

25. Bryce Harlow, Memorandum for the Record, January 30, 1958, Folder: Staff Notes January 1958, Ann Whitman File, DDE Diary Series, Box 30, Eisenhower Library.

26. Parmet, *Eisenhower and the American Crusades*, p. 287.

27. Ibid.

28. Ibid.

29. Hughes, *The Ordeal of Power*, p. 126.

30. Parmet, *Eisenhower and the American Crusades*, p. 287.

31. Ibid., p. 288.

32. Ibid.

33. Ambrose, *Eisenhower: The President*, p. 650.

34. Richard F. Fenno, Jr., *The President's Cabinet* (New York: Vintage Books, paperback edition, 1959), pp. 44–45.

35. Ibid., p. 41.

36. Bradley H. Patterson, Jr., interviewed by Paul L. Hopper, September 19, 1968, Oral History Interview #225, p. 7, Eisenhower Library.

37. Ibid., p. 28.

38. Bradley H. Patterson, "An Overview of the White House," in Kenneth W. Thompson, ed., *Portraits of American Presidents Volume III: The Eisenhower Presidency* (Lanham, Md.: University Press of America, 1984), p. 127.

39. Dwight D. Eisenhower, Oral History Interview by Philip A. Crowl, p. 14, Eisenhower Library.

40. Patterson, "An Overview of the White House," p. 119.

41. Memorandum from Bradley Patterson to Dwight D. Eisenhower, February 11, 1960, Folder: Proposals to Improve Cabinet Procedures, White House Office, Cabinet Secretariat Records, Box 33, Eisenhower Library.

42. Patterson, Oral History Interview, p. 11.

43. Bradley H. Patterson, Jr., *The President's Cabinet: Issues and Questions* (Washington, D.C.: American Society for Public Administration, 1976), p. 108.

44. Ibid., p. 111.

45. Ibid., p. 112.

46. Hughes, *The Ordeal of Power*, pp. 135–136.

47. Herbert Brownell, Oral History Interview, pp. 37–38, Eisenhower Library.

48. Excerpt of Cabinet Discussion, January 16, 1959, Folder: Cabinet Meeting January 16, 1959, Ann Whitman File, Cabinet Series, Box 12, Eisenhower Library.

49. Theodore Sorensen, *Kennedy* (New York: Harper and Row, 1965), p. 283.

50. Richard Tanner Johnson, *Managing the White House* (New York: Harper and Row, 1974), p. xx.

51. Lester M. Salamon, "The President and Policy Making," reprinted in Robert E. DiClerico, ed., *Analyzing the Presidency* (Guilford, Conn.: Dushkin Publishing Group, 1985), p. 212.

52. Richard P. Nathan, *The Plot that Failed: Nixon and the Administrative Presidency* (New York: John Wiley and Sons, 1975).

53. Ibid., p. 46.

54. Ibid., p. 53.

55. R. Gordon Hoxie, "Staffing the Ford and Carter Presidencies," in Bradley D. Nash et al., *Organizing and Staffing the Presidency* (New York: Center for the Study of the Presidency, 1980), p. 50.

56. Ibid.

57. Dom Bonafede, "The Collapse of Cabinet Government?" *National Journal*, April 22, 1978, p. 641.

58. These policy differences are outlined by R. Gordon Hoxie in his essay, "Staffing the Ford and Carter Presidencies," pp. 74–75.

59. Ibid., p. 76.

60. Betty Glad, *Jimmy Carter: In Search of the Great White House* (New York: W. W. Norton, 1980), p. 448.

61. Stephen Hess, *Organizing the Presidency* (Washington, D.C.: Brookings Institution, 1976), p. 8.

62. Hoxie, "Staffing the Ford and Carter Presidencies," p. 45.

63. Ibid.

64. Interview with Bradley Patterson, Jr., Grand Rapids, Michigan, November 1, 1985.

65. Alexander Haig, Excerpts from *Caveat: Realism, Reagan and Foreign Policy* (New York: Macmillan, 1984), reprinted in *Time*, April 2, 1984, p. 51.

4

The Eisenhower
National Security Council
Reappraised

The resignation of Secretary of State Alexander Haig on June 25, 1982, provided a dramatic climax to one facet of the seemingly perennial struggle for control over foreign and national security policy waged between the White House–centered staff of the National Security Council and the once preeminent State Department. In the midst of the now customary feuding among Cabinet Secretaries, Assistants to the President for National Security Affairs, and White House staff, it is constructive to take a closer look at the comparatively tranquil Eisenhower years when the two principal advisory and administrative organs—the Cabinet and the National Security Council—worked in tandem with remarkable success in providing an orderly and effective forum for presidential policy-making. Certainly Eisenhower himself must be credited with providing the leadership necessary to blend the often disparate elements of the nation's foreign affairs and defense establishment into a cohesive framework, conducive to teamwork rather than the type of factionalism and jurisdictional rivalry that has so often pervaded modern administrations. But equally important in explaining the relative harmony between the White House and the Cabinet departments is recognition of the contribution made by certain organizational features of the Eisenhower era. In the discussion that follows, we will focus on the interaction between the President's personal style of leadership and the organizational setting in which his principal advisory bodies operated.

We will begin with a brief summary of previous scholarship on Eisenhower's National Security Council system, focusing on some of the alleged weaknesses cited by critics with regard to Council operations. Drawing on recently declassified materials, we will then turn to a detailed examination of the Eisenhower NSC system, reconstructing with greater precision than has hitherto been possible the actual operations of the Council under Eisenhower's leadership. Finally, in Chapters 6 and 7 we will examine post-Eisenhower practices in comparative fashion, with an eye toward presenting a prescription for improving policy processes based on the Eisenhower experience.

TRADITIONAL ASSESSMENTS OF
NATIONAL SECURITY POLICY-MAKING
DURING THE EISENHOWER YEARS

On the basis of previous analyses by scholars, one might conclude that national security policy-making processes during Eisenhower's Presidency were static, inflexible, and incapable of producing broad consideration of policy alternatives. The National Security Council presented a popular target for administration critics. Members of the Council were often depicted as compliant and courteous rather than probing—exhibiting a reluctance to highlight differences of opinion in front of the President.[1] Some writers believed that the Council functioned as a legislative committee, with members going beyond an advisory capacity and actually voting on issues. It was suggested that Eisenhower's decisions (frequently characterized as Council decisions) were based not on deliberate measuring of opposing views against each other, "but on a blurred generalization in which the opportunity for choice had been submerged by the desire for compromise."[2] Approved statements were allegedly so broad that they did not address specific problems adequately. The vagueness was sufficient to allow each protagonist of a different line of action to find justification for his own view.[3]

Beyond these perceived weaknesses in Council operations, the President himself was portrayed as a reluctant decision-maker who was more interested in achieving consensus than in tackling complex problems head-on. Richard Neustadt, in his classic work *Presidential Power*, noted that "Eisenhower, seemingly, preferred to let subordinates proceed upon the lowest common denominators of agreement than to have their quarrels—and issues and details—pushed up to him."[4]

Richard Tanner Johnson, in his widely cited study on presidential management styles, suggested that Eisenhower undermined his own authority by using his elaborate administrative machinery as a protective shield. In comparing the decision-making styles of Truman and Eisenhower, Johnson wrote:

> While both Truman and Eisenhower respected staff machinery and utilized what we have called the formalistic approach, Truman's machinery was geared as an aggressive apparatus for acquiring and conveying information to the top: in contrast, Eisenhower arrayed his staff machinery like a shield. Truman wanted alternatives to choose from. Eisenhower wanted

a recommendation to ratify. When Ike could not work through his set procedures, or when the shield failed him or when his associates quarreled or confronted him with a difficult choice, he grew disheartened and angry.[5]

Eisenhower's formalistic approach to decision-making was characterized by "the absence of thorough-going deliberations in formulating policy."[6] Eisenhower, by Johnson's account, "usually remained silent in the discussion" of issues at NSC meetings.[7] Indeed, the President "was often a hazy figure in the background of the decisions of his Administration; he delegated broad authority to his advisors and backed them up." The more Eisenhower delegated authority, Richard Neustadt cautioned, "the less he knew, and the less he knew, the less confidence he felt in his own judgment."[8]

With the use of newly available archival evidence, a more enlightened account of Eisenhower's national security policy-making can now be constructed. Traditional scholarship notwithstanding, the Eisenhower system brought about routinization without excessive rigidity and fostered broad advice rather than watered-down bureaucratic consensus. Eisenhower, as we shall see, encouraged and demanded statesmanlike advice from his department heads. The President simply would not tolerate unbridled parochialism—a fact that was crystal clear to all who served in his administration. Finally, contrary to the dogmatic beliefs of his critics and those of his successor in office, new documentation makes it clear that Eisenhower was not a captive of his own elaborate NSC machinery. Rather, the President was remarkably adept at gathering advice and information from a variety of sources and at drawing upon this broad base of information to make decisions that were at times boldly detached from the counsel of administration insiders.

DEVELOPMENT OF THE EISENHOWER NSC: AN OVERVIEW

The origins of the National Security Council can be traced to the problems brought about by the lack of an established coordinating mechanism for national security policy formulation during World War II. In a report to Secretary of the Navy James Forrestal, written in 1945, Ferdinand Eberstadt proposed the establishment of a coordinating body that would enable the President to benefit from systematic interdepartmental staff work. Eberstadt suggested that the creation of a council system would enhance national security policy-making by ensuring regular consultation by future Presidents with their principal civilian and military advisors. The National Security Act of 1947, as passed by Congress, incorporated many of Eberstadt's ideas. The act formally created the National Security Council to "advise the President with respect to the integration of domestic, foreign, and military policies relating to the national security."[9]

During the campaign of 1952, Eisenhower pledged to utilize the National Security Council more extensively and effectively than he thought had been the case under Truman's leadership. In a speech delivered in San Francisco on October 8, 1952, Eisenhower affirmed his intent to use the NSC as the primary means of imparting presidential direction and overall coherence to the activities of the departments and agencies.[10]

In one of the first steps taken to effectuate his campaign pledge, the President-elect asked General Robert Cutler, a Harvard-trained attorney and Boston banker, to direct a thorough study of the NSC mechanism as it had been utilized by Truman with recommendations for making better use of the Council in the formulation, coordination, and implementation of policy. In this task, Cutler was assisted by an NSC Study Group that consisted of such individuals as Paul Nitze, Allen Dulles, Arthur Flemming, and Professor W. Y. Elliott.

On February 19, 1953, a few weeks after Eisenhower had taken office, General George C. Marshall submitted a memorandum to the President in which he detailed what he believed to be key weaknesses in the Truman NSC system along with suggestions for improving its operations in the new administration. Marshall depicted the Truman NSC as "a meeting of busy men who had no time to pay to the business before them."[11] The General expressed concern that members of the Council were "not prepared" and "took refuge either in non-participation or in protecting their own departments."[12] In addition to these problems, Marshall observed that "there was too much compromise before the papers came to the NSC" and that they "failed to state pros and cons."[13] The papers "presented a fait accompli, to be accepted or rejected or modified a little. The papers never presented alternatives to decide upon."[14] Marshall proposed that steps be taken to make the Council a truly deliberative body, with various options and objections discussed at meetings.

Marshall was also convinced from his experience on the Truman NSC that no permanent staff of the Council could possibly take the place of a staff representative of the agencies.

These Senior Staff men must be active in their agencies and in the stream of things in order to be useful. Men like that must wrestle out the papers. Occasionally civilian-permanent staff groups can do ad hoc jobs. But they must not preempt or appear to compete with the agencies' representatives— if they do, friction will result.[15]

Eisenhower's NSC Study Group, in findings similar to General Marshall's, expressed the belief that those officials who are charged with day-to-day operations in their respective departments and agencies are the persons best qualified to assist in the formulation of security policies that they will ultimately be asked to carry out. In this way,

> each interested and affected Department and Agency shares in formulating the recommendations which go to the Council, has full opportunity to be heard at the Planning Board and Council levels, and has the right to have succinctly stated and reported at the Council levels any disagreement which it may have with such recommendations.[16]

To bring a balance to Council proceedings, the President issued a clear admonition against departmentalism and parochialism. The Council was to be viewed as

> a corporate body, composed of individuals advising the President in their own right rather than representatives of their respective departments and agencies. Their function should be to seek, with their background of experience, the most statesmanlike solution to the problems of national security, rather than to reach solutions which represent merely a compromise of departmental positions.[17]

Beyond the emphasis placed on departmental representation, tempered by a statesmanlike perspective, the NSC Study Group set forth several other proposals that served as important guidelines in establishing the Eisenhower system. Foremost among them, the NSC was to be a highly active organization, characterized by regular and frequent meetings, full agenda, and vigorous discussion of major issues.[18] Council debate was to be facilitated by thorough interdepartmental discussion and preparation of "precisely worded, carefully studied, and well-presented" papers, prepared by representatives of the departments and agencies who were involved in the operationalization of national security policy.

Another prominent objective of Council operations under Eisenhower was to give greater emphasis to budgetary considerations in all national security policy-making. During the Truman years the defense budget had been drawn up by the Department of Defense and then given to the President, who worked out the final amount with the Bureau of the Budget.[19] Instead of bringing in representatives of the Treasury Department and Bureau of the Budget after the fact, Eisenhower insisted that they take part in NSC planning discussions. To determine the financial implications of a policy proposal, a budget appendix was required at the end of each proposal submitted by the Planning Board to the Council. In early June 1953 the Director of the Bureau of the Budget became a standing-request participant of the Council and was represented at all Planning Board meetings by a Bureau official.

ORGANIZATION OF THE EISENHOWER NSC

Under Eisenhower's leadership, the National Security Council became the principal forum for the formulation and implementation of national security policy. He created the position of Special Assistant to the President for National Security Affairs, expanded the professional staff of the NSC, and established two major NSC adjuncts: the Planning Board and the Operations Coordinating Board.[20] Through these mechanisms, Eisenhower "institutionalized the NSC and gave it clear lines of responsibility and authority."[21]

To assist the President in administering the NSC, Eisenhower's Special Assistant for National Security Affairs was named the principal executive officer of the Council with responsibilities for (1) determining (subject to the President's approval) the Council agenda, (2) briefing the President in advance of Council meetings, (3) presenting matters for discussion at Council meetings, and (4) supervising the overall operations of the NSC staff and Council.[22] In these activities, the Special Assistant was expected to serve as a neutral facilitator and coordinator, not as a policy advocate. As presidential scholar R. Gordon Hoxie notes, the Special Assistant's low profile was consistent with Eisenhower's emphasis on "teamwork" as an indispensable element in the administration's national security organization.

> He made clear at the outset that under his personal direction the Secretary of State was to be the "channel of authority within the executive branch in foreign policy." It would have been unconscionable to Eisenhower (as to Dulles) that the Special Assistant for National Security Affairs, who served as the executive officer in vitalizing the NSC, could in any way come between the President and the Secretary of State. Eisenhower made the Secretary of State, the Secretary of Defense, and the Secretary of the Treasury a triumvirate to review national security plans and operations on the premise that diplomatic, military and economic affairs were necessarily related.[23]

THE PLANNING BOARD AND POLICY FORMULATION

The Planning Board became an integral part of the Eisenhower NSC system, meeting 640 times in the first five years of the administration. The Board incorporated Eisenhower's desire for continuous policy planning. It normally met twice a week for sessions lasting three or four hours. Board members devoted most of their time to debating, refining, and drafting policy papers for consideration by the President and the Council.

There were four principal categories of policy papers considered by the Council. First and most important were overall policy papers, which covered a wide range of national security problems and contained related political, economic, and military strategy. Second were papers covering individual foreign countries or larger geographical regions. A third category of papers dealt with "functional" policies such as atomic energy, regulation and control of armaments, and international trade. The final category of papers dealt with organization policies relating to the Council itself.[24]

NSC papers were usually assigned by the Planning Board to the department or agency with primary responsibility for implementation of the policy under consideration. The responsible agency had the freedom to call on all other NSC agencies for assistance in producing a draft of the policy report. Frequently, the CIA had input on policy papers because of its role as spokesman for the intelligence community. Likewise, the Treasury Department and Bureau of the Budget were likely to have substantial input on the many policy papers requiring an evaluation of costs and resources.[25]

A typical NSC paper contained several sections: a "General Consideration" of the problem at hand; a list of "Objectives" of U.S. security policy; a statement of options, or "Courses of Action," dealing with methods of achieving the stated goals, often subdivided into categories such as political, economic, and military; and a final section consisting of a "Financial Appendix" detailing the estimated costs of putting a new program or policy into effect.[26]

Upon completion of the first draft, the policy paper was presented to the Planning Board for open discussion. The Special Assistant to the President, who chaired all Planning Board meetings, opened consideration of a paper with his own criticisms and comments, based on extensive work by his staff. The paper was then placed before the entire Board for input and debate. From all accounts, these debates were generally spirited and rigorous. S. Everett Gleason, a career civil servant who served on the staff of the NSC under both Truman and Eisenhower, described the procedure of the Planning Board as informal and democratic.

Any Planning Board member is free to speak to any issue which may arise whether or not this issue is within the precise sphere of his department's official responsibility or is presumed to be his area of expertise.[27]

Most reports were discussed at several sessions of the Planning Board and revised between meetings on the basis of the Board's discussions. A conscientious effort was made to ensure that differences of opinion were not glossed over. Where disagreements existed, policy "splits" were written into the Planning Board drafts prior to submission to the Council for debate and resolution. Far more than representing mere verbal quibbles, the splits in the policy papers reflected genuine differences with respect to intelligence estimates or policy recommendations.[28]

Ralph Reid, who was appointed to the Planning Board of the NSC in 1954 as the Bureau of the Budget's representative, had this to say about Planning Board operations:

> I read so often that the policy recommendations that went to President Eisenhower were necessarily bland and represented unanimity of feeling, and from my point of view, exactly the reverse was true. According to the ground rules under which we operated, any member of the board was entitled to suggest an alternative, a turn of phrase, an alternative recommendation, and alternative conclusion. . . .
>
> As a result of this, . . . essentially every NSC paper which came before the Council had in it a variety of alternatives which represented imagination, innovation, and not—occasionally, just sheer disbelief in some of the intelligence papers that were presented as a basis for the introduction of the paper.[29]

Reid recalled one instance in which he himself took issue with an intelligence estimate in a Planning Board paper focusing on Japan. The paper, as drafted by the Planning Board, concluded that economic conditions in Japan were heading downhill and would likely result in the ascendancy of one of the left-wing parties in Japan. Reid, who had studied Japanese and Chinese politics at Harvard's Yenching Institute while completing his doctorate, registered strong disagreement with the intelligence estimate and a formal split was recorded in the Planning Board paper. When the National Security Council took up the matter, the President agreed with Reid that the intelligence estimate was faulty and requested that the paper be reworked.[30]

On the surface, it would seem unlikely that the Bureau of the Budget's representative on the NSC Planning Board would play an active role in debate regarding the political future of Japan. But Ralph Reid's role in the issue serves to underscore the fact that policy differences were not limited to departmental lines. Indeed, it was not uncommon for the State Department representative to take a split on a financial matter or for a Defense Department representative to take a split on a commercial matter, and so on down the line. Such diversity, unimpeded by departmental parochialism, reflected the President's desire "to see the fullest range of alternatives presented to him."[31]

Policy splits of the type described by Gleason and Reid were written into the NSC papers prior to submission to the President and the Council. An average of two out of every three papers submitted to the President for consideration in the NSC contained such splits.[32] These differences were stated sharply and succinctly, usually in parallel columns in the draft paper sent forward to the Council. In the annual restatement of basic national security policy, it was customary to find from six to twelve differences of opinion stated. Such differences were fully debated and ultimately resolved at the Council level.[33] One policy paper was forwarded to the NSC with a total of nineteen splits and required five successive Council meetings before final approval could be reached.[34] As Special Assistant Robert Cutler suggests,

> difficult or minor differences were not "swept under the rug." The purpose, to the contrary, was to provoke discussion, at the Planning Board and at the Council levels, to the end that all interested in the issues should have an opportunity to be heard in presentation and rebuttal before the decision was made by the President. In fact, this quality especially distinguished the operation of the Council under President Eisenhower. . . . The Council was, indeed, a forum for vigorous discussion of conflicting views on alternative issues of security policy.[35]

The potential for departmental and agency biases dominating Planning Board discussions was further offset by the fact that the Special Assistant to the President for National Security Affairs chaired the Board. Not only did the chairman of the principal policy-formulating staff have no departmental ties, his close staff relationship with the President allowed him to remain fully cognizant of his outlook and concerns.

The papers prepared by the Planning Board were distributed at least ten days prior to the Council meeting in which they were discussed, thus ensuring that the Under Secretaries or Assistant Secretaries who had participated in Planning Board discussions would have an opportunity to brief the heads of their departments with regard to issues that would be brought before the Council. Robert Bowie, who served as the State Department's representative on the Planning Board, observes that the preparatory staff meetings held at the State Department provided an opportunity "for thrashing out positions and expressing competing views, before the Secretary, so that he could reach a judgment about what position he wanted to take at the NSC meeting the next day."[36] Then, in the Council meeting, the principal advisors to the President confronted one another. Consequently, Bowie notes, the President "got a pretty good exposition of the competing points of view within the Executive branch."[37]

The observations of Gleason, Bowie, Reid, and other members of the administration suggest that departmental representatives were not prisoners of their departments. Indeed, the advantages of active departmental representation far outweighed the potential disadvantages during the Eisenhower years. For one thing, the utilization of department and agency representatives on the Planning Board tempered the policy advice passed on to the President with a realistic appreciation for the operational capabilities and limitations of the departments concerned. Furthermore, the fact that the Eisenhower NSC machinery included many high-ranking personnel from the departments did not, as is commonly assumed, preclude a government-wide perspective. For as political scientist Paul Hammond suggests, active participation by departmental heads and their representatives strengthens rather than weakens policy-making.

Indeed, their status within their own agency can be enhanced by their participation in the NSC. The fact that the department head has demands placed upon him in the NSC to rise above departmental viewpoints can be a part of that enhanced status, for all the more must he be reckoned with as the President's spokesman within his own agency. Furthermore, the staff mechanisms of the NSC can make substantial inroads upon the obstacles to effective NSC operation. . . . The momentum of staff work, by having available facts and arguments from the previous consideration of the same or similar subjects, can more effectively evoke current information from the departments and evaluate current departmental judgments and arguments. For instance, simply to record and keep the positions of an agency on file, together with the evidence it provides on a particular subject over time, can build up a record which would at least limit its freedom of maneuver and might force it, increasingly, to discuss the subject on its merits. At the same time, the determination of the Chief Executive to make use of the NSC can in some cases force his agency heads to make use of it also. Finally, there is a *prima facie* argument that the greater the speed and flexibility, which the NSC and its staff mechanisms develop— specifically, the more continuous their review of established policies becomes—the more the gap between secret plans and political realities is likely to be closed.[38]

By systematically reviewing national policy together, Planning Board members provided insurance against a sudden crisis unexpectedly arising in the world.[39] Through the Planning Board and NSC mechanism, "Eisenhower himself was happily occupied with what he liked to do best: the orderly process of reasoning and analysis."[40] The thoroughly prepared and commonly understood facts and recommendations of the

Planning Board papers provided a foundation for decisive and lasting results, with records available for future consultation by all concerned.

THE ROLE OF THE NSC SUPPORT STAFF

Standing apart from the Planning Board with its policy-formulating role was the support staff of the NSC, which consisted of an Executive Secretary and several professional assistants. Whereas the Planning Board was composed of individuals from the departments and agencies responsible for developing policy ideas for consideration by the Council, the staff of the NSC was a permanent, career-oriented cadre of professionals charged with preserving continuity. Hence, whereas the Planning Board often served as an agent for change, the staff was designed to foster the type of "institutional memory" often associated with the Foreign Service of the State Department. Its task, in the words of one participant, was "to remember, not to recommend."[41]

The NSC staff reviewed policy papers with respect to coherence, completeness, and applicability in light of past experience. Through integrated evaluation of the status of all national security programs, the staff identified gaps in national security policy and brought to the attention of the Council important issues or anticipated developments that were not receiving sufficient attention.[42]

In a sense, the NSC staff emulated the qualities of "neutral competence" often associated with high-ranking civil servants at the Bureau of the Budget. The staff provided a government-wide perspective, untainted by the parochial outlook that occasionally surfaced among departmental and agency representatives on the Planning Board. "At the very least," write Clark and Legere, "its existence meant that there was available to the President (through the Special Assistant) an independent source of analysis of departmental recommendations."[43] A similar balance was struck within the Operations Coordinating Board between permanent staff officers, who provided continuity in operations, and staff officers on assignment from the Board's member agencies, who contributed expert advice based on departmental experience.

Eisenhower believed that the support staff, unlike the Planning Board and Council, would remain relatively stable in its composition across different administrations. Over time, however, the professional staff of the NSC has become increasingly politicized. More and more, the views of the staff have come to resemble the particular outlook and perspective of the President's Assistant for National Security Affairs. Generally speaking, there are fewer departmental and agency representatives, less government experience, and more of an academic perspective on national security issues than during the Eisenhower years. The ramifications of these trends will be discussed in greater depth in Chapter 6.

REGULAR MEETINGS AS A CORNERSTONE OF POLICY DEVELOPMENT

Soon after Eisenhower took office, his advisory panel on national security stressed the importance of direct presidential participation in the successful operation of the National Security Council. Although President Truman presided at the first NSC meeting and at occasional meetings thereafter, he did not regularly attend sessions of the Council until the beginning of the Korean War. His abstention was based in part upon the concern that his presence might inhibit free discussion, and in part because he questioned whether Congress had the constitutional authority to require the President to seek advice from the statutory members of the NSC before reaching decisions on certain subjects.

Truman's early absence from the Council table deprived him of the opportunity to hear first-hand the views of Council members, to ask questions of them, and to engage personally in the interchange of ideas. Even when Truman was present, at least one participant, General George Marshall, believed that "he was not a force at the table to bring out discussion."[44]

In recognition of the importance of active presidential participation in Council affairs, Eisenhower's NSC Study Group recommended that the President should attend Council meetings as regularly as possible, and as chairman "should ask for views around the table; exercise leadership so as to bring out conflicts and so that all agencies which later have to do the job will feel they have participated."[45]

Regularly scheduled, well-attended, and presidentially directed Council meetings became a hallmark of the Eisenhower era, but, for some, these features gave the appearance of excessive routinization and formalism. Yet these ingredients served an invaluable "clearing-house" function for the administration by providing a regularized forum in which the President's principal advisors on national security were brought up to date, through briefings, policy reports, and open discussion of the most important issues of the day.

Special Assistant Robert Cutler notes that the clearing-house aspect of the Council was especially valuable in the early stages of the Eisenhower administration.[46] Regular meetings of the Council afforded those personnel without previous government experience an opportunity to gain first-hand knowledge of how the Washington bureaucracy operates along with detailed information on national security policy. Participants were also exposed on a regular basis to the President's own thinking on policy. This exposure combined with written directives prepared on the basis of the President's statements left less latitude for bureaucratic improvisation at the implementation stage. According to Dillon Anderson, a prominent NSC participant, Eisenhower wanted the department heads who had the responsibility for carrying out policy to have the opportunity to advise him before he decided what policy would be. The President "invited a lot of give and take" from departmental representatives before making his decision. But having participated in a decision by stating their views, representatives from the departments "damn well knew what it was and there'd be no fuzzing up as to what the President's decision had been."[47]

Despite the important advantages associated with frequent utilization of the NSC as a policy forum, Presidents in the post-Eisenhower era have not followed suit in employing the Council on a regular basis. Even in the comparatively active Nixon and Ford administrations, the Council was convened only 125 times,[48] or about one-third the number of meetings that took place during the comparable eight-year period of the Eisenhower Presidency. Indeed, during Eisenhower's tenure as Chief Executive, there were 366 regular and special meetings of the National Security Council. The President presided over 329 of these meetings— nearly 90 percent of the total.[49]

It comes as no surprise, in light of the Eisenhower experience, that one of the principal recommendations of President Jimmy Carter's reorganization study on "National Security Policy Integration" called for more carefully structured meetings of the National Security Council and more precise mechanisms for recording and carrying out agreements. The "Odeen Report," named after Chairman Philip Odeen, argued that more full meetings of the type utilized by Eisenhower would keep officials from the departments informed about policy, thus making policies more bureaucratically enforceable.[50]

ATTENDANCE AT COUNCIL MEETINGS

As Special Assistant to the President for National Security Affairs, Robert Cutler was keenly aware of the problems that could arise when Council meetings became too large. There is a point, he observed, at which a group turns into a "town meeting. . . . Once this invisible line is passed, people do not discuss and debate; they remain silent or talk for the record."[51] Consequently, Cutler and the President agreed in March 1953 that, "as a general rule, not more than eight persons who participate in discussions should attend Council meetings."

Despite efforts to limit attendance, White House records show that an average of twenty or more individuals were allowed to attend Council meetings.[52] All told, however, there were only about eleven or twelve actual participants in Council debate at a typical meeting. This figure reflects the fact that there were several types of attendees at Council meetings: statutory members, general standing request members, ad hoc standing request members, White House staff, and observers who were not seated at the Council table.

When Eisenhower took office, the NSC consisted of five statutory members: the President, Vice President, Secretary of State, Secretary of Defense, and Director of the Office of Civil Defense Mobilization. Attending all Council meetings in an advisory capacity were the Chairman of the Joint Chiefs of Staff and the Director of the Central Intelligence Agency. In addition to these members, Eisenhower designated three general standing request officers: the Director of the Bureau of the Budget and the Secretary of the Treasury (whose status as members reflected the importance attached by the President to the economic ramifications of national security policy), and the Chairman of the Atomic Energy Commission. Among others regularly attending Council meetings were the President's Special Assistant for National Security Affairs, the Executive Secretary, the Deputy Executive Secretary of the NSC, and five others who held standing invitations to Council meetings.

In a report dated April 1, 1955, Robert Cutler admonished the President to resist the "constant pressure from the outside to increase the number of persons regularly attending Council meetings."[53] Cutler argued that it was necessary to limit attendance "in the interest of security, but even more in the interest of keeping the size of the meeting at a level where intimate, frank, fruitful discussion can take place."[54]

Dillon Anderson, who succeeded Cutler as Special Assistant to the President for National Security Affairs, notes that the President himself shared Cutler's concern for regulating attendance at Council meetings.

I think he felt that the larger the crowd, the less free people would be to speak, and the less effective the NSC would be as an instrumentality for airing different viewpoints before he had these great decisions to make. Somewhere there is an optimum size, and he thought that certain people were essential to be there, and beyond that he didn't want it enlarged, and if he saw around the table more people than he had expected there, pretty soon after the meeting I'd have to explain to him why they were there, though he did give me the privilege of including people when it seemed appropriate because the subject called for their expertise. But he also gave me the privilege of saying it was his direction that only the regular members attend.[55]

In line with his philosophy of limited attendance, Eisenhower rejected the proposal that the secretaries of the armed services should be in regular attendance at Council meetings. Moreover, he did not believe that it was necessary to have the Joint Chiefs of Staff present, although they were invited on an ad hoc basis. There were exceptions, however, to the rule of limited attendance, particularly when the Council held important background meetings. One such meeting took place in the spring of 1955, when John Von Neumann made a presentation on the development of ballistic missiles that lasted for more than four hours.[56]

In recognition of the fact that small meetings were often more conducive to frank and intimate discussions, the President frequently met informally with a handful of selected advisors and officials to discuss policy in the privacy of the Oval Office. The President found these meetings to be a useful adjunct to formal Council meetings, but he never considered such meetings to be a substitute for the broad-ranging discussions of the full Council.

AGENDA-SETTING FOR COUNCIL MEETINGS

The major departments and agencies involved in the formulation of national security policy frequently generated ideas for the policy agenda from studies and forward planning. Agenda items often arose from the deliberations of the Council itself, through Planning Board discussions, from Cabinet meetings, or from an important official in government. In some cases, ideas for the Council agenda came directly from the President—from his own pondering of a subject, or from a conference or outside communication.

The formal agenda of the Council was determined jointly among the President, his Special Assistant for National Security Affairs, and the Executive Secretary of the Council. Those attending Council meetings were given plenty of advance notice with regard to the topics that would be discussed. The agenda was circulated ten days in advance, followed by Planning Board papers supporting each agenda item.

In advance of each meeting, the Special Assistant briefed the President with regard to the content and background of the items scheduled for Council discussion. Special Assistant Dillon Anderson describes his briefing sessions with the President in this way:

> I always went to the President the day before the meeting and took the [Planning Board] papers with me and went over them with him. He would have them before him and I would have them before me and I would talk and he would scan, and I would take from 15 to 30 minutes depending on the complexity of the paper or papers, and the questions that he would

ask me. The object, of course, was to alert him to the questions that were coming up and give him time to ponder them in advance. These were perfectly wonderful sessions because, as we proceeded, he would stop, get up, and he seemed always to feel that he was doing his thinking best when he was walking, because he used to walk the floor and talk, and talking helped him to generate related thoughts, and he would pound the desk sometimes on these subjects and I would thus be able to have a pretty good feel as to his views on a subject before it was discussed in the National Security Council.[57]

Once items were placed on the agenda, the Special Assistant and the President made sure that members stuck to the business at hand unless there were compelling reasons for departing from it. When asked whether a prominent member of the Council such as John Foster Dulles could steer the debate away from the formal agenda, White House staffer Bernard Shanley responded:

Eisenhower ran the show, and he was very meticulous about staff work. Foster wouldn't dare try to avoid the issue or go off on tangents because the boss would bring him right back again. Because he not only presided, but it was his decision to make and he made them.[58]

Sticking closely to the agenda certainly seemed to yield tangible results in terms of the amount of business conducted by the Council. In its first two years, the Eisenhower administration recorded actions on 656 of the items considered at NSC meetings.[59] Comparatively speaking, this was a huge workload; the Truman administration, for instance, recorded action on only 699 matters in the entire five-year period of the Council's existence.

THE FORMAT OF NSC MEETINGS: AN OVERVIEW

The typical NSC meeting during the Eisenhower years began with a briefing by the Director of the Central Intelligence Agency, Allen Dulles. This briefing usually focused on the world situation or on the intelligence background to problems that were about to be discussed by the Council. Admiral Arthur Radford frequently followed the intelligence briefings with a short military report on behalf of the Joint Chiefs of Staff. The next item on the agenda often consisted of a Progress Report on policy implementation by the Operations Coordinating Board. These reports were designed to keep the Council informed on the status of previously approved policies. The Progress Reports were prepared on the basis of "Record of Action" documents, which consisted of the official decisions of the Council as recorded by the Executive Secretary and his deputy.

At the conclusion of these various presentations, the Special Assistant for National Security Affairs would move directly to consideration of each policy paper prepared by the Planning Board. The Special Assistant would summarize the paper for the Council, paying careful attention to the splits of opinion contained in the paper. The Special Assistant would then customarily open discussion on each of the important issues addressed in the policy paper. It was not uncommon for the President to take control of the meeting at this point by making comments and addressing questions to other members of the Council. Lively discussion and a vigorous exchange of views highlighted many of the NSC meetings.

Contrary to what has so often been reported, decisions in the Eisenhower NSC were not made on the basis of voting or a counting of hands. As Special Assistant Dillon Anderson notes:

> While he [Eisenhower] welcomed the use of the NSC mechanism, as an advisory body, or a sort of a super-staff for him in the delineation of our national security policy, he nevertheless felt that the onus and responsibility for decision lay exclusively with him and he therefore did not ever use the voting procedure that seemed to have been contemplated in the act of Congress.[60]

The President would usually reach tentative decisions at some point during the NSC meeting. Unless he chose to defer his decision for a day or two of reflection, a "Record of Action" statement was drafted by the Executive Secretary or his assistant, expressing as accurately as possible the President's policy views on issues that had been resolved in the Council. The Record of Action was prepared and submitted to the President within forty-eight hours of the Council meeting. The President would then review and amend the Record of Action as he deemed necessary. Once the corrected Record of Action was signed by the President, it became an official statement of policy to be adopted by the executive branch. The Record of Action papers, roughly four to ten pages in length, were submitted to all members of the Council as well as to officials charged with the implementation of a given policy.

THE OPERATIONS COORDINATING BOARD: POLICY IMPLEMENTATION IN A DYNAMIC SYSTEM

After decisions were made by the President and communicated to the departments and agencies via Record of Action statements, the implementation of policies became the responsibility of the Operations

Coordinating Board (OCB). This important NSC adjunct was created by Executive Order on September 2, 1953, to coordinate the implementation of NSC policies "in an imaginative and effective manner and in accordance with the Council's wishes."[61] In addition, the OCB was charged with reporting on the progress that appropriate departments and agencies had made in carrying out NSC policies. The objective of the OCB, in the words of Sherman Adams, was to prevent the execution of a policy from "falling between the chairs. It was meticulous hard work, the follow-up that ensued after decisions had been made."[62]

The OCB did not have the authority to direct or order agencies and departments to implement policies in a particular fashion. Rather, its plans, actions, and recommendations were based on agreement among the chiefs or deputy chiefs of the major departments. Hence, the OCB relied on collegiality and consensus-building to shape implementation processes.

Prior to the creation of the OCB, the implementation of policy directives from the NSC had been entrusted to one department or agency, normally the State Department. Although other departments and agencies were nearly always involved in the implementation of policy, arrangements for coordination were generally ad hoc in nature.[63]

The OCB was initially chaired by the Under Secretary of State. The Board's other members included the Deputy Secretary of Defense, the Director of Central Intelligence, the Director of the United States Information Agency and a representative of the President. Heads of other agencies were invited to send a representative to OCB meetings when the OCB was dealing with matters bearing directly on their responsibilities. Membership on the OCB was constituted at the Under Secretary level to ensure that Board members would have sufficient authority within their respective agencies to direct the implementation of agreements reached within the OCB.

Formal weekly meetings of the OCB were preceded by an informal luncheon at 1:00 P.M. every Wednesday. At the luncheon meeting, members were free to bring up any matters that they considered appropriate for discussion. No agenda was utilized, although members of the Board frequently gave advance notice of topics they wished to discuss.[64]

Although the Planning Board was sometimes criticized for relying heavily on the use of staff papers, OCB discussions at these informal luncheon meetings were seldom conducted on the basis of such papers. Rather, the luncheons served as a forum in which OCB members consulted informally with other high-ranking government officials on a wide spectrum of concerns related to the Board's activities. Agreements were reached during the luncheon on some matters. Others were referred to an appropriate OCB working group for study and recommendations.

Still others were referred to relevant agencies for decision outside the OCB framework.

Following the informal luncheons, the OCB would convene for its formal meeting at 2:15 P.M. In contrast to the luncheons, the formal OCB meetings were guided by a written agenda. Operation plans for implementing national security policy were discussed, revised, and approved at these meetings. The chairman of the working group responsible for preparing operation plans, along with an Assistant Secretary from the agency charged with implementing the policies under consideration, were usually in attendance to answer questions and report on developments.

Operation plans usually contained a section listing the objectives of a given policy, a statement of actions agreed upon, an enumeration of agency responsibilities for implementation, statements of the agency programs for carrying out the plan as prepared by the agencies responsible for implementation, and a section on proposed actions on which there was no agreement between the agencies.[65] Preparation of operation plans helped participating departments and agencies identify, clarify, and resolve differences of policy interpretation or operating responsibility. By exposing operating difficulties, the plans provided a basis for practical recommendations for more effective implementation of policies. Once approved, operation plans set forth useful guidelines for agency operations in Washington and abroad, with particular attention focused on activities that required interagency coordination.

In addition to preparing plans for the operationalization of policy, the OCB was required to report to the National Security Council on the progress of the departments and agencies in implementing policies. These "Reports to the NSC" were submitted every six months and included information on actions taken to implement policy along with a discussion of difficulties in operations that impeded the attainment of objectives authorized by the NSC.[66] Supplementing these detailed semi-annual reviews were weekly progress reports that provided ideas for change or modification of policies.[67]

The Operations Coordinating Board was not a rigidly structured organization. Rather, it was a subject of study and revision throughout Eisenhower's term of office. Near the end of his first term, for example, a study was initiated by the President to analyze the OCB with an eye toward recommendations for reorganization and improvement. The study, which was directed by Nelson Rockefeller, recommended that the OCB be given command authority. It also recommended that the Special Assistant to the President for National Security Affairs be made the Chairman of the Board and that he be backed by an independent staff.[68]

Rockefeller's report drew special attention to the difficulty of trying to distinguish, in practice, between policy and operations. An attempt had been made to draw such a distinction by physically separating the Planning Board and the Operations Coordinating Board. In a memorandum to Sherman Adams, White House aide William Jackson summarized the problem:

> Situations . . . are brought into OCB and other interdepartmental mechanisms for discussion and possible resolution under the assumption that these are within the scope of "coordination" and "operations" although they really represent situations in which a policy decision has to be made. One of the basic difficulties with the OCB has been that its role in these cases which involve policy conflicts has not been defined.[69]

In recognition of the problems brought about by separating the activities of the Planning Board and the Operations Coordinating Board, President Eisenhower issued an Executive Order on January 7, 1957, that designated Special Assistant Robert Cutler as a representative of the President on the OCB and as Vice Chairman of the Board. The merger of Cutler's responsibilities as Chairman of the Planning Board and Vice Chairman of the OCB offered growing recognition of the important interrelationship between policy formulation and policy implementation.

On February 25, 1957, Eisenhower issued a revised Executive Order that, for the first time, formally placed the OCB within the structure of the NSC. The White House press release announcing this formal merger stated that the time had come to establish "a closer relation between the formulation and the carrying out of security policies."[70] In line with this action, the offices of the OCB staff were moved into the Executive Office Building in space adjacent to the offices of the NSC staff.[71]

A final step toward integration of the OCB into the NSC framework was taken on January 13, 1960, when Eisenhower designated his Special Assistant for National Security Affairs, Gordon Gray, as the new Chairman of the OCB. In his letter to Gray confirming the appointment, Eisenhower wrote:

> In view of your continuing responsibility as the principal supervisory officer of the work of the National Security Council in formulating national security policies including those assigned by me to the OCB for coordination, you are in a position to provide impartial and objective guidance and leadership to the Board.
>
> This new assignment is one step which I feel should be taken toward enabling the President to look to one office for staff assistance in the whole range of national security affairs.[72]

In a letter written on January 19, 1960, Secretary of State Christian Herter extended his personal congratulations to Gordon Gray for his new role as OCB Chairman. Although the appointment of Gray meant that a State Department representative would no longer chair the OCB, Herter expressed hope that Gray would continue to utilize the State Department's facilities for OCB luncheons and Board meetings. "In this way," Herter wrote, "perhaps, I may be able to drop in on your luncheon meetings from time to time."[73]

In his response to Herter, Gray underscored his intention to continue the harmonious working relationship between the White House and State Department that had characterized the Eisenhower years.

> I will keep constantly in mind the predominant interest and responsibility of the State Department in most of the matters which come before the Board.
>
> Your gracious offer for the use of the Board of the Department's facilities for luncheons and Board meetings is accepted with alacrity. Please know that it would give all of the members of the Board the greatest personal pleasure if you will drop in on luncheon meetings from time to time, and beyond that, it would give us added incentive to do our work well.[74]

In a transition memorandum written one year after he became Chairman of the OCB, Gray noted that the change had been an improvement for a variety of reasons. By naming the Special Assistant as Chairman, the President had in effect eliminated a situation in which a protagonist was also expected to be an "impartial chairman."[75] Furthermore, the new arrangement allowed for more direct involvement of the President in OCB affairs through his Special Assistant.[76]

In a letter to the President written during the final days of the administration, Gray noted:

> The Board is an evolving mechanism, changing its procedures and organization as it gains in experience and in response to changes in the world situation.
>
> In the eyes of the highest officers of the departments that do business through the Board, it has become an increasingly effective mechanism.[77]

Gray's letter to Eisenhower captures the dynamic quality of the Eisenhower NSC system, which, though highly structured, was nonetheless flexible and adaptive.

As with the Planning Board of the NSC, departmental representation on the Operations Coordinating Board did not preclude a government-wide perspective. The NSC structure under Eisenhower blended the expertise of the career bureaucracy with the skillful coordination of a low-profile presidential staff.

In Chapter 5, we will turn our attention to Eisenhower's national security decision-making. The discussion will focus on Eisenhower's utilization of the formal NSC apparatus, and on his efforts to augment Council machinery with advice and information from sources outside the NSC setting.

NOTES

1. Paul Y. Hammond summarizes the arguments of critics in his article, "The National Security Council: An Interpretation and Appraisal," *American Political Science Review*, December 1960, reprinted in Alan A. Altshuler, *The Politics of the Federal Bureaucracy* (New York: Dodd, Mead and Co., 1975), p. 147.

2. Stanley L. Falk, "The National Security Council Under Truman, Eisenhower and Kennedy," *Political Science Quarterly*, vol. 79, no. 3, September 1964, p. 424.

3. Ibid.

4. Richard E. Neustadt, *Presidential Power: The Politics of Leadership* (New York: John Wiley and Sons, 1976), p. 229.

5. Richard Tanner Johnson, *Managing the White House* (New York: Harper and Row, 1974), p. 96.

6. Ibid., p. 81.

7. Ibid., p. 92.

8. Neustadt, quoted in James David Barber, *The Presidential Character: Predicting Performance in the White House*, 2nd ed. (Englewood Cliffs, N.J.: Prentice-Hall, 1977), p. 163.

9. Eberstadt, quoted in Charles W. Kegley, Jr., and Eugene R. Wittkopf, *American Foreign Policy: Pattern and Process* (New York: St. Martin's Press, 1979), p. 248.

10. Keith C. Clark and Laurence J. Legere, eds., *The President and the Management of National Security* (New York: Praeger Publishers, 1969), p. 60.

11. Memorandum from George Marshall to Dwight D. Eisenhower, February 19, 1953, Folder: NSC Organization and Functions (5), White House Office, Office of the Special Assistant for National Security Affairs, NSC Series, Administrative Subseries, Box 6, Eisenhower Library.

12. Ibid.

13. Ibid.

14. Ibid.

15. Ibid.

16. Robert Cutler, Comments on Speech by Senator Jackson, June 5, 1959, p. 7, Folder: NSC Investigation (Jackson Resolution), Staff Files, Bryce Harlow, Box 17, Eisenhower Library.

17. Memorandum for the NSC from James Lay, Jr., February 25, 1960, Folder: NSC Memorandum, Staff Files, Bryce Harlow, Box 17, Eisenhower Library.

18. James Lay, Jr., "An Organizational History of the NSC," p. 29, Folder: NSC (1), Papers of Dwight D. Eisenhower as President of the United States, Ann Whitman File, Administration Series, Box 30, Eisenhower Library.

19. Virgil Pinkley compares budgetary processes under Truman and Eisenhower in *Eisenhower Declassified* (Old Tappan, N.J.: Fleming H. Revell Company, 1979), p. 277.

20. R. Gordon Hoxie, "The National Security Council," *Presidential Studies Quarterly*, vol. 12, Winter 1982, p. 109.

21. Ibid.

22. Lay, "An Organizational History of the NSC," p. 33.

23. R. Gordon Hoxie, *Command Decision and the Presidency: A Study of National Security Policy and Organization* (New York: Reader's Digest Press, 1977), p. 254.

24. Lay, "An Organizational History of the NSC," p. 12.

25. S. Everett Gleason, Draft of a Speech on NSC presented at the National War College, August 31, 1954, p. 13, Folder: National Security Council (1), Papers of S. Everett Gleason, Box 2, Harry S. Truman Library.

26. Ibid.

27. Ibid., pp. 14–15.

28. Ibid., p. 8.

29. Ralph Reid, Oral History Interview, pp. 6–7, Eisenhower Library.

30. Ibid., p. 8.

31. Ibid., p. 7.

32. "The National Security Council and Its Critics," Folder: National Security Council Investigation (Jackson Resolution), Staff Files, Bryce Harlow, Box 17, Eisenhower Library.

33. Ibid.

34. Stephen Hess, *Organizing the Presidency* (Washington, D.C.: Brookings Institution, 1976), p. 73.

35. "The National Security Council and Its Critics," Eisenhower Library.

36. Robert Bowie, Columbia Oral History Interview, p. 16, Eisenhower Library.

37. Ibid.

38. Hammond, "The National Security Council: An Interpretation and Appraisal," reprinted in Altshuler, *The Politics of the Federal Bureaucracy*, p. 154.

39. Peter Lyon, *Eisenhower: Portrait of the Hero* (Boston: Little, Brown, 1974), p. 504.

40. Ibid.

41. Gleason, Draft of a Speech on NSC, p. 9.

42. Lay, "An Organizational History of the NSC," p. 34.

43. Clark and Legere, *The President and the Management of National Security*, p. 64.

44. Memorandum from George Marshall to Dwight D. Eisenhower, February 19, 1953, Eisenhower Library.

45. Notes of Study Group Conference, February 17, 1953, p. 2, Folder: NSC Organization & Function (5), White House Office, Office of Special Assistant for National Security Affairs, NSC Series, Administration Subseries, Box 6, Eisenhower Library.

46. Robert Cutler, Report to the President, April 1, 1955, Folder: April 1955 (1), White House Office, Office of the Special Assistant for National Security Affairs, Special Assistant Series, Chronological Subseries, Box 1, Eisenhower Library.

47. Dillon Anderson, Columbia Oral History Interview, p. 18, Eisenhower Library.

48. Dick Kirschten, "Beyond the Vance-Brzezinski Clash Lurks an NSC Under Fire," *National Journal*, May 17, 1980, p. 816.

49. Dwight D. Eisenhower to Gordon Gray, Press Release, January 13, 1961, Folder: Final Reports (2), Papers of Dwight D. Eisenhower as President of the United States, Ann Whitman File, Transition Series, Box 3, Eisenhower Library.

50. Kirschten, "Beyond the Vance-Brzezinski Clash," p. 816.

51. Robert Cutler, "The Development of the National Security Council," *Foreign Affairs*, vol. 34, 1956, p. 453.

52. "The National Security Council and Its Critics," Eisenhower Library.

53. Robert Cutler, Report to the President, April 1, 1955, Eisenhower Library.

54. Ibid.

55. Dillon Anderson, Oral History Interview, p. 67, Eisenhower Library.

56. Ibid., pp. 54–55.

57. Ibid., p. 65.

58. Bernard Shanley, Oral History Interview, p. 101, Eisenhower Library.

59. Robert Cutler, Report to the President, April 1, 1955, Eisenhower Library.

60. Dillon Anderson, Oral History Interview, p. 109, Eisenhower Library.

61. Gleason, Draft of a Speech on NSC, p. 1.

62. Sherman Adams, Columbia Oral History Interview, Part 3, p. 154, Eisenhower Library.

63. Clark and Legere, *The President and the Management of National Security*, p. 65.

64. Lay, Jr., "An Organizational History of the NSC," p. 54.

65. Ibid., p. 56.

66. Ibid., p. 57.

67. Cutler, "The Development of the National Security Council," p. 450.

68. William Jackson to Sherman Adams, Memorandum of April 2, 1956, on "The Role of the OCB," Folder: William Jackson (1) October 1954–March 1961, White House Office: Office of the Staff Secretary, White House Subseries, Box 3, Eisenhower Library.

69. Ibid., p. 3.

70. Lay, Jr., "An Organizational History of the NSC," p. 53.

71. Ibid., p. 59.

72. Ibid., p. 54.

73. Christian Herter to Gordon Gray, Letter of January 19, 1960, Folder: OCB (1) April 1958–April 1960, White House Office: Office of the Special Assistant for National Security Affairs, Records 1952–1961, OCB Series, Administrative Subseries, Eisenhower Library.

74. Gordon Gray to Christian Herter, Letter of January 22, 1960, Folder: OCB (1) April 1958–April 1960, White House Office: Office of the Special

Assistant for National Security Affairs, Records 1952–1961, OCB Series, Administrative Subseries, Eisenhower Library.

75. Memorandum for the Record, January 11, 1961, p. 4, Folder: Memos Staff Re: Change of Administration (3), Papers of Dwight D. Eisenhower as President of the United States, Ann Whitman File, Transition Series, Box 7, Eisenhower Library.

76. Ibid.

77. Gordon Gray to Dwight D. Eisenhower, Letter of January 13, 1961, Folder: Final Reports (2), Papers of Dwight D. Eisenhower as President of the United States, Ann Whitman File, Transition Series, Box 7, Eisenhower Library.

5

Eisenhower's National Security Decision-Making

FORMAL AND INFORMAL SOURCES OF ADVICE AND INFORMATION

Eisenhower's National Security Council system was organized to satisfy the President's desire for systematic presentation of alternative viewpoints. In defending his reliance on the formal components of his decision-making apparatus, Eisenhower said:

> I have been forced to make decisions, some of them of a critical character, for a good many years, and I know of only one way in which you can be sure that you have done your best to make a wise decision. That is to get all of the people who have a partial and definable responsibility in this particular field, whatever it may be. Get them with their different viewpoints in front of you, and listen to them debate.
>
> I do not believe in bringing them in one at a time, and therefore being more impressed with the most recent one you hear than by earlier ones. You must get courageous men, men of strong views, and let them debate and argue with each other. You listen, and you see if there is anything that has been brought up, any idea that changes your own view or enriches your view or adds to it. Then you start studying. Sometimes a case becomes so simple that you can make a decision right then. Or you may go back and wait two or three days, if time is not of the essence. But you make it.[1]

Although the Council system itself was designed to facilitate thorough consideration of issues, the blend of personalities on the Council undoubtedly played a major role in fostering the type of bold and imaginative debate encouraged by the President. Dillon Anderson, who served as Eisenhower's second Special Assistant for National Security Affairs, suggests that the broad experience and strong convictions of Council members combined to produce balanced, broad-ranging discussions incorporating a multiplicity of viewpoints and ideas.

> Foster Dulles in the foreign field had very great influence. . . . George Humphrey, just by sheer force of his intellect and the strength of his personality, was always a strong voice, and I don't mean to say that either Foster Dulles or George Humphrey did most of the talking, but when they spoke they were strong contributors. . . .
>
> [Secretary of Defense] Charles Wilson's greatest contribution used to be asking questions. He would often ask a question that would sort of blow a proposition out of the water. . . .
>
> Radford was a powerful participant of course. Radford brought the whole military assessment to things, and he was a strong contributor. . . .
>
> Dick Nixon's contribution . . . was very great, and as a good lawyer and a good politician, he adhered to the area where he was expected to be expert. . . . He usually commented upon the political feasibility, domestic political feasibility, of this policy or that. . . . His comments I always thought were given well and in seemly fashion, expressing a judgment as to how such a program or policy might be received by the Congressional leaders, or ultimately by the Congress. And this would seem to be right on the button.[2]

At a legislative leaders conference just four months after he had taken office, Eisenhower said, "More and more, we find that the central body in making policy is the NSC. Its sessions are long, bitter, and tough. Out of that sort of discussion we're trying to hammer policy."[3]

In his memoirs, Robert Cutler provides us with a glimpse of one such Council meeting near the end of the Korean War. This meeting, as recollected by Cutler, dealt with "a many-faceted tangle of issues" featuring a debate over the introduction of nuclear weapons into the Korean conflict.

> Secretary Dulles and Admiral Radford presented opposing views for thirty-five minutes. First one and then the other addressed the Council in quiet earnestness, the head of the President—and all our heads—turning from left to right like watchers at a tennis match, as each man spoke. The issue and the presentation was charged with drama.[4]

Meetings of the type described by Cutler explain why the President was perplexed by the charge that he disliked controversy and preferred a watered-down consensus to heated debate of an issue. As Eisenhower put it:

I have never in my life, except on a court martial, seen a vote to decide a question. Some people have alleged that my way of making decisions— and this was actually quoted—was to insist on unanimity, and if there was a divided or minority opinion, I'd send all of them back and say, "Get it unanimous." Then I'd adopt it. Well, I could not think of anything more ridiculous and more wide of the mark than this. All my life is a refutation of such a theory, and why someone dreamed it up, I don't know.

As a matter of fact, there was a writer who speculated on exactly how much my assistants made my decisions for me or helped me, or how much I deferred to them. Well, this is one of those things where you become inarticulate when you try to refute it. . . .

Now this one writer of whom I spoke, he certainly never came to see me. He never came to any man who was really close to me. Yet he wrote with great authority. And so did some columnists. . . .

When really scholarly people reach conclusions on somebody else's book or column as their authority—they don't seem to me to be very true to the scholarly tradition. They ought to go to better sources than that.[5]

Turning to better sources does indeed provide us with a vastly different impression regarding Council operations. Declassified minutes of the National Security Council meeting of August 30, 1956,[6] for example, illustrate the Council's invaluable role in promoting forward planning, facilitating open debate, and assisting the President in crystallizing policy options. The topics discussed on August 30 were numerous and diverse. The meeting began with a discussion of the Suez Canal situation. After a report by the Secretary of State on the London Conference, Admiral Arthur Radford presented a Joint Chiefs of Staff study analyzing eight possible military courses of action in the event that war broke out over the Canal. The general conclusion reached by the Joint Chiefs of Staff was that the most desirable course of action for the United States would be strong public, political, and logistic support for Great Britain and France, without direct military intervention by the United States in support of these countries against Egypt. Although the merits of the proposals of the Joint Chiefs were rejected in later meetings of the NSC, the discussion on August 30 alerted Council members and the President to possible alternative courses of action and underscored the seriousness of the situation in Egypt. Indeed, the President noted that the Suez situation was "so grave that it must be watched hourly."[7]

In addition to anticipating possible military contingencies, Council discussion focused attention on two other key issues: the evacuation of American civilians in Egypt and concern for continued access to Saudi

Arabian oil. Admiral Radford informed the President that a plan for the evacuation of American citizens was already being finalized. Similarly, Arthur Flemming assured Council members that the Office of Defense Mobilization was moving ahead with plans for dealing with the oil situation in the event of trouble in the Suez Canal.

After discussing the Suez situation and other significant world developments, the Council turned its attention to a far-ranging discussion of NSC Planning Board Paper 5612, which focused on "U.S. Policy in Mainland Southeast Asia." The ensuing debates were significant in that they identified finely honed differences of opinion between various advisors on the Council. At least four major "splits" can be discerned in the debates of the August 30 meeting. Although these differences were not always dramatic, they unequivocally demonstrate the fact that important policy disagreements were not glossed over as has often been charged. Instead, alternative viewpoints were set forth in lucid fashion by the Planning Board and subjected to what Robert Cutler has described as the "acid bath" of Council debate.

The Joint Chiefs of Staff (JCS) registered two important splits regarding the Planning Board document at the August 30 meeting. The first point of disagreement centered on a provision in paragraph 2 of the document, which stated that "the loss of the Southeast Asian mainland could thus destroy the possibility of establishing an equipoise of power in Asia."[8] The Joint Chiefs believed that this sentence improperly implied that "establishing an equipoise of power in Asia" was or should be the U.S. objective in the area."[9] The President indicated his approval of an alteration in the wording of the sentence to read: "The loss of Southeast Asia mainland could thus have far-reaching consequences seriously adverse to U.S. security interests."[10] In accepting the recommendation of the Joint Chiefs, the President agreed that the "equipoise of power" language could be construed broadly to reflect an American commitment to maintaining a balance of power in the area.

After granting his approval to alternative language for paragraph 2 of the Planning Board document, the President and the Council members turned their attention to another, more critical, change proposed by the Joint Chiefs of Staff in the wording of paragraph 19. This paragraph provided for the use of military force in Southeast Asia under the condition

> that the taking of military action shall be subject to prior submission to and approval by the Congress unless the emergency is so great that immediate action is necessary to save a vital interest of the United States.[11]

The Joint Chiefs proposed that this statement be reworded to read:

The Congress should be requested to give to the President advance authority to act quickly in times of crises, including the use of armed forces. The grant of such authority should be publicized.[12]

Hence, the Joint Chiefs sought to solicit from Congress a "Gulf of Tonkin"–styled resolution long before its time, and without the pretext of a Tonkin Gulf–like incident. The Chiefs argued that full knowledge that the President had been given authority by Congress to act, with military force if necessary, would serve as a strong deterrent to Communist aggression. But although the President agreed with the Chiefs' objection to the equipoise language in an earlier paragraph of the document, he did not accept the second change for fear that the language of the paragraph, if accepted as government policy, might "commit the United States to military intervention in Southeast Asia too readily."[13]

Secretary of State Dulles, addressing himself to Special Assistant Dillon Anderson, asked for clarification of paragraph 19:

Was it conceivable that under this paragraph as presently worded, U.S. armed forces could intervene to assist a state of mainland Southeast Asia without having either a mandate from the UN or the cover of the SEATO treaty? If this were the case, then the purport of paragraph 19 went beyond anything that could be described as constitutional.[14]

Anderson explained to Dulles that, in his view,

military action by the United States, as set forth in paragraph 19, would not take place prior to submission to and approval by the Congress, unless the emergency was so great that immediate action was necessary to protect our vital interests.[15]

The minutes show, however, that Anderson's response did not satisfy Dulles. The Secretary of State reemphasized that

if the paragraph conceivably could mean that the President could decide to intervene with our armed forces in the absence of any cover of UN or SEATO action, such a move went beyond the constitutional powers of the Presidency.[16]

The President agreed with Dulles' argument, stating that he did not believe that he could constitutionally go as far as paragraph 19 would suggest if it were modified to include the proposed language of the Joint Chiefs of Staff. More importantly, perhaps, in language fore-shadowing the spirit of the War Powers Act of 1973, Eisenhower said:

except in the event of a direct attack on the United States itself or the
armed forces of the United States, we could not possibly go to war without
a declaration of war by the Congress.[17]

In rejecting the language presented by the Joint Chiefs, Eisenhower
reiterated his belief that no concept of the vital interests of the United
States would justify intervention with military force except a direct
attack on the United States or on U.S. forces.[18]

Eisenhower's insistence on consulting Congress stemmed from his
constitutional interpretation that the legislature must share in any decision
to commit American troops or initiate military action abroad. Although
it is true that Congress granted the President extensive authority in this
realm under the Formosa Resolution of 1955 (as it did two years later
with regard to the Middle East), Eisenhower's actions comported closely
with his constitutional philosophy of restraint as expressed at the Council
meeting of August 30. His handling of the crisis in the Formosa Straits
suggests that the President did not interpret the Resolution to constitute
a "blank check" for presidential action, as Lyndon Johnson would later
view his authority under the Tonkin Gulf Resolution. Rather, as Alexander
George and Richard Smoke suggest, Eisenhower's practice of seeking
congressional endorsement in advance of his intended commitments and
actions exhibited "an element of shrewd manipulation of the norms of
crisis bipartisanship as well as respect for the necessary role of Congress
in foreign policy."[19]

After concluding the debate over the President's prerogatives regarding
the use of military force in Southeast Asia, the Council discussed and
resolved several other important issues during the August 30 meeting.
One important split involved different positions on behalf of the State
Department and the Defense Department with regard to the question
of distinguishing between allied and neutral nations in the administration
of military and economic aid.

The essence of the State Department position on the trade issue was
that it did not wish to lay down as a fixed policy statement the principle
of preferential treatment for countries formally aligned with the United
States. Secretary of State Dulles noted:

It might well happen that some country aligned with the United States
in some kind of collective security pact would not actually be in need of
military or economic assistance; whereas some other country which was
in a neutralist posture might need our help to prevent itself from being
absorbed into the Communist orbit.[20]

Responding to Dulles, Acting Secretary of Defense Reuben Robertson
expressed concern that if the United States proceeded "to give military

assistance to neutral nations such as Burma, nations allied with us will assume that this assistance will be given to Burma at their expense."[21] Admiral Radford added that it was the view of Congress that the United States should give military assistance only to dependable allies.

Dulles then insisted that paragraph 11 of the policy paper under consideration should not consist of a fixed rule or statement of policy that would actually prevent the United States from providing military assistance to neutral countries such as Burma if it proved to be in the strategic interest of the nation to do so.

The President stated that although he was sympathetic to Secretary Dulles' desire to avoid an iron-clad rule, he also agreed with the Defense Department that, "other things being equal, the United States should extend preferential treatment to allies over neutrals."[22]

The debate over the question of preferential treatment to allies over neutrals prompted Dulles to offer a modification in the wording of the Defense Department's language to make it clear that although preferential treatment would "normally" be given, there would be room for exceptions. Eisenhower approved Dulles' proposal, and the Record of Action incorporated the more flexible language as government policy.

Among other splits of opinion debated by the Council on August 30 were provisions concerning the degree of support that the United States should provide to the armed forces of Laos and the type of aid, if any, that should be extended to Burma. The former issue pitted the Defense Department and the Joint Chiefs of Staff against representatives of the State Department, the Office of Defense Mobilization, and the Bureau of the Budget. The issue of aid to Burma found the State Department and the Office of Defense Mobilization opposing the Treasury Department, the Bureau of the Budget, and the Joint Chiefs. These divisions clearly illustrate the diversity of coalitions on the Council. When added to the previously discussed debates of the Council, they also reveal the depth of the discussions that took place at a typical Council meeting.

The minutes of the NSC meeting of August 30, 1956, provide important insights with regard to the Council's role in debating and refining issues and in assisting the President in resolving complex problems through consideration of policy options. For a closer look at the President's pivotal role at Council meetings, we will find it instructive to turn for a moment to records of the 363rd Council meeting, which took place on April 24, 1958.[23] The minutes to this meeting illustrate Eisenhower's rather formidable skill for raising probing questions, pinpointing central issues, and facilitating critical debate in his efforts to arrive at sound decisions.

The April 24 meeting began with a presentation by William H. Holaday, the Director of Guided Missiles. Holaday's report included a recommendation that the number of Intermediate-Range Ballistic Missiles (IRBMs) be increased from 8 to 12 squadrons (120 to 180 missiles) by 1963. Eisenhower questioned the wisdom of increasing the number of first-generation IRBMs to 180, given that much more would be known about the effectiveness of first-generation THOR and JUPITER missiles by 1960. It may be, the President argued, that "some time about 1960 we may have to say that we are going to scrap some of these missiles."[24] Eisenhower was particularly concerned that improved second-generation IRBMs would be available in the not-so-distant future, making the purchase of more first-generation missiles a questionable investment. James Killian, the President's Science Advisor, voiced the opinion that the question of second-generation missiles raised by the President was indeed the key question in the debate.

After addressing the issue of producing more first-generation IRBMs, the President questioned Holaday about the reasons for producing two types of aerodynamic missiles known as MACE and REGULUS. Holaday offered the explanation that REGULUS missiles were ship launched, whereas the MACE series was land based. Apparently not satisfied with Holaday's explanation, the President asked whether REGULUS could not be launched from the land as well as from ships. Holaday responded that REGULUS could be used as a land-based missile but that it would be more costly than the MACE system to use in a land-based capacity.

The President then suggested that REGULUS missiles be modified so that they could be used on land or at sea, and that the MACE program be discarded. Secretary of Defense Donald Quarles interjected that MACE had a special guidance system that made it particularly effective for tactical use, whereas REGULUS was adapted to radio control and was not as effective for shifting land operations. The notes of the NSC discussion indicate that Eisenhower remained skeptical about the need for both systems, despite Quarles' explanation. In line with the general thrust of his questions, the President said:

> It would seem that we must anticipate some very hard thinking if in four or five years' time we are to avoid presenting a bill to the public for these military programs which will create unheard of inflation in the United States.[25]

Secretary of State Dulles lent support to the President's arguments in a manner that provides a striking contrast to traditional images of the Secretary's zeal for prosecuting the Cold War. Dulles prefaced his comments to Council members by challenging the notion that the United States should strive to be the greatest military power in the world. The Secretary of State was particularly concerned that most discussions of the Council seemed to suggest that the United States should have the most and the best of everything. "Was there no group in government," Dulles asked, "which ever thought of the right kind of ceiling on our military capabilities?"[26]

Dulles noted that the President had often quoted George Washington regarding the desirability that the United States possess a "respectable military posture." The Secretary of State suggested that a ceiling should be imposed when the government had reached a level of "respectable" military readiness. "In the field of military capabilities," Dulles told Council members, "enough is enough."[27] Failure to recognize this fact would lead to a situation in which all of the nation's productive capability would be centered in the military establishment. The President voiced agreement with Dulles, adding that too much defense spending "could reduce the United States to being a garrison state or ruin the free economy of the nation."[28]

Although in the end Eisenhower approved the Defense Department's proposal for increasing the operational capability of IRBMs from 8 to 12 squadrons, he did so only after satisfying himself that the request was neither premature nor unnecessarily redundant. Eisenhower's decision appears to have surprised Special Assistant Robert Cutler, who expected on the basis of the remarks made by both the President and the Secretary of State that approval would be withheld or at least delayed pending further study. But as was characteristic of Eisenhower's approach to decision-making, his tough questions and comments reflected a commitment to weighing the broader implications of policies under consideration by the Council while simultaneously testing the strength of conviction of the policy advocates themselves. As presidential aide Robert Bowie suggests: "Eisenhower often directed probing questions at Council members, not so much to play devil's advocate, as to make sure the person had given careful thought to the problem at hand."[29]

Despite his approval of the Defense Department's IRBM proposal, the President, by "thinking aloud" before Council members, left no illusion regarding the thorough scrutiny that would be given to questions of military procurement. Records of White House meetings held outside the formal Council setting further illustrate the President's active leadership role in combating parochialism and steering debate toward the broader economic and security interests of the nation. At a conference on the defense budget on March 29, 1956, for example, Eisenhower raised several questions about duplication of research and development among the three branches of the armed services.[30] The President opened the meeting, which was attended by three representatives from the Defense Department and three from the Bureau of the Budget, by expressing concern that "nothing in the defense budget is ever eliminated."[31] Noting that this was hardly a new phenomenon, the President added that it took the Army fifty years to get rid of horses after they had become obsolete.

In a White House meeting with the Joint Chiefs of Staff the following day, Eisenhower said that although he did not expect the Chiefs to abandon their basic convictions or conclusions about security needs, he did expect that activities "will be conducted on a spartan basis, and with awareness of the essentiality of a sound economy to true security."[32] He warned the Chiefs of the adverse effects of fluctuations that would result from attempting too much for a short period and then having to cut back deeply.

In line with his desire to relate national security policies to projected costs and to the potential impact on the economy, Eisenhower instituted the requirement, early in his administration, that a financial appendix appear at the end of all proposals submitted to the NSC for consideration. The financial appendix, by placing a new burden on departments to justify their programs on economic as well as security grounds, became a subject of controversy in the administration. The Special Assistant to the Joint Chiefs of Staff for National Security Affairs, Lieutenant General F. W. Farrell, expressed his displeasure with the requirement in a letter to Robert Cutler written in June of 1957:

> While recognition of the financial facts of life is extremely important, it seems to me that the Planning Board could well overplay its Watch Dog of the Treasury role. . . . It is essential to realize that NSC documents have significance other than as budget safeguards. . . . We should not take it on ourselves to do all the Budget Bureau's work for it.[33]

Cutler responded to General Farrell with a lucid defense of the budget practices of the NSC's Planning Board:

> In its planning operations, the Planning Board should be just as much concerned with the effect of defense plans on the economy as with defense plans on themselves. To have this concern, and constantly exercise it, is not solely a Budget [Bureau] function. Budget is not an originator but an appraiser and executioner. The Planning Board, to adequately serve President Eisenhower, must integrate the economic as fully into every policy as the politico-military. The Planning Board is not a planner for the ideal, but for the intensely practical.[34]

Cutler's letter to Farrell accurately captured the President's commitment to hard-nosed economic analyses in judging the acceptability of national security policy proposals. Undoubtedly, the resulting integration of domestic and economic considerations is of fundamental importance in explaining Eisenhower's success in keeping the defense budget from spiraling out of control in the Cold War environment of the 1950s.

THE QUEMOY-MATSU CRISIS:
A CASE OF MULTIPLE ADVOCACY

Eisenhower found the National Security Council to be an invaluable forum for debate and deliberation, not only in formulating long-term foreign policy objectives, but also in responding to international crises. Such was the case during the Quemoy-Matsu crisis of 1954–1955, when the President faced the question of whether to commit U.S. forces to the defense of islands off the shore of mainland China that were occupied by Chiang Kai-shek's Nationalist forces.

In early September 1954, Communist Chinese artillery opened fire on Quemoy Island in what was construed by some of the President's advisors as a prelude to a full-scale attack on the Quemoy, Matsu, and Tachen islands, followed by an invasion of Formosa. Although many administration insiders registered alarm, Eisenhower remained poised in his assessment of the Formosa situation. At the peak of tensions in late March 1955, the President recorded in his diary:

> Lately there has been a very definite feeling among the members of the Cabinet, often openly expressed, that within a month we will actually be fighting in the Formosa straits. It is, of course, entirely possible that this is true, because the Red Chinese appear to be completely reckless, arrogant, possibly over-confident, and completely indifferent as to human losses.
>
> Nevertheless, I believe hostilities are not so imminent as is indicated by the forebodings of a number of my associates. It is clear that this gloomy outlook has been communicated to others because a number of articles in the papers state that the Administration is rather expecting hostilities within a month.
>
> I have so often been through these periods of strain that I have become accustomed to the fact that most of the calamities that we anticipate really never occur.[35]

Eisenhower's diary entry of March 26 accurately captures his dispassionate approach to decision-making throughout the Quemoy-Matsu episode. During the initial stages of the crisis, amid conflicting assertions from his top advisors, Eisenhower ordered a "ground estimate" so that he could make an independent assessment of military factors.[36] Drawing on White House records, Bennett Rushkoff indicates that the President was equally concerned with the political implications of possible American involvement. In a phone conversation on September 6, 1954, for example, Eisenhower and General Bedell Smith

> agreed that the United States would be putting its prestige on the line by becoming directly involved in the defense of Quemoy. As a result, they concluded that U.S. forces "should not go in unless we can defend it." Eisenhower even questioned the advisability of the United States evacuating Nationalist troops from Quemoy in the face of a major onslaught, because he felt that "once we get tied up in any one of these things our prestige is so completely involved."[37]

One week after his phone conversation with Bedell Smith, Eisenhower convened a special Sunday meeting of the National Security Council at Lowry Air Force Base, in Denver, Colorado, to discuss the Formosa matter. The September 12 meeting was attended by sixteen of the President's top advisors, including four Cabinet officers. The record of discussion for the September 12 meeting indicates that a broad spectrum of ideas was discussed and debated by the Council.[38]

Early in the meeting, Secretary of Defense Charles Wilson raised the provocative question of "whether we should continue supporting Chiang in stirring up hell with Communist China."[39] There is "a difference," Wilson noted, "between the position regarding Formosa and the Pescadores, which were formerly Japanese, and the offshore islands, which are involved in finishing up the civil war in China." Furthermore, the Secretary of Defense asserted, an American commitment to defend the offshore islands "will result in a war with Communist China." Such wars, Wilson cautioned,

> are traditionally hard to stop. . . . China would constantly accuse us of expanding the war, and there would be continuing questions as to how far we had to expand it. . . . The Communist Chinese could accept substantial attrition of their forces and therefore force us to expand the war. . . . We should know how we could end such a war before we started it.[40]

President Eisenhower, sharing Wilson's concern about a long-term commitment, noted that "if the Communists, by making faces and raising hell, can tie down U.S. forces, they will use that device everywhere."[41] The President added that he was "personally against making too many promises to hold areas around the world and then having to stay there to defend them."[42] Quemoy, the President suggested, "was not really important except psychologically."[43]

Admiral Arthur Radford, Chairman of the Joint Chiefs of Staff, disagreed with the President's assessment, stating that there were "military reasons for holding the islands of considerable importance."[44] Radford added that the Joint Chiefs of Staff "had not envisaged a stalemate situation with the U.S. forces tied down."[45] If the Chinese Communists attacked the offshore islands, Radford noted, "we would use mostly our carriers which were in the area in normal training and rotation." Radford, the record of discussion shows, "did not feel that we would get into a general war with Communist China if we undertook to repulse attacks of the kind under consideration."[46]

Presidential advisor Harold Stassen voiced agreement with Radford and the Joint Chiefs of Staff, stating: "If we show the Communists we are going to slap them down, we will be able to hold our position in the Far East. . . . We have got to show strength and determination."[47] Responding to Stassen, the President admonished his advisors to "get one thing clear in their heads, and that is that they are talking about war."[48]

With regard to possible military action, Special Assistant Robert Cutler asked whether the United States "would have to go into Communist China in retaliation, if the Chinese Communists attack our carriers." Admiral Radford suggested that the United States "could prevent the loss of the Tachens and Matsu Islands without hitting Communist China, but could not defend Quemoy without an attack on the mainland." Radford added that the minute the United States knew "that the Chinese Communists were about to launch an air attack on Quemoy, we should go after the airfields in China from which they would launch such an attack."[49]

The President noted that action of the type described by Radford would require congressional authorization, since such action would constitute war. "If Congressional authorization were not obtained," the President asserted, "there would be logical grounds for impeachment. Whatever we do must be done in a Constitutional manner."[50]

Near the end of the meeting, Secretary of State Dulles said that he thought it "important that we not ignore the United Nations in this situation."[51] Dulles suggested that thought be given "to taking the offshore island situation to the UN Security Council to obtain an injunction to maintain the status quo, on the theory that what the Communist Chinese were proclaiming was not directed only against Quemoy but also against Formosa."[52] Elaborating on this proposal, Dulles noted that

we would take it to the UN as in incipient aggression. The fact that the Communists would claim that this was civil war would not be effective, since they made the same claim in Korea and all the other UN nations disagreed. This could be presented under Article V of the UN Charter in order to prevent an aggravation of the world situation and to maintain the status quo pending further study.[53]

The record of discussion indicates that the Secretary of State

felt that no final decision should be made today, either to go to the defense of the islands or not, until the consequences of his proposal had been studied. Secretary Dulles said that information he had obtained close to the horse's mouth was a feeling that as a result of the Chinese Nationalist reaction at Quemoy and the uncertainty as to U.S. action, we do not need to anticipate a critical situation regarding the offshore islands for some time. This, therefore, gives us more time to consider the question.[54]

The President "heartily endorsed" Dulles' proposal for further reflection on the idea of taking the matter before the United Nations. He also discussed the importance of public opinion as a factor that should be considered in shaping the administration's decisions. The memorandum of discussion of the September 12 meeting provides an insightful summary of the President's closing remarks to the Council.

The President said that he did not believe that we could put the proposition of going to war over with the American people at this time. The West Coast might agree, but his letters from the farm areas elsewhere constantly say don't send our boys to war. It will be a big job to explain to the American people the importance of these islands to U.S. security. Moreover, if we shuck the UN, and say we are going to be the world's policeman, we had better get ready to go to war, because we'll get it. The President said that while he was in general agreement with everything that had been said, we must enlist world support and the approval of the American people.[55]

In January 1955, some five months after the Chinese Communists fired upon Quemoy, the administration focused on the separate but related issue of whether or not to evacuate the group of offshore islands known as the Tachens, where a Nationalist infantry division was stationed. Concern for the defense of the Tachen Islands was heightened when Chinese Communist forces seized one island near the Tachen group known as Ichiang on January 18, 1955. Air and sea attacks of mounting intensity were reported against the Tachen Islands themselves during the period of hostilities.

The President and his top advisors debated the question of whether to defend or evacuate the Tachen Islands at the 232nd meeting of the

National Security Council on January 20, 1955. Secretary of State Dulles opened the discussion by noting that it was "fundamentally unsound," in his view, "for the United States to try to assist the Chinese Nationalists to hold the northern groups of islands. The Tachens and the other islands in this area were simply too difficult to defend. On the other hand, Quemoy and the Matsu group could be readily protected by U.S. air power, including such air power based on Formosa."[56]

The President suggested that a decision by the United States to give up the Tachen Islands

> would at least have the merit of showing the world that the United States was trying to maintain a decent posture. At the same time, the proposed policy would make clear that this U.S. concession with respect to the Tachens would not mean that the United States was prepared to make any concessions with respect to Formosa and the Pescadores.[57]

The President noted that the particular problem with respect to the defense of the Tachens was "the lack of a safe port for our ships in this area. . . . It would be very difficult for us to sustain the garrisons in the Tachen Islands." The President suggested that "an announcement of a decision to evacuate the Tachens garrison, together with a statement of our determination to hold Formosa and the islands 'in front of it' [Quemoy and the Matsus], would appear to be the best course of action."[58]

Secretary of the Treasury George Humphrey disagreed with the President, stating that he had great difficulty understanding, and even more difficulty justifying, the proposal to retain the Quemoys when they "were set right down in the middle of a Chinese Communist harbor."[59]

Responding to Secretary Humphrey's misgivings, John Foster Dulles said:

> As long as the Chinese Communists insist that they are going to take Quemoy as part of their operations for the ultimate seizure of Formosa, all this put Quemoy in a very different light. If we wait until we have lost all these islands, and much of our prestige as well, we would be fighting at a terrible disadvantage.[60]

The real question, Secretary Humphrey persisted, was where to draw the defense line, and "why Quemoy should be included within it."[61] Voicing strong agreement with the Secretary of the Treasury, Secretary of Defense Wilson stated that he had believed, even before the Denver meeting of the National Security Council on September 12, 1954, "that the only reasonable hope of stabilizing the situation in the Far East was a determination by the United States to hold Formosa and the Pesca- dores."[62] There could be no "cooling off of the hot situation" vis-à-vis Communist China, Wilson explained,

> so long as these other close-in islands remained in the hands of the Chinese Nationalists. To let them remain in Nationalist hands was simply to invite Chinese Communist military action against them. Accordingly, if we make a move now, we should get the Chinese Nationalist garrisons off just as many of these small islands as we can, and should explain that the sole reason that we are assisting in holding any of the islands at all is that they are vital to the defense of Formosa.[63]

The Secretary of Defense concluded his remarks by noting that it would be "foolish to fight a terrible war with Communist China simply in order to hold all these little islands. . . . We should defend only Formosa and the Pescadores and let the others go."[64]

The Secretary of State responded that he did not disagree with the position taken by Secretaries Humphrey and Wilson "over the long period," but that timing was of critical importance. "This was certainly not the moment or the occasion," Dulles cautioned, "to inform the Chinese Nationalists that we would not assist them to hold any of the offshore islands." To do so at present, the Secretary of State suggested, would have "a catastrophic effect on Chinese Nationalist morale." However, if later on the situation "cooled down and the Chinese Communists renounced their intention of seizing Formosa, the United States would then be in a position to give up these other islands," as Secretaries Humphrey and Wilson were recommending.[65]

Arthur Flemming, the Director of the Office of Defense Mobilization, added that "while of course we did not wish to become involved in a war with Communist China over Quemoy, neither did we wish to get involved in such a war over Formosa. We therefore must be sure that in trying to avoid the first we do not bring on the second."[66] Concurring with Flemming, the President underscored the psychological significance of Quemoy, suggesting that "we probably couldn't hold Formosa if Chiang Kai-shek gives up in despair before Formosa is attacked."

Later in the meeting, the Council discussed the "reliability and the fighting spirit of the Chinese Nationalist garrison on the Tachen Islands." CIA Director Allen Dulles described morale as "rather poor" as a result of the Chinese Communist attack. Admiral Radford, on the other hand, thought that morale "seemed very good" when he had discussed it on his recent trip. He also believed that the defense position on the Tachen Islands was "so strong" that it would "cost the Communists a lot to take it."[67] Harold Stassen noted, however, that "once the Chinese Communists begin their attacks, they would almost certainly expend whatever resources were necessary to seize these islands."[68]

Vice President Richard Nixon inquired as to the mechanics "of making clear our new intentions regarding the offshore islands."[69] The Secretary of State suggested that the President should consider an announcement in the form of a message to Congress. In preparing the message, Dulles said:

> The precise details would not be spelled out, but the President's statement would convey the idea that some of these islands would be evacuated and that others would be held because they were related to our determination to defend Formosa. The Presidential statement would likewise make reference to action in the UN and to the desirability of a ceasefire.[70]

The National Security Council reconvened at 9 A.M. the following morning, January 21, 1955, to review Dulles' draft of the proposed presidential message to Congress. The draft message included the following passage:

> In the light of the announced plans of the Chinese Communists to retake Formosa by force, it is essential for the United States to make sure that war does not occur by reason of any possible miscalculations of our intentions. In the interest of peace, the United States must remove any doubt regarding our intentions or our willingness to fight, if necessary, to preserve our vital interests in Formosa and the Pescadores. This requires not only Presidential action but also Congressional action.[71]

In asking for a resolution of support from Congress, the message was careful not to imply that the President lacked constitutional authority to act. "Authority for some of the actions which might be required," the President said, "would be inherent in the authority of the Commander-in-Chief."[72] But a "suitable congressional resolution" would "clearly and publicly establish the authority of the President" to act in whatever fashion might be necessary.[73] "I do not suggest," the President noted, "that the United States enlarge its defensive obligations beyond Formosa and the Pescadores." The danger of attack against them, however, compelled consideration of "closely related localities and actions which, under current conditions, might determine the failure or the success of such attack."[74]

On the afternoon of January 21, the President met with Admiral Radford, Admiral Robert Carney, General Nathan Twining, and General Lemuel Shepherd to inform them of the proposed message to Congress.

Admiral Carney expressed the view that the presidential message advocated an evacuation of the Tachen Islands, which he and the other members of the Joint Chiefs believed would be both unwise and difficult.[75] Carney argued that it would be better to defend or reinforce the Tachens than to withdraw from them.[76] White House records show, however, that the President was not persuaded by the arguments of the Joint Chiefs.

In an incisive analysis of the Quemoy-Matsu crisis, Bennett Rushkoff explains why the President remained steadfast in his decision regarding the Tachens.

> One advantage of Eisenhower's professional background was that he did not have to accept the statements of his military advisers unquestioningly. In fact, at the meeting of January 21, he probed beyond the Chiefs' general assertions and expanded the scope of the discussion to include some of the more basic military considerations that were relevant to his decision. For example, . . . on the matter of reinforcing the islands, the President observed that while supplying the troops and civilians with food would not be a problem, supplying sufficient amounts of ammunition could be difficult. . . .
>
> He was a military man, and his military judgments were as valid as those of the Chiefs. Thus, not only could Eisenhower reject the advice of the Chiefs on political grounds, he could also reject it on military grounds.[77]

Hence, despite the advice of the Joint Chiefs to extend the United States' commitment to include the Tachen Islands, the President submitted his message to Congress, unchanged, just three days after the January 21 meeting. By the end of the week, both the House of Representatives and the Senate had passed resolutions authorizing the President "to employ the armed forces of the United States as he deems necessary for the purpose of securing and protecting Formosa and the Pescadores against armed attack."[78] As Eisenhower would later note in his memoirs: "I stuck to my proposed message, the purpose of which was to inform the Chinese Communists of the United States' intentions, to dispel doubts in foreign capitals that the United States was acting on constitutional grounds, and to bolster Chinese Nationalist morale."[79]

In an examination of Eisenhower's correspondence during the crisis, Fred Greenstein affirms that the President, in making his decisions, carefully assessed all of the complex political and military issues surrounding the offshore islands controversy.[80] A letter written by Eisenhower to his one-time Chief of Staff, Alfred Gruenther, on February 1, 1955, is particularly revealing of Eisenhower's ability to frame the key issues in their broader political context. "If one were assessing the situation strictly in military terms," Eisenhower wrote,

> a clear distinction could be drawn between the defense of Formosa and the defense of the so-called offshore islands. Not only are two different military problems presented, but in the one case [Formosa] we are talking about territories the control of which has passed from nation to nation through the years—and in the other case [Quemoy-Matsu], about territories that have always been a part of the Chinese mainland both politically and, in effect, geographically. If there were no other factors to consider, you and I, for example, would study the problem and would permit no advance by the Communists beyond the offshore islands, but that in any struggle involving only the territory of those islands, we would see no reason for American intervention.[81]

Eisenhower recognized, however, that the political dimensions of the problem complicated matters. If the United States were to adopt a policy of non-intervention in the case of an attack on the offshore islands, it "would infuriate the Chinese Nationalists." If, on the other hand, the United States were to "state flatly" that it would defend the Quemoy and Matsu islands, the policy "would frighten Europe and of course . . . infuriate the Chinese Communists."[82]

One political factor that weighed heavily in Eisenhower's calculus during the early stages of the Quemoy-Matsu problem was the morale of the Nationalist forces. Although the President had pushed for evacuation of the Tachen Islands against the advice of the Joint Chiefs, he believed as late as February 1955 that evacuation of the Quemoy and Matsu islands had to be weighed against the likely psychological damage to the morale of Nationalist troops. Consistent with this concern, Secretary of State Dulles confirmed on March 15 that the United States would in fact participate in the defense of the offshore islands if it became clear that an assault on the islands was the first stage of an attempt to conquer Formosa.[83] By late March, however, Eisenhower had begun orchestrating a shift away from the earlier commitment to defend the islands. In a letter to Winston Churchill, Eisenhower wrote that he "would personally be very happy" if Chiang decided that an evacuation of the offshore islands was desirable.[84] The shift in American policy became official on April 5, 1955, when Eisenhower sent a memorandum to Dulles outlining a plan for persuading Chiang Kai-shek to transform the offshore islands into outposts. The memorandum stated that the world should be made aware "that neither Chiang nor ourselves is committed to full-out defense of Quemoy and Matsu."[85]

The turnabout in American policy regarding the overall defense of the offshore islands appears to have resulted from the cumulative impact of advice given to the President from sources inside and outside the White House. Internally, as we have noted, George Humphrey and Charles Wilson were outspoken in their belief that the offshore islands should not be included in the defense commitment of the United States. Externally, Winston Churchill was among those who urged the President to disentangle the primary issue of protecting Formosa from the secondary issue of holding the offshore islands. In a letter of February 15, 1955, Churchill argued that no decisive relationship existed between the offshore islands and protection of Formosa from invasion. Churchill was confident that the United States could easily "drown any Chinese would-be invaders of Formosa," no matter where they came from. Churchill suggested that the United States should provide Chiang the protection of its shield but not the use of its sword.[86]

Some three weeks after Churchill's letter, Anthony Eden urged in a speech in the House of Commons that the Nationalists should withdraw from Quemoy and Matsu, and that the Communists should agree to abstain from attacking them or Formosa. This arrangement, Eden suggested, could be followed by discussion of the political issues that would produce a peaceful settlement.[87]

Eisenhower's emphasis on protecting the morale of the Nationalist forces seems to have been tempered by the pleas of Churchill, Eden, and those members of the National Security Council who advocated that the United States should abandon its commitment to the defense of the offshore islands. In military terms, Eisenhower had already reached a similar conclusion in his phone conversation with Bedell Smith of September 6, 1954, and in his letter to Alfred Gruenther of February 1, 1955. The President continued, however, to defend the American commitment to the defense of Quemoy and Matsu on political grounds, until Secretary of State Dulles himself conveyed to the President a nagging doubt about how loyal Chiang's troops would be if attacked. Dulles rendered his negative assessment on March 10 after returning from two weeks in Southeast Asia and the Western Pacific. The Secretary of State's report disturbed the President greatly. "The United States," he noted at a White House meeting, "cannot possibly save the Nationalists if they don't want to be saved. The Secretary's report of military morale on Formosa puts the problem in a different light."[88]

Eisenhower's decision-making throughout the Quemoy-Matsu episode was marked by calm deliberation; thorough consideration of important political and military issues; an ability to make independent judgments in the face of strong conflicting assertions among top advisors; and, perhaps most important, the flexibility to shift course in midstream after the accumulated wisdom of counsel from those inside and outside the administration seemed to warrant a modification in the U.S. commitment to the Nationalists. The prudence of Eisenhower's midcourse adjustment in American policy became evident, at least temporarily, in late April 1955, when Communist Chinese Premier Chou En-lai proclaimed that his country was willing to open negotiations with the United States so that the two nations could settle their differences without war.[89]

THE AUGMENTATION OF FORMAL NSC CHANNELS

When the offshore island controversy resurfaced in the summer of 1958, Eisenhower, at the prompting of Special Assistant for National Security Affairs Gordon Gray, found it desirable to augment formal NSC channels. At a meeting with the President on August 11, 1958, Gray noted that the Council's standard operating procedures did not promote timely consideration of the issues generated by the controversy.[90] He mentioned to the President that he had initially discussed the offshore island problem with the Planning Board on August 4, but that if normal procedures were followed (i.e., discussion in the Planning Board, drafting by Board Assistants, further discussion by the Planning Board, and the customary ten-day review by the Joint Chiefs of Staff), the item would probably not come before the Council until August 28. Gray also used the occasion to voice concern that the number of people attending both NSC and Planning Board meetings was beginning to have a stifling effect on debate.

In discussing these problems with Gray, the President indicated that the Special Assistant should not be bound by rigid procedures. He then instructed Gray to bypass normal channels whenever he thought that a matter deserved timely attention by the Council, even if elaborate coordination had not been achieved. With regard to the Taiwan problem, Eisenhower informed Gray that he would like to schedule a restricted meeting in his office three days later, on August 14. The President also gave Gray the authority, whenever he deemed it necessary, to schedule meetings restricted to the statutory members of the Council, plus selected individuals, to consider problems of great consequence. As an example, the President suggested that a discussion of the cessation of nuclear testing would involve John McCone and Lewis Strauss, the current and former heads of the Atomic Energy Commission, and James Killian, the President's Science Advisor. Special meetings of this type were to take place at 9:00 A.M. (one-half hour before regular Council meetings) and would augment the regular weekly deliberations of the Council.[91]

Staff Secretary Andrew Goodpaster worked closely with Gordon Gray in coordinating these meetings as an adjunct to formal Council meetings.

Goodpaster suggests that these meetings were often used by the President to help focus on key policy questions that would be addressed at ensuing Council meetings.[92] White House records indicate that a substantial number of these meetings took place in the Oval Office. During the months of May and June 1959, for example, the President held at least six small-group advisory meetings and several additional meetings with his Special Assistant for National Security Affairs to discuss pressing problems.[93] As the schedule in Appendix 2 indicates, these meetings dealt with a wide array of important issues, including test suspension of nuclear weapons, the Berlin problem, nuclear-powered aircraft, and the Jackson Committee report on NSC operations. Attendance at these meetings was strictly limited relative to regular NSC meetings, with a maximum of ten individuals invited to participate.

In addition to these small, informal meetings in the President's office, Eisenhower made fairly extensive use of outside consultants to supplement formal NSC machinery. During the first two years of the administration, the President utilized outside consultant groups on at least six different occasions. These groups dealt with such topics as continental defense policy, petroleum policy, and basic national security policy.

Within a month following his inauguration, the President invited seven individuals from different walks of life and different regions of the nation to act as consultants to the NSC. This group, which became known in administration circles as the "Seven Wise Men," included, among others, the President of Cornell University, the Head of Pacific Gas and Electric, and a prominent scientist from St. Louis who had played a major role in the Manhattan Project.[94] By design, these men were all Washington outsiders who were completely disassociated with the departments. All seven were given security clearances and received intensive briefings from CIA, military, and State Department officials. Eisenhower called upon this group of advisors to provide a fresh perspective, untainted by bureaucratic biases.

Some critics have suggested that the reports of outside consultants and panels were filed away and not acted upon, but this clearly was not the case. Rather, the reports of advisory groups were critically reviewed by the NSC Planning Board before being sent to the Council for consideration and action. The President and the Council would approve, modify, or reject reports in part or in whole. Recommendations of the Technological Capabilities Panel (1954–1955), for example, were presented by Chairman James Killian of the Massachusetts Institute of Technology, at a long Council meeting. Various portions of the recommendations were considered and acted upon at fourteen subsequent Council meetings.[95]

One of the most influential outside advisory groups assembled by Eisenhower was the Securities Resources (Gaither) Committee (1957–1958). The Gaither Committee—named for its Chairman, H. Rowan Gaither, Jr., the Chairman of the Boards of the Ford Foundation and the RAND Corporation—was created by Eisenhower in 1957 at the advice of his Special Assistant for National Security Affairs, Robert Cutler. In addition to Gaither, the committee included Robert C. Sprague, an industrialist and an expert on continental defense; William C. Foster, a former Deputy Secretary of Defense and an expert on defense organization; James A. Perkins and William Webster, who had studied civil defense extensively; Jerome Wiesner, an expert on weapons systems evaluation who later served as a science advisor in the Kennedy administration; and five other men who brought additional technical competence as well as expertise in history and economics.[96] The report produced by the Gaither Committee was undoubtedly the most comprehensive study of national security ever produced by an ad hoc civilian group.

The findings of the Gaither Committee were presented by the Chairman of the Committee and his principal assistants on November 7, 1957, to one of the largest gatherings in the history of the National Security Council. At the President's request, more than forty people gathered in the White House for the presentation and ensuing discussion. Portions of the Committee's recommendations were acted upon at thirteen subsequent Council meetings.

One consequence of the Gaither Panel's report was to put more emphasis on the alert and dispersal of Strategic Air Command bombers in order to lessen their vulnerability to a Soviet attack.[97] In a detailed study of the Gaither Committee's work, political scientist Morton Halperin concluded:

The Committee Report provided clear, well-reasoned statements of the problems of vulnerability and limited war, of the role of dispersal and hardening [of missile systems], and of the problems and opportunities of civil defense. It undoubtedly made a major contribution to the understanding of these problems by top officials. . . . The Committee also advanced a number of new policy proposals, particularly in the field of defense reorganization, which were not likely to come from the armed services. . . . The Committee thus fulfilled its primary purpose of providing an additional source of information for the President, unencumbered by future or past policy responsibility.[98]

Eisenhower's outside advisory panels generated new ideas in the area of arms control as well. The famous Open-Skies proposal for American and Soviet aerial inspection of each other's territories was formulated by an administration advisory group known as the Quantico Panel. At the encouragement of the President, Nelson Rockefeller set up and directed the Quantico Panel to explore various ideas for recommendations that the United States might submit at the Geneva Summit Conference in July 1955 with regard to arms control. The Quantico Panel "groped for a formula that would allow the U.S. to retain its nuclear arsenal while making it clear that its primary purpose was peace."[99] The Quantico report went to the President on June 10, 1955, and he read it with enthusiasm. Although the proposal was not accepted by the Soviets, it was one of the many innovative and far-reaching proposals that evolved from Eisenhower's utilization of advisors and consultants, who served the President from outside the formal channels of the administration's national security machinery.

CONCLUSION

Under Eisenhower's leadership, the National Security Council provided an important forum for identifying key issues and facilitating systematic analyses of policy options. Formal meetings assisted the President in his decision-making by exposing him to a broad array of information and advice. More important, perhaps, Council members were exposed on a weekly basis to the President's own thinking on national security issues and to his policy directives once decisions had been made.

Clearly, Eisenhower's decision-making style was not passive or disinterested, as some of the scholarship on his Presidency has suggested. Rather, it was deliberate, contemplative, and well informed—at times boldly detached from the counsel of administration insiders, but always mindful of the importance of free and open debate in arriving at sound decisions.

Studies of Eisenhower's advisory processes in the field of national security policy seldom make reference to the President's efforts to augment formal Council machinery with informal advisory channels. Yet the administration was marked by a far more dynamic and flexible character than has commonly been assumed. White House records demonstrate that the President utilized a variety of sources to gather and assess information. Advisory groups such as the Quantico Panel, the Gaither Committee, and the "Seven Wise Men" epitomize Eisenhower's efforts to go beyond established governmental channels by deliberately seeking the opinions and expertise of prominent individuals outside the government setting.

Far from fostering a rigid or stifling organizational approach to national security policy-making, the President and his advisors sought on a continual basis to improve the formal machinery of the National Security Council. The President's use of ad hoc advisory meetings during the second Quemoy-Matsu crisis and the evolution of the Operations Coordinating Board toward greater integration between policy formulation and operations are but two examples of the innovative and dynamic quality of Eisenhower's administrative apparatus.

In light of the unquestionable value of the NSC system during the Eisenhower years, it is ironic that misinformed assessments of Council operations not only survived relatively unchallenged but also contributed to the demise of the system itself during the Kennedy and Johnson years. The consequences of the deinstitutionalization of policy-making processes in the post-Eisenhower period will be the focus of our discussion in Chapter 6.

NOTES

1. Dwight D. Eisenhower, Columbia Oral History Interview, July 20, 1967, p. 103, Eisenhower Library.

2. Dillon Anderson, Oral History Interview, pp. 46–49, Eisenhower Library.

3. Eisenhower, quoted in Peter Lyon, *Eisenhower: Portrait of the Hero* (Boston: Little, Brown, 1974), p. 503.

4. Robert Cutler, *No Time for Rest* (Boston: Little, Brown, 1966), p. 305.

5. Dwight D. Eisenhower, Columbia Oral History Interview, July 20, 1967, p. 103, Eisenhower Library.

6. Memorandum of Discussion at the 295th Meeting of the National Security Council on August 30, 1956, dated August 31, 1956, Folder: 295th Meeting of NSC, Papers of Dwight D. Eisenhower as President of the United States, Ann Whitman File, NSC Series, Box 8, Eisenhower Library.

7. Ibid., p. 6.

8. Ibid., p. 10.

9. Ibid.

10. Ibid.

11. Ibid., p. 13.

12. Ibid.

13. Ibid.

14. Ibid., p. 14.

15. Ibid.

16. Ibid.

17. Ibid.

18. Ibid., p. 15.

19. Alexander George and Richard Smoke, *Deterrence in American Foreign Policy: Theory and Practice* (New York: Columbia University Press, 1974), p. 289.

20. Memorandum of Discussion at the 295th Meeting of the National Security Council on August 30, 1956, p. 11.

21. Ibid., p. 12.

22. Ibid., p. 11.

23. Memorandum of Discussion at the 363rd Meeting of the National Security Council on April 24, 1958, dated April 25, 1958, Folder: 363rd Meeting of NSC, Papers of Dwight D. Eisenhower as President of the United States, Ann Whitman File, NSC Series, Box 10, Eisenhower Library.

24. Ibid., p. 2.

25. Ibid., p. 4.

26. Ibid., p. 5.

27. Ibid.

28. Ibid.

29. Robert Bowie, Columbia Oral History Interview, p. 13, Eisenhower Library.

30. Notes of Meeting in President's Office, March 29, 1956, Folder: March 1956 Diary (1), Papers of Dwight D. Eisenhower as President of the United States, Ann Whitman File, Ann Whitman Diary Series, Box 8, Eisenhower Library.

31. Ibid.

32. Memorandum by Goodpaster on Conference with the President on March 30, 1956, dated April 2, 1956, Folder: April 1956—Goodpaster, Papers of Dwight D. Eisenhower as President of the United States, Ann Whitman File, Dwight D. Eisenhower Diaries, Box 15, Eisenhower Library.

33. Memorandum from Lieutenant General F. W. Farrell to Robert Cutler, June 21, 1957, Folder: General Robert Cutler, Vol. I-1, White House Office, Office of the Staff Secretary, White House Subseries, Box 2, Eisenhower Library.

34. Memorandum from Robert Cutler to Lieutenant General Francis Farrell, June 25, 1957, Folder: General Robert Cutler Vol. I-1, White House Office, Office of the Staff Secretary, White House Subseries, Box 2, Eisenhower Library.

35. Dwight D. Eisenhower, diary entry of March 26, 1955, Folder: ACW Diary, March 1955 (2), Papers of Dwight D. Eisenhower as President of the United States, Ann Whitman File, Ann Whitman Diary Series, Box 4, Eisenhower Library.

36. Bennett Rushkoff offers an illuminating examination of the differences among Eisenhower's chief military advisors in "Eisenhower, Dulles, and the Quemoy-Matsu Crisis, 1954–55," *Political Science Quarterly*, vol. 96, 1981, pp. 465–480.

37. Ibid., p. 467.

38. Memorandum of Discussion at the 214th Meeting of the National Security Council, Sunday, September 12, 1954, Folder: 214th Meeting of NSC, Papers of Dwight D. Eisenhower as President of the United States, Ann Whitman File, NSC Series, Box 6, Eisenhower Library.

39. Ibid., p. 6.

40. Ibid.

41. Ibid., p. 7.

42. Ibid.

43. Ibid., p. 6.

44. Ibid.

45. Ibid., p. 7.

46. Ibid.

47. Ibid., p. 8.

48. Ibid.

49. Ibid.

50. Ibid.

51. Ibid., p. 10.

52. Ibid., p. 9.

53. Ibid.

54. Ibid., p. 10.

55. Ibid., p. 11.

56. Memorandum of Discussion at the 232nd Meeting of the National Security Council, January 20, 1955, reprinted in *Foreign Relations of the United States, 1955-1957, vol. II, China* (Washington, D.C.: U.S. Government Printing Office, 1986), p. 71.

57. Ibid., p. 74.

58. Ibid.

59. Ibid., pp. 75–76.

60. Ibid., p. 76.

61. Ibid.

62. Ibid.

63. Ibid., pp. 76–77.

64. Ibid., p. 77.

65. Ibid.

66. Ibid., p. 78.

67. Ibid., p. 80.

68. Ibid.

69. Ibid., p. 78.

70. Ibid.

71. Draft Message from the President to the Congress, reprinted in *Foreign Relations of the United States, 1955-1957, vol. II*, pp. 81–82.

72. Dwight D. Eisenhower, *The White House Years: Mandate for Change* (Garden City, N.Y.: Doubleday and Company, 1963), p. 468.

73. Ibid.

74. Ibid.

75. Ibid.

76. Rushkoff, "Eisenhower, Dulles, and the Quemoy-Matsu Crisis, 1954–55," p. 471.

77. Ibid.

78. Eisenhower, *Mandate*, p. 469.

79. Ibid., p. 467.

80. Fred I. Greenstein, *The Hidden-Hand Presidency: Eisenhower as Leader* (New York: Basic Books, 1982), pp. 20–24.

81. Ibid., p. 22.

82. Ibid.

83. Rushkoff, "Eisenhower, Dulles, and the Quemoy-Matsu Crisis, 1954–55," pp. 475–476.

84. Ibid.

85. This memorandum is published in full in Eisenhower, *Mandate*, p. 611.

86. Ibid., p. 472.

87. Ibid., p. 475.

88. Ibid., p. 476.

89. Rushkoff, "Eisenhower, Dulles, and the Quemoy-Matsu Crisis, 1954–55," p. 479.

90. Gordon Gray, Memorandum of Conversation with the President, August 11, 1958, Folder: Meetings with the President 1958 (4), White House Office, Office of the Special Assistant for National Security Affairs, Presidential Subseries, Box 3, Eisenhower Library.

91. Ibid.

92. Interview with General Andrew Goodpaster by Phillip G. Henderson, Institute for Defense Analyses, October 7, 1983.

93. List of Meetings with the President, Folder: Meetings with the President 1959 (1), White House Office, Office of the Special Assistant for National Security Affairs, Presidential Subseries, Box 4, Eisenhower Library.

94. Dillon Anderson, Columbia Oral History Interview, pp. 19–20, Eisenhower Library. The "Seven Wise Men" included Dillon Anderson; Jim Black, head of Pacific Gas and Electric; Eugene Holman, Chairman of Standard of New Jersey; and Charles A. Thomas, a scientist from St. Louis and head of Monsanto Company. Although names for the remaining members of the group were omitted from Anderson's oral history interview, records of a special meeting of the National Security Council on March 31, 1953, indicate that the other three were John Cowles, Deane W. Malott, and David B. Robertson.

95. Robert Cutler, Comments on Speech by Senator Jackson, June 5, 1959, p. 7, Eisenhower Library.

96. Morton H. Halperin, "The Gaither Committee and the Policy Process," in Morton H. Halperin and Arnold Kanter, eds., *Readings in American Foreign Policy: A Bureaucratic Perspective* (Boston: Little, Brown, 1973), p. 277.

97. William Bragg Ewald, Jr., *Eisenhower the President: Crucial Days, 1951–1960* (Englewood Cliffs, N.J.: Prentice-Hall, 1981), p. 250.

98. Halperin, "The Gaither Committee and the Policy Process," p. 299.

99. Robert J. Donovan, *Eisenhower: The Inside Story* (New York: Harper, 1956), p. 345.

6

The Deinstitutionalization of the Eisenhower NSC System

CAUSES AND CONSEQUENCES

The election of John F. Kennedy to the Presidency in November 1960 marked the beginning of the end of the highly organized and institutionalized National Security Council apparatus that had flourished under Eisenhower's leadership. The youthful President-elect did not share Eisenhower's appreciation for the virtues of formal organization, both in fostering a comprehensive approach to policy-making and in promoting the spirit of teamwork among representatives of the departments and members of the White House staff. Consequently, Kennedy was favorably disposed toward the recommendations of a newly released report by the Senate Subcommittee on National Policy Machinery, which called for a substantial overhaul of the NSC system as it had existed under Eisenhower.

The Jackson Subcommittee, named for its chairman, Senator Henry M. (Scoop) Jackson of Washington, had been established by Senate resolution in July 1959 "to study the effectiveness of the existing government organizations and procedures for formulating and executing national security policy in the contest with world communism."[1] The Subcommittee suggested in its preliminary report that the Eisenhower NSC system was static, overstaffed, and unresponsive to questions of national security posed by the Soviet threat.[2] In order to respond more directly to the perceived threat posed by the Soviet Union, the Jackson Subcommittee proposed that steps be taken by the new administration to "deinstitutionalize" and "humanize" policy-making processes.[3]

Kennedy shared with Jackson the belief that American security vis-à-vis the Soviet Union had been weakened during the Eisenhower years. Indeed, during the presidential campaign of 1960, Kennedy charged that the Eisenhower administration had left the nation with a "missile gap" favoring the Soviet Union.[4] Hence, the Jackson Subcommittee recommendations, which were predicated upon strengthening the United States' defense posture, converged with Kennedy's own outlook (as well as with his highly personalized style of leadership) to make the demise of Eisenhower's NSC system inevitable.

The rationale used by Kennedy administration insiders to justify the dismantling of the Eisenhower system was predicated, in large part, upon inaccurate assessments of Council operations and misleading appraisals concerning the Council's impact on policy-making. Ironically, many of these misperceptions can be traced directly to the Jackson Subcommittee reports of 1960 and 1961.

In this chapter we will focus on the causes and consequences of the dramatic restructuring of national security policy-making processes in the post-Eisenhower era on the premise that the systematic, well coordinated, and department oriented approach to policy-making utilized by Eisenhower offered many advantages over the informal, ad hoc, and White House–centered approach to policy-making that followed.

BACKGROUND TO THE
JACKSON SUBCOMMITTEE REPORT

For all the negative publicity that the Jackson Subcommittee generated with regard to the organization and operations of the Eisenhower NSC, it seems clear in retrospect that Senator Jackson, himself, was concerned with the operations of the Council only insofar as they had failed to produce the policy outcomes that he found desirable. Indeed, Eisenhower's Special Assistant, Gordon Gray, was probably not far off the mark in a paper that he prepared for the American Political Science Association's annual meeting in 1959, in which he wrote: "I suspect that the unhappiness of any knowledgeable person with respect to the NSC and its procedures really derives, not from a concern about how the machinery works, but [from] what it produces."[5]

The principal shortcoming of Eisenhower's NSC apparatus, in Jackson's view, was that it had not formulated a broad enough strategy and committed sufficient resources to winning the Cold War. On April 16, 1959, Jackson outlined the deficiencies of Eisenhower administration policies in a speech to the National War College entitled "How Shall We Forge a Strategy for Survival?"[6] Jackson told his audience that the United States was "losing the Cold War" and suggested that the nation should spend whatever amount of money was necessary for defense to win a bold and decisive lead in the race for new weapons systems. The Senator suggested that the Eisenhower administration had fallen victim to a "budgetary fetish" and that there should never be an arbitrary budget ceiling on defense spending. Although Jackson acknowledged that Congress and the American public knew only "bits and pieces" of NSC policy papers, he was convinced on the basis of this fragmentary evidence that the Eisenhower NSC mechanism "has not produced, and cannot produce as now operated, a coherent and purposeful national program which sets forth what the United States has to do to survive."[7]

On the presumption that faulty organization had somehow contributed to the perceived sluggishness of national security policies during the Eisenhower years, Senator Jackson introduced a resolution in the summer of 1959 that led to the creation of the Subcommittee on National Policy Machinery. In October 1959, Jackson wrote: "The fundamental issue before the Subcommittee is this: How can we best organize for the long pull to generate the sustained national effort which will be needed to win out in the Cold War?"[8] Among other areas of inquiry, Jackson wanted to know whether the NSC had fully considered the psychological impact of "permitting the Russians to be first with the ICBM, first in orbiting a satellite, first in sending a rocket beyond the moon?"[9] The Senator also wondered if the NSC under Eisenhower's leadership had prepared a paper analyzing alternative means by which the United States could support and finance an increased defense program.

Clearly, then, Senator Jackson's chief criticisms of the Eisenhower NSC system were premised on an assumption, shared by Kennedy, that the United States' defense capability, particularly its strategic arsenal, had lagged dangerously behind that of the Soviet Union during Eisenhower's Presidency. But as Kennedy's close advisor and confidant, Theodore Sorensen, would later record, the assertions of Jackson and Kennedy proved to be incorrect.

> Contrary to the charges made by some Democrats in 1960, the Eisenhower administration's official intelligence estimates of Soviet missile prospects were not revised downward for political or budgetary reasons. . . .
> Eisenhower was right in downgrading the "missile gap" dangers in 1960. . . .
> Kennedy's error in 1960 on the "missile gap" had been the result of the public's being informed too little and too late—even after the facts were certain—about a danger which he had in good faith overstated.[10]

As with the "missile gap" charge, some of the Jackson Subcommittee's conclusions concerning the National Security Council itself are inconsistent with information now available regarding the actual operations of the Council under Eisenhower's leadership. Indeed, some of the Subcommittee's proposals were formulated to remedy problems that, in retrospect, were far less pronounced than the Jackson Subcommittee reports suggested. The Subcommittee recommended, for example, that the NSC should offer a clear expression of alternate courses of action and "not spare the President the necessity of choice."[11] But, as noted in Chapter 4, the preponderance of evidence available today, ranging from the frequent "splits" appearing in the Planning Board's policy papers to the broad debate and diverse options evidenced in the declassified records of NSC meetings, suggests that the Council was performing precisely such a function throughout Eisenhower's tenure as President.

Of course, some of the criticisms raised by the Jackson Subcommittee were well founded. The charge, for example, that a steady diet of Planning Board papers could at times bog down the Council with too much paperwork was the subject of serious debate within the administration itself. Eisenhower, for instance, became restless with what at times seemed to be excessive reliance on NSC papers. In a letter to Special Assistant Robert Cutler dated April 2, 1958, the President suggested that he would like to consider alternatives to the format of Council meetings.[12] The President hinted that the Council should not become consumed in the study of papers prepared by the Planning Board. Instead, he preferred that the Planning Board more often follow the lead of Council discussions. In this way, the President hoped to facilitate more discussion of provocative issues that required high-level thought.[13]

In a letter to John Foster Dulles written on May 2, 1958, Cutler acknowledged that the President was somewhat dissatisfied with Council procedures, but he defended the continued reliance on policy papers to facilitate debate.

> Sometimes the President seems to me to feel that too much NSC time is spent in considering written papers and not enough in free discussion of broad issues. I have done, and intend to do, all I can to stimulate free discussion. . . . But it is also my firm conviction that there is no substitute, if we are to have an orderly conduct of government, for consideration at the apex of government of carefully prepared written statements, upon the basis of which decisions are made for guidance to the Executive Branch.[14]

Having recognized that reliance on Planning Board papers occasionally restricted the scope of the Council's focus, the President sought to broaden his base of information through greater use of small, informal meetings in the Oval Office and greater reliance on outside consultants and advisors. Although Council operations were particularly flexible in this regard during the last two years of Eisenhower's Presidency, the

Jackson Subcommittee reports do not make reference to such adaptive features of Eisenhower's advisory system.

Some recommendations of the Jackson Subcommittee, while focusing attention on legitimate problems or deficiencies in Council operations, offered solutions that posed a cure worse than the disease itself. Noting that the distinction between planning and operations had been overdrawn in the Eisenhower administration, for example, the Subcommittee proposed to remedy the problem by completely abolishing the Operations Coordinating Board. By incorporating the OCB within the NSC framework and designating the President's Special Assistant for National Security Affairs as the new Chairman of the OCB, the Eisenhower administration had taken great strides to ameliorate the problems that can arise from drawing too sharp a distinction between policy formulation and policy implementation. Yet the administration wisely sought to prevent the obliteration of the planning and operations distinction altogether, lest there be a temptation to abandon the planning phase of policy-making entirely or, even worse, to preclude the departments from having input on policies that they would be asked to enforce.

JOHN F. KENNEDY AND THE DEMISE OF THE EISENHOWER SYSTEM

In its report to John F. Kennedy, the Jackson Subcommittee suggested that the President-elect could use the NSC either as "an intimate forum" to meet "with his chief advisors in searching discussion and debate of a limited number of critical problems" or as "the apex of a comprehensive and highly institutionalized system for generating policy proposals and following through on Presidentially approved decisions."[15] Based on its study, the Subcommittee concluded that the "real worth of the Council to a President" lay in the former course.[16] The report specifically criticized the Eisenhower NSC system for "over-institutionalization, and over-reliance on the Planning Board and OCB."[17] Hence, the Subcommittee proposed that the formal NSC staff should be reduced and that a small presidential staff, working "outside the system," should closely assist the Chief Executive by providing information, suggesting "policy initiatives," and "spotting gaps in policy execution."[18]

With the recommendations of Senate colleague Henry M. Jackson fresh at hand, Kennedy sought from the start to supplant Eisenhower's formal administrative apparatus with a highly personalized style of leadership. Kennedy's approach to organizing the government for national security policy-making presented a striking contrast to that of his predecessor. For as Kennedy's close aide and advisor Theodore Sorensen commented:

Kennedy brought to the White House unusual first-hand knowledge of the foreign, domestic, legislative and political arenas but no experience in the Executive Branch. He was always more interested in policy than in administration, and would later admit that "it is a tremendous change to go from being a Senator to being President. . . ." He continued to reshape executive procedures throughout his term, but from the outset he abandoned the notion of a collective, institutionalized Presidency.[19]

Rather than follow Eisenhower's example in administering the Presidency, Kennedy was intent on reviving the highly informal approach to executive management that had been utilized by Franklin Roosevelt. Yet, it is unlikely that Roosevelt himself could have dealt successfully with the federal government of the 1960s with the same free-wheeling management style that had served him so well in the 1930s.[20] Washington had not only gotten bigger; it had also undergone important political changes. Agencies that had been created and staffed by Roosevelt with New Deal loyalists in the 1930s had evolved into entrenched bureaucracies, complete with standard operating procedures, consolidated interest group ties, and independent bases of support within powerful committees in Congress.

Despite these changes, Kennedy persisted in his belief that the informal management style of the Roosevelt era would serve him equally well in dealing with the bloated bureaucracy of the 1960s. With open disdain for Eisenhower's efforts to institutionalize departmental representation through such mechanisms as the Planning Board and Operations Coordinating Board, Kennedy sought to "deinstitutionalize" and "humanize" policy-making processes in accordance with the recommendations of the Jackson Subcommittee on National Policy Machinery. Hence, by Sorensen's account, Kennedy

abolished the practice of White House staff meetings and weekly Cabinet meetings. He abolished the pyramid structure of the White House staff, the Assistant President-Sherman Adams-type job, the staff secretary, the Cabinet secretariat, the NSC Planning Board and the Operations Coordinating Board, all of which imposed, in his view, needless paperwork and machinery between the President and his responsible officers. . . . He paid little attention to organization charts and chains of command which diluted and distributed his authority.[21]

These actions were taken despite pleas from Eisenhower and his associates not to act too hastily in abandoning the organizational innovations of the previous eight years. Gordon Gray, Eisenhower's Special Assistant for National Security Affairs during the final months of the administration, advised his successor, McGeorge Bundy, to avoid hasty decisions to abolish the machinery developed by Eisenhower. In a White House memorandum, Gray summarized his remarks to the incoming Special Assistant:

> I confessed some personal bias for I said that I felt that my reaction to the suggestion that the OCB be abolished would be perhaps the same as his to the suggestion that now the College of Arts and Sciences at Harvard be abolished. . . . I constantly reiterated that I was simply asking for avoidance of hasty decisions and that the main point was that the functions assigned to the OCB were vital in Government and that it did not make sense to me to abolish the agency and then find it necessary to recreate it. This could be an unhappy waste of time and resources. I said even the suggestion that it might be abolished had an eroding effect on the structure, especially in the lower echelons of the department.[22]

Cognizant of the Jackson Subcommittee's criticisms of Council operations, Eisenhower himself made special efforts during the transition period to brief the President-elect on the importance that he attached to the formal machinery of the Council in shaping national security policy. In a transition meeting on December 6, 1960, Eisenhower attempted to impress upon Kennedy the importance of the NSC as a policy-making forum. In a transition memorandum, Eisenhower summarized his remarks to the incoming President:

> I explained to him in detail the purpose and work habits of the Security Council, together with its two principal supporting agencies—the Planning Board and the Operations Coordinating Board. I said that the National Security Council had become the most important weekly meeting of the government; that we normally worked from an agenda, but that any member could present his frank opinion on any subject, even on those that were not on the formal agenda. I made clear to him that conferences in the White House are not conducted as Committee meetings in the Legislative Branch. There is no voting by members and each group has one purpose only—to advise the President on the facts of particular problems and to make to him such recommendations as each member may deem applicable. I described how "splits" in Planning Board papers were handled.[23]

Eisenhower encouraged Kennedy to avoid any reorganization of the National Security Council or White House staff until the President-elect had become well acquainted with the current setup—but apparently to no avail. Not only were the Planning Board and Operations Coordinating Board abolished, but the National Security Council itself seemed to fall into disfavor with the new President. As Theodore Sorensen notes in his memoirs:

> At times he [Kennedy] made minor decisions in full NSC meetings or pretended to make major ones actually settled earlier. . . . He strongly preferred to make all major decisions with far fewer people present, often only the officer to whom he was communicating the decision. . . .
>
> For brief periods of time, during or after a crisis, the President would hold NSC meetings somewhat more regularly, partly as a means of getting on record the views of every responsible officer (who might otherwise complain that he wasn't consulted and wouldn't have approved), but mostly to silence outside critics who equated machinery with efficiency.[24]

In 1961, a Kennedy aide mentioned to former Special Assistant Robert Cutler that the administration's intention had been first to dismantle the Council machinery that Eisenhower had developed and then to build new Council machinery of the kind President Kennedy wanted. But the aide candidly admitted, "We've been so damn busy since we got down here, Bobby, that we've never had time to get on with the second step."[25]

Sorensen acknowledges that the lack of formal decision-making processes led to difficulties at times. In his assessment of the administration's advisory processes during the Bay of Pigs, for example, Sorensen notes that

> [o]nly the CIA and the Joint Chiefs had an opportunity to study and ponder the details of the plan. Only a small number of officials and advisors even knew of its existence; and in meetings with the President and this limited number, memoranda of operation were distributed at the beginning of each session and collected at the end, making virtually impossible any systematic criticism or alternatives. . . . No strong voice of opposition was raised in any of the key meetings, and no realistic alternatives were presented. . . . No realistic appraisal was made of the chances for success or the consequences of failure.[26]

Sorensen concedes that the gaps in planning "arose in part because the new administration had not fully organized itself for crisis planning." And although Kennedy himself believed that "no amount of formal NSC, Operations Coordinating Board or Cabinet meetings would have made any difference," Sorensen suggests that not all of the President's associates agreed with this assessment.[27]

General Maxwell Taylor is among those who faulted Kennedy's national security policy processes for producing the decisions that led to the Bay of Pigs fiasco. General Taylor believed that it was a lack of bureaucratic procedure and expertise that doomed the landing. The military was blamed for an operation it did not control. It was asked to advise from the sidelines with only partial glimpses of the total plan.[28]

Under Kennedy's highly informal approach to policy-making, the same individuals who planned the operation were the ones who judged its chances of success.[29] The Cuban desk specialists at the State Department who received information from the island on a regular basis were not even asked to comment on the feasibility of the venture.[30] Historian Arthur Schlesinger, Jr., who served as an advisor to the President during the Bay of Pigs planning, suggests that the "need-to-know" standard whereby no one was told of the project unless it became operationally necessary "had the idiotic effect of excluding much of the expertise of government at a time when every alert newspaperman knew something was afoot."[31] In place of the probing skepticism and wide-ranging debates that characterized Eisenhower's National Security Council meetings, the Kennedy administration meetings on Cuba took place, by Schlesinger's account, "in a curious atmosphere of assumed consensus."[32]

Bernard Shanley, who served as Special Counsel in the Eisenhower administration, suggests that Kennedy's advisory processes failed him in the Bay of Pigs case precisely because of the lack of a formal administrative apparatus of the type utilized by Eisenhower to channel departmental input. By abolishing the Planning Board and the Operations Coordinating Board, Shanley suggests, Kennedy in effect destroyed the backbone of the NSC: "The staff work was just not done properly, so when these issues came before the National Security Council, they were not properly staffed or prepared for decision."[33]

General Maxwell Taylor expressed dismay that White House organization and operations changed very little, even after the Bay of Pigs.

> As an old military type, I was accustomed to the support of a highly professional staff trained to prepare careful analyses of issues in advance of decisions and to take meticulous care of classified information. I was shocked at the disorderly and careless ways of the new White House staff. . . . When important new problems arose, they were usually assigned to ad hoc task forces with members drawn from the White House staff and other departments. These task forces did their work, filed their reports, and then dissolved into bureaucratic limbo without leaving a trace or contributing to the permanent base of governmental experience.[34]

On a similar note, *Foreign Affairs* editor William Bundy suggests that "there were clearly cases" after the Bay of Pigs fiasco "where the lack of a process of systematic review and discussion caused real trouble."[35]

The Skybolt decision of late 1962 and the initial actions encouraging the overthrow of Diem in the fall of 1963 are two such instances cited by Bundy. Although the processes used by Kennedy suited his style, they were, in Bundy's words, "flawed and idiosyncratic."[36]

Lyndon Johnson, like Kennedy, did not allow the NSC to take on the institutional role it had assumed under Eisenhower.[37] Consequently, the bureaucracy charged with enforcing administration decisions was cut off from the process of policy formulation and consultation on implementation. In place of the formal Planning Board and OCB meetings utilized by Eisenhower to bring participants into the policy-making arena, Johnson relied on informal mechanisms such as the famous "Tuesday lunches" to iron out policy. Townsend Hoopes suggests that the informality of the Johnson system exacted a heavy price with regard to policy outcomes.

> The decisions and actions that marked our large-scale military entry into the Vietnam War in early 1965 reflected the piecemeal consideration of interrelated issues, . . . the natural consequence of a fragmented NSC and a general inattention to long-range policy planning. Consultation, even knowledge of the basic facts, was confined to a tight circle of Presidential advisors, and there appears to have been little systematic debate outside that group.[38]

Reflecting on his many years of experience in the foreign affairs community, William Bundy offered this assessment of policy-making processes under Johnson:

> The well-known Tuesday lunches used by the President to shape war and negotiating strategy were, in my considered judgment, a procedural abomination—rambling, lacking in a formal agenda or clear conclusions, infinitely wearing to the participants, and confusing to those at the second level who then had to take supporting actions.[39]

The reluctance of Kennedy and Johnson to follow Eisenhower's lead in utilizing formal planning and coordinating bodies under the auspices of the National Security Council was predicated, in part, upon a general feeling that the State Department was too unwieldy and too slow in responding to presidential initiatives in foreign affairs. Sorensen suggests that Kennedy

> was discouraged with the State Department almost as soon as he took office. He felt that it too often seemed to have a built-in inertia which deadened initiative and that its tendency toward excessive delay obscured determination. It had too many voices and too little vigor.[40]

Kennedy's discontent with the State Department was reflected in the greatly expanded activities of the President's Special Assistant for National Security Affairs, McGeorge Bundy, and his staff. Consistent with the recommendations of the Jackson Subcommittee on National Policy Machinery, Kennedy departed from Eisenhower's reliance on professional support staff from the departments and agencies to build a more intimate—and, consequently, more heavily politicized—staff under Bundy's direction.

In sharp contrast to his predecessors in the Eisenhower administration, Bundy became an active formulator of policies and an active representative of the President in the actual conduct of national security affairs.[41] The latter role included such activities as inspection trips to Vietnam on behalf of the President. Over time, Bundy and his successor, Walt Rostow, added yet another role to the National Security Assistant's repertoire— that of presidential spokesman.[42]

The activities of Bundy and Rostow went well beyond the charter of authority granted by Eisenhower. Indeed, Eisenhower's first Special Assistant for National Security Affairs, Robert Cutler, was so little seen or heard in Washington that Samuel Lubell entitled his February 1954 *Saturday Evening Post* article on the Special Assistant "The Mystery Man of the White House."[43] Cutler offered a cogent explanation for this characterization in his memoirs.

> Before I came to the White House I had been speaking a great deal on a variety of subjects. But an "anonymous" Assistant to the President has no charter to speak for his chief in public. The President and I made an early arrangement, from which I never departed except on the President's permission, that as to my official duties (other than to explain mechanical aspects of the Council) I should keep my trap shut. No speeches, no public appearances, no talking with reporters.[44]

Eisenhower's second Special Assistant for National Security Affairs, Dillon Anderson, shared with Cutler a low-profile approach to serving the President.

> I undertook to indicate to him the policy alternatives and the differences, if any, in the departmental views. But I became mindful early in the game that the only way I could be of continuing service to him was to keep out of an effort to suggest policy to him. . . . I could have plugged my own views. But I felt it was not the right thing for me to try to get in between the President and his Secretary of State on foreign policy matters. . . . And during my period of service there I enjoyed the most cordial relations with Foster Dulles, and with Wilson and with Radford, because

they knew that I was not trying to use my proximity to the President to end-run them on any of their subjects.[45]

In the midst of his service to Eisenhower, Robert Cutler prophetically warned against efforts by future Presidents either to expand the policy role of the Special Assistant for National Security Affairs or to enlarge his staff.

> Since the Special Assistant has direct access to the President, an NSC staff operation of the kind suggested would tend to intervene between the President and his Cabinet members, who are responsible to him for executing his policies. Grave damage could be done to our form of government were there an interruption in the line of responsibility from the President to his Cabinet.
> For the foregoing reasons, I have opposed the interposition at the apex of government, responsive to the President's Special Assistant of a large staff which would concern itself with the formulation of national security policy. The Special Assistant may need a few more staff assistants. . . . But I would think it inadvisable formally to give him greater responsibilities or formally to increase his functional prestige.[46]

Despite Cutler's admonition against efforts to base the formulation of foreign and national security policy in the White House, the Kennedy and Johnson administrations expanded the policy role of the Special Assistant and his staff far beyond the functions envisioned by Eisenhower. And, as will be shown below, despite a dramatic restructuring of the National Security Council during the Nixon years, White House control over policy-making processes became even more pronounced with time.

KISSINGER ASCENDANT: THE NATIONAL SECURITY COUNCIL UNDER RICHARD NIXON

In a campaign speech on October 24, 1968, Richard Nixon vowed to restore the National Security Council to its preeminent role in national security planning.[47] Nixon asserted that "most of our serious reverses abroad" could be attributed to "the inability or disinclination of President Eisenhower's successors to make use of this important Council."[48]

Shortly after the 1968 election, Nixon instructed his newly appointed Special Assistant for National Security Affairs, Henry Kissinger, to begin work on revitalizing the Council as the primary channel for shaping national security policy. Kissinger's dissatisfaction with the "catch-as-catch-can talkfests" that had characterized policy-making processes during the Kennedy and Johnson years found expression in a statement issued by Nelson Rockefeller on June 21, 1968, in the midst of his campaign for the Republican nomination.

> There exists no regular staff procedure for arriving at decisions; instead, ad hoc groups are formed as the need arises. No staff agency to monitor the carrying out of decisions is available. There is no focal point for long-range planning on an interagency basis. Without a central administrative focus, foreign policy turns into a series of unrelated decisions—crisis-oriented, ad hoc, and after-the-fact in nature. We become the prisoners of events.[49]

Compounding these problems was the tendency, brought about by the informality of unprepared meetings, "to be obliging to the President and cooperative with one's colleagues," which "may vitiate the articulation of real choices."[50] Kissinger set out to correct these and other perceived weaknesses in policy-making by dramatically restructuring the NSC system.

The newly organized NSC system was expanded to include an elaborate web of policy committees and a staff of some 120 assistants.[51] A Senior Review Group was established to review papers submitted by the departments in much the same fashion as the Planning Board of the Eisenhower years had done. Membership on the Senior Review Group was constituted at the assistant secretary level but soon became dominated by Kissinger himself. A special panel known as the Washington Special Actions Group (WSAG) was formed in April 1969 to handle crises and provide contingency planning for world developments. In all, there were six such committees in the Nixon NSC system, with Kissinger the central figure in all aspects of the Council's work.

The appearance of formalism in the Nixon NSC stemmed largely from the sheer number of subsidiary organizations.[52] In practice, Kissinger's prescription for restoring the NSC to the preeminence that it had enjoyed in the Eisenhower years fell short of the mark. Instead of reviving the Council's central role in policy-making, the Nixon system, which centered on Kissinger and his staff, continued the post-Eisenhower trend toward White House domination of policy processes—but without the Eisenhower era's spirit of teamwork and emphasis on departmental participation.

By Kissinger's account, Nixon considered William Rogers an ideal choice for the position of Secretary of State because Rogers' unfamiliarity with foreign affairs "guaranteed that policy direction would remain in the White House."[53] Kissinger records in his memoirs that he soon became a beneficiary of Nixon's distrust of the career bureaucracy and, to an extent, of his distrust of the Cabinet itself.

Ironically, one reason why the President entrusted me with so much responsibility and so many missions was because I was more under his control than his Cabinet. Since I was little known at the outset, it was also his way of ensuring that at least some credit would go to the White House. Nixon compounded his problem by an administrative style so indirect and a choice of Cabinet colleagues with whom his personal relationship was so complex (to describe it most charitably) that a sense of real teamwork never developed. This was especially the case with respect to his Secretary of State.[54]

Conflict between the White House and State Department manifested itself even before the new administration took office when the President-elect and his Special Assistant for National Security Affairs moved to abolish the Senior Interdepartmental Group (SIG), which had been established by Lyndon Johnson in 1967. The Senior Interdepartmental Group was set up both to review the options that were to be presented to the NSC and to follow up on decisions reached by the Council. The mechanism, which was chaired by the Under Secretary of State, represented a last-ditch effort by President Johnson to establish some of the coordination that had been performed by Eisenhower's NSC machinery but had been so lacking throughout the previous seven years.

The State Department considered the Senior Interdepartmental Group system "a major bureaucratic triumph" because, in Kissinger's words, "it formally enshrined the Department's preeminence in foreign policy."[55] In his memoirs, Kissinger acknowledges that the battle over the Senior Interdepartmental Group had great symbolic significance.

It made no difference that the National Security Council had rarely met in the Johnson administration and therefore there had been little for the Senior Interdepartmental Group to do. Nor did it matter that the follow-up to the Tuesday lunches, where decisions were made, was outside the SIG structure. To the State Department, its preeminence, however hollow and formalistic, was a crucial symbol. And it was not wrong, given the Washington tendency to identify the reality of power with its appearance.[56]

In a post-election meeting with Kissinger, Nixon noted that because of the Foreign Service's "ineradicable hostility to him," he would not consider preserving the Senior Interdepartmental Group. Kissinger's notes of the meeting conveyed the message clearly: "Influence of State Department establishment must be reduced."[57]

Secretary of State designate William Rogers voiced strong opposition to the proposal to abolish the Senior Interdepartmental Group and to the perceived diminution of the role of the State Department—but to no avail. The battle over the Senior Interdepartmental Group set the tone for future White House–State Department relations. "Nixon increasingly moved sensitive negotiations into the White House where he could supervise them directly, get the credit personally, and avoid the bureaucratic disputes or inertia that he found so distasteful."[58]

Over time, the Nixon NSC system became more informal than had originally been envisioned.[59] Crucial issues were maneuvered to committees chaired by Kissinger. The frequency of full NSC meetings diminished from thirty-seven in 1969 to twenty-one in 1970, and to a mere ten meetings in the first nine months of 1971.[60] Ultimately, as Charles Kegley and Eugene Wittkopf observed:

> The NSC committee system commanded by Kissinger grew to be more important than the NSC itself. . . . Thus, despite Nixon's avowed intention to make the NSC "the principal forum for the consideration of policy issues" requiring Presidential decision, in fact the Council "looked more and more like the Kennedy NSC, like a pro forma body which symbolizes a serious approach to policy-making and legitimizes staff work done in its name." In effect, the formal National Security Council as well as the established foreign policy departments and agencies became subservient to the NSC committee system.[61]

Although Eisenhower had used the NSC to coordinate policy with the permanent career officials in the departments, the Kissinger-led NSC staff sought at times to circumvent the departments. In his memoirs, Kissinger describes one such instance that came about during the India-Pakistan crisis of 1971. The crisis, according to Kissinger, was marked by "a bureaucratic stalemate in which White House and State Department representatives dealt with each other as competing sovereign entities, not members of the same team."[62] With White House NSC staffers purportedly expressing "a degree of condescension for the work of the traditional departments," Foreign Service personnel felt "underutilized and distrusted by the Nixon administration," and morale reached a low ebb during the early 1970s.[63]

Despite the many problems posed by White House centralization of policy processes, some observers found the Nixon system preferable to the largely ad hoc approach to policy-making of his predecessors. In an early assessment, John Leacacos wrote in *Foreign Policy* that

> Nixon has been better served by his more formalized national security advisory system than either Lyndon Johnson or John F. Kennedy were served by their informal systems. . . . The product of all the memos and meetings, questionnaires and options is the refined raw material of Presidential decision-making, the identification of what opportunities and escape-hatches are open to the nation's leadership.[64]

The appointment of Kissinger as Secretary of State in September 1973 restored to the State Department some of the policy-making preeminence that had dissipated during the preceding twelve years. The role of the State Department was enhanced even further during Gerald Ford's Presidency. Conscious of the struggles in earlier years between the White House and State, Ford moved to restore a more harmonious working relationship between the two bodies by appointing Lieutenant General Brent Scowcroft as his Assistant for National Security Affairs. Scowcroft's highly professional demeanor and low-profile approach to coordination revived the spirit of teamwork that had characterized the Eisenhower years. Personality conflicts did arise in the Ford administration, but they were limited primarily to interdepartmental feuding between State and Defense rather than the once bitter White House–State Department rifts that had plagued Ford's predecessor.

THE CASE OF CONFLICTING SIGNALS: NATIONAL SECURITY POLICY-MAKING DURING THE CARTER YEARS

Although the administration of Gerald Ford witnessed a brief return to the Eisenhower standard of a low-profile Assistant for National Security Affairs, Jimmy Carter was quick to revive the practice, which had become so pronounced during the Nixon years, of appointing a highly visible National Security Advisor. Indeed, Zbigniew Brzezinski, in his memoirs, boldly asserts that an activist President needs a conceptualizer or policy advocate in the White House.[65] Brzezinski concedes, however, that his dual role of "protagonist as well as coordinator of policy" fueled the image of an administration "in which the National Security Advisor overshadowed the Secretary of State," with "adverse consequences not only for me personally but more significantly for the President himself."[66]

Kenneth W. Thompson, in his incisive review of Brzezinski's memoirs, suggests that the principal lesson of the Security Advisor's account is that "no Secretary of State could possibly be the President's principal advisor on foreign policy under the organizational system Brzezinski describes."[67] For, as Thompson notes,

[i]n organizing his power, Brzezinski is frank to say that he saw the President as many as six times a day, summarized discussions with Secretaries Vance or Brown including his disagreements with their recommendations, conveyed messages from the President to the Secretaries, sent the President a weekly NSC Report ("a highly personal and private document for the President alone"), used the SCC [Special Coordination Committee] . . . " to shape our policy toward the Persian Gulf, on European

security issues, on strategic matters, as well as in determining our response to Soviet aggression," . . . outlined all major Presidential speeches on foreign policy, cleared with relevant NSC staff all major cables with policy implications, approved foreign travel by Cabinet members, and established the Situation Room as the locale where most decision-making in the joint area of national security policy took place.[68]

Indeed, Carter's foreign policy decision-making system was, in Brzezinski's own words, "formally the most centralized of all in the postwar era," with the National Security Advisor himself at the hub of that system.[69]

By entrusting his National Security Advisor with such vast authority, President Carter, like Nixon before him, set the stage for marked conflict between Brzezinski and Secretary of State Cyrus Vance. Such conflict manifested itself most clearly in the sensitive area of Soviet-American relations.

Appearing on NBC's "Meet the Press" on May 28, 1978, Brzezinski bluntly accused Moscow of worldwide activities that were incompatible "with the code of détente" and stated that Cuban military activities in Africa were "intolerable to international peace."[70] Declaring that Soviet-Cuban activities should not be "cost free," Brzezinski openly advocated an American response through covert action in such places as Angola. The National Security Advisor also took a hard line on negotiations in the Strategic Arms Limitation Talks (SALT), under the rationale that there should be linkage between arms control and Soviet behavior in Africa and in the rest of the world.

In Paris, on June 14 (less than three weeks after Brzezinski's "Meet the Press" appearance), Secretary of State Vance made a policy statement that was sharply at odds with Brzezinski's earlier pronouncements, particularly with regard to American policy toward Angola. Following White House clearance and discussions with European allies, Vance authorized a senior American diplomat to visit the Angolan capital of Luanda to improve lines of communication and cooperation with the Soviet and Cuban-backed government there. These actions were followed by testimony before the House International Relations Committee in which Vance asserted that U.S. policy in Africa was "positive" and "affirmative." The Secretary of State dismissed the notion of linkage between Soviet-backed Cuban adventurism in Africa and the SALT negotiations. When asked by members of the committee who spoke for the administration—the Secretary of State or the President's National Security Advisor—Vance assured the committee members that he alone spoke for the President.

In a major foreign policy address delivered at the U.S. Naval Academy in Annapolis on June 7, 1978, President Carter attempted to reconcile the apparent contradictions between his two chief spokesmen in foreign affairs. The speech, according to chief White House speechwriter James Fallows, "was intended to set the record straight on U.S. policy toward the Soviet Union, which was then very muddied because of the varied comments coming from Brzezinski and Vance."[71] In preparing the speech, however, Carter unwittingly exacerbated the problems that had arisen from having two principal foreign policy spokesmen rather than one. After soliciting memoranda from Vance and Brzezinski with suggestions for the tone and content of the speech, Carter, by Fallows' account,

> assembled the speech essentially by stapling Vance's memo to Brzezinski's without examining the tensions between them. When he finished rewording the memos, the speech was done. It had an obvious break in the middle, like the splice in a film. . . . The *Washington Post's* story the next morning was titled "Two Different Speeches," an accurate and obvious interpretation, but one that galled Carter and those around him.[72]

Underlying the personality clash between Vance and Brzezinski was an equally important but relatively unnoticed institutional problem. An internal study on "National Security Policy Integration," which had been authorized by Carter in August 1977, cited "weaknesses in current organization and procedures" in the Carter White House's national security advisory apparatus as an instrumental cause of the "widespread perception that the administration lacks coherence in policy and action."[73] The internal study, directed by Philip Odeen, a policy analyst with thirteen years of experience in the Defense Department and on the National Security Council, emphasized that organizational structures and procedures, more than personalities, were at the root of the Carter administration's problems.

The Odeen report suggested that the National Security Council staff, under Brzezinski's leadership, had become so preoccupied with making policy that its role in helping the President plan for crises and in following up on policies at the implementation stage had been significantly weakened.[74] The report suggested that Brzezinski and his staff had failed to strike a balance between their "personal advisory role" to the President and their less glamorous "institutional responsibilities."[75] Though crediting the NSC staff for "serving the President well, according to his style and desires," the report suggested that it might be time for the President to adapt his own style to meet the changing needs of his administration. "The main issue," the report concluded, "is whether the role [of the NSC staff] should shift now that the administration has largely completed its policy formulation stage and must focus more on putting the President's policies into effect."[76] Noting that there were problems in reaching decisions, as well as a lack of "the bureaucratic discipline" necessary for enabling a staff to close ranks behind a decision after it is made, the Odeen report recommended that the President utilize "a planned decision process" involving more carefully structured meetings and more precise mechanisms for recording decisions.[77]

The Odeen report underscored the point that beneath the surface appearances of a formal administrative apparatus, important decisions were frequently made by a small group of Carter's intimates—often by agency heads who met at breakfast or lunch. The Vance, Brown, and Brzezinski breakfast meetings on Fridays were not unlike Lyndon Johnson's famous Tuesday lunches. The result of such informality, noted the Odeen report, is that officials "come away with differing perceptions of just what the agreement was."[78] The informality of the Carter system became the focus of media attention in the aftermath of the ill-fated hostage rescue attempt in Iran when it became clear that the rescue mission had been decided upon in the absence of Secretary of State Vance, who had been outspoken in his private criticism of the plan.

William Bundy is probably correct in suggesting that

> it is unlikely that historians or future practitioners of foreign policy will find the Carter administration anything but a negative example of method and process. . . . As in other briefer periods of such disarray, the moral is simple: a President who cannot impose teamwork on his senior advisors will be in deep and recurrent trouble.[79]

CONCLUSION

In 1961, the Senate Subcommittee on National Policy Machinery, in reviewing the origins of the National Security Council, concluded that the purpose of the Council was "at least as much to make the Presidency serve the needs of the departments as to make the latter serve the former."[80] Ironically, although Eisenhower's NSC system had come under heavy criticism by the Senate Subcommittee, it came closer to meeting this goal than any succeeding administration. Although the Eisenhower NSC staff consisted largely of career officials directed by a Special Assistant for National Security Affairs who was instructed by the President to serve as a neutral facilitator and coordinator of advice and information, the post-Eisenhower experience has been strikingly different. Indeed, although the Senate Subcommittee on National Policy Machinery warned explicitly against efforts to base foreign policy coordination on a "super-staff" in the White House,[81] the practice of nearly all post-Eisenhower administrations has been geared toward precisely this type of centralization. The Kennedy administration, for example, while describing the Secretary of State as the "agent of coordination in all our major policies toward other nations,"[82] in practice created a White House–centered foreign policy staff that at times rivaled the State Department for control over the direction of foreign and national security policy. Paradoxically, the subordination of the State Department was accompanied by the dismantling of the formal National Security Council machinery of the Eisenhower era. By 1963, the National Security Council had become, in the words of one Kennedy staffer, "little more than a name."[83]

The NSC witnessed some semblance of an institutional revival in the Nixon and post-Nixon years, but the trend toward White House centralization of policy processes, which so characterized the Kennedy and Johnson years, became an ingrained feature of modern administrations as well. This trend has been accompanied by a corresponding surge in policy entrepreneurship among prominent NSC staff. No longer are Assistants to the President for National Security Affairs neutral coordinators with a passion for anonymity. Instead, they have become policy advocates who often find themselves in direct confrontation, not just with the Secretary of State but with the Secretary of Defense and other department and agency heads as well. Increasingly, Presidents find themselves in a self-imposed quandary over whom to listen to.

Against this backdrop of dramatic change in the complexion of modern national security advisory processes, the Eisenhower experience takes on greater significance than ever before. For one of the principal lessons that can be drawn from the Eisenhower years is that the idiosyncrasies and machinations of an individual or small group cannot easily short-circuit or override a well organized and institutionalized advisory system. This is especially true when the advisory system has as its primary mission the systematic presentation of national security issues in a forum conducive to probing discussion and an open exchange of ideas.

More than any of his successors, Eisenhower realized the importance of respecting the authority of the executive departments by resisting the tendency to centralize and isolate policy-making in the White House. Nowhere was this more clear than in the explicit limits he placed on the role of the Special Assistant to the President for National Security Affairs. Eisenhower, as Gordon Hoxie has noted, would not have countenanced a staff assistant with all the authority in national security policy tendered Henry Kissinger or, for that matter, Bundy, Rostow, or Brzezinski.[84] Instead of a "super-staff" in the White House, Eisenhower sought to institutionalize the role of the departments through such mechanisms as the NSC Planning Board and the Operations Coordinating Board.

No President since Eisenhower has utilized the NSC as extensively, and only occasionally have Presidents used this body as effectively in the formulation and implementation of policy. It seems clear, in retrospect, that Eisenhower's formal advisory processes are better suited to the multiple demands placed on modern Presidents than the informal, ad hoc approach to policy-making utilized by some of his successors.

NOTES

1. U.S. Senate Background Memorandum on Study of National Policy Machinery, October 1959, Folder: NSC Investigation (Jackson Resolution) Staff Files, Bryce Harlow, Box 17, Eisenhower Library.

2. Ibid.

3. I. M. Destler, *Presidents, Bureaucrats, and Foreign Policy: The Politics of Organizational Reform* (Princeton, N.J.: Princeton University Press, paperback edition, 1974), p. 96.

4. Theodore Sorensen, *Kennedy* (New York: Harper and Row, 1965), pp. 610–613.

5. Gray, quoted in Stanley L. Falk, "The National Security Council Under Truman, Eisenhower and Kennedy," *Political Science Quarterly*, vol. 79, no. 3, September 1964, p. 426.

6. Comments by Robert Cutler on Speech by Senator Henry M. Jackson, Folder: NSC Investigation (Jackson Resolution) Staff Files, Bryce Harlow, Box 17, Eisenhower Library.

7. U.S. Senate Background Memorandum on Study of National Policy Machinery, October 1959, Eisenhower Library.

8. Ibid.

9. Ibid.

10. Sorensen, *Kennedy*, pp. 610–613.

11. Falk, "The National Security Council Under Truman, Eisenhower and Kennedy," pp. 427–428.

12. Robert Cutler to Dwight D. Eisenhower, letter of April 2, 1958, Folder: ACW Diary, April 1958 (2), Dwight D. Eisenhower Papers as President of the United States, 1953–1961, Ann Whitman File: Diary Series, Box 10, Eisenhower Library.

13. Ibid.

14. Robert Cutler to John Foster Dulles, letter of May 2, 1958, Folder: General Robert Cutler Vol. I (2), White House Office: Office of the Staff Secretary, White House Subseries, Eisenhower Library.

15. Falk, "The National Security Council Under Truman, Eisenhower and Kennedy," p. 427.

16. Ibid.

17. Harold Seidman, *Politics, Position, and Power: The Dynamics of Federal Organization*, 3rd ed. (New York: Oxford University Press, 1980), p. 202.

18. Falk, "The National Security Council Under Truman, Eisenhower and Kennedy," p. 428.

19. Sorensen, *Kennedy*, p. 281.

20. Garry Wills argues this point persuasively in "The Kennedy Imprisonment, Part I," *Atlantic Monthly*, January 1982, p. 38.

21. Sorensen, *Kennedy*, p. 281.

22. Gordon Gray, Memorandum for the Record, January 11, 1961, p. 11, Folder: Memos Staff Re: Change Administration (3), Dwight D. Eisenhower Papers as President of the United States, 1953–1961, Ann Whitman File, Transition Series, Box 7, Eisenhower Library.

23. Dwight D. Eisenhower, Memorandum for the Record of December 6th, 1960, meeting with President-elect Kennedy, Folder: Memos Staff Re: Change of Administration (1), Dwight D. Eisenhower Papers as President of the United States, Ann C. Whitman File, Transition Series, Box 1, Eisenhower Library.

24. Sorensen, *Kennedy*, pp. 284–285.

25. Robert Cutler, *No Time for Rest* (Boston: Little, Brown, 1966), pp. 295–296.

26. Sorensen, *Kennedy*, p. 304.

27. Ibid., p. 305.

28. Garry Wills, "The Kennedy Imprisonment, Part II," *Atlantic Monthly*, February 1982, p. 54.

29. Arthur M. Schlesinger, Jr., *A Thousand Days: John F. Kennedy in the White House* (Greenwich, Conn.: Fawcett Publications, paperback edition, 1965), p. 233.

30. Ibid.

31. Ibid.

32. Ibid., p. 235.

33. Bernard Shanley, Oral History Interview #2, interviewed by Dave Horrocks, May 16, 1975, Eisenhower Library.

34. Taylor, quoted in Wills, "The Kennedy Imprisonment, Part II," p. 54.

35. William P. Bundy, "The National Security Process," *International Security*, vol. 7, no. 3, Winter 1982-1983, p. 100.

36. Ibid.

37. R. Gordon Hoxie, *Command Decision and the Presidency: A Study of National Security Policy and Organization* (New York: Reader's Digest Press, 1977), p. 330.

38. Hoopes, quoted in Charles W. Kegley, Jr., and Eugene R. Wittkopf, *American Foreign Policy: Pattern and Process* (New York: St. Martin's Press, 1979), p. 253.

39. Bundy, "The National Security Process," p. 101.

40. Sorensen, *Kennedy*, p. 287.

41. John W. Kessel, *Presidential Parties* (Homewood, Ill.: Dorsey Press, 1984), pp. 118–119. For a detailed discussion of these roles, see Alexander L. George, *Presidential Decisionmaking in Foreign Policy: The Effective Use of Information and Advice* (Boulder, Colo.: Westview Press, 1980), especially Chapter 11.

42. Kessel, *Presidential Parties*, p. 119.

43. Cutler, *No Time for Rest*, p. 294.

44. Ibid., pp. 295–296.

45. Dillon Anderson, Columbia Oral History Interview, Part 2, pp. 69–70, Eisenhower Library.

46. Robert Cutler, "The Development of the National Security Council," *Foreign Affairs*, vol. 34, 1956, p. 457.

47. Henry Kissinger, *White House Years* (Boston: Little, Brown, 1979), p. 38.

48. Ibid.

49. Ibid., p. 39.

50. Ibid., p. 40.

51. Hoxie, *Command Decision and the Presidency*, p. 331.

52. Ibid., p. 333.

53. Kissinger, *White House Years*, p. 26.

54. Ibid., pp. 25–26.

55. Ibid., p. 42.

56. Ibid.

57. Ibid., p. 43.

58. Ibid., p. 29.

59. John P. Leacacos, "Kissinger's Apparat," *Foreign Policy*, 5, Winter 1971-1972, p. 5.

60. Ibid.

61. Kegley and Wittkopf, *American Foreign Policy: Pattern and Process*, p. 257.

62. Kissinger, *White House Years*, p. 887.

63. Leacacos, "Kissinger's Apparat," pp. 5, 18.

64. Ibid., pp. 23–24.

65. Kenneth W. Thompson, review of *Power and Principle*, by Zbigniew Brzezinski, in *Presidential Studies Quarterly*, vol. 13, Fall 1983, pp. 666–668.

66. Ibid.

67. Ibid.

68. Ibid.

69. Ibid.

70. *Washington Post*, June 2, 1978, p. A-22.

71. James Fallows, "The Passionless Presidency: The Trouble with Jimmy Carter's Administration," *Atlantic Monthly*, May 1979, p. 43.

72. Ibid.

73. Dick Kirschten, "Beyond the Vance-Brzezinski Clash Lurks an NSC Under Fire," *National Journal*, May 17, 1980, p. 814.

74. Ibid.

75. Ibid.

76. Ibid.

77. Ibid., p. 816.

78. Ibid.

79. Bundy, "The National Security Process," p. 104.

80. Destler, *Presidents, Bureaucrats and Foreign Policy*, pp. 84–85.

81. Ibid., p. 2.

82. Ibid.

83. Ibid., p. 100.

84. Hoxie, *Command Decision and the Presidency*, p. 331.

7

The Reagan Administration and the Iran-Contra Affair

PROLOGUE TO REFORM

Ronald Reagan's Presidency may provide the most compelling evidence yet of the need for a return to the systematic, broadly consultative, and well managed decision-making processes of the Eisenhower years. For it was in the absence of such processes that the administration embarked upon the disastrous initiatives now known as the Iran-Contra affair. The policy of selling arms to Iran and the ensuing diversion of funds from the arms sales to the Contras of Nicaragua offer a telling indictment of policy-making processes (or lack thereof) during the second term of the Reagan administration. Indeed, the entire Iran-Contra debacle may well have been avoided had there been an Eisenhower-like adherence to thorough staffing, careful planning, and frequent debate among the President's top foreign policy advisors.

New insights regarding the Iran-Contra affair will likely come forth in the months and years ahead. Already, however, there exists an unusually rich array of materials for shaping our assessments. The Tower Commission report, which is based largely on declassified White House documents, and the subsequent testimony of key participants before the joint House and Senate committees investigating the affair provide revealing insights into the flawed approach to policy-making that characterized the Iran-Contra initiatives.

The policy-making climate that gave rise to the Iran-Contra affair can perhaps best be understood if we review the conflicts over the conduct of foreign policy that appeared in the very first days of the Reagan administration. Indeed, it seems clear, in retrospect, that the early infighting among members of the administration set a tone of rivalry and discord that would have adverse consequences for months and years to come.

147

THE QUEST FOR CONTROL:
HAIG VERSUS THE WHITE HOUSE STAFF

Ronald Reagan entered the White House determined to avoid the kind of battling between the White House and State Department that had plagued the Nixon and Carter administrations. He proclaimed that his Secretary of State would be "the chief formulator and spokesman for foreign policy in this administration."[1] He was equally emphatic about his intention to downgrade the role of the White House National Security Advisor. In a pre-inaugural interview, the President-elect made it clear that he intended to utilize his National Security Advisor exclusively as a staff coordinator in the Eisenhower mold. "I think of the NSC as a kind of liaison," Reagan said, "to correlate what comes in from the State Department for the benefit of a President."[2] The President-elect added, "I think that the White House advisor should not be a rival of the Secretary of State, as he has been so much in the past. The National Security Advisor has seemed to be almost in competition with the Secretary of State, and I want that changed. Policy remains between the Secretary of State and the President."[3]

At a meeting two weeks before the inauguration, Secretary of State designate Alexander Haig and the President-elect agreed that the National Security Advisor and NSC staff "would have no independent contact with the press and that contacts with visiting foreign dignitaries should be the sole province of the Department of State."[4]

Despite the downgrading of the role of the President's National Security Advisor, there were signs of tension between the White House staff and the State Department in the first days of the administration. The problems began at a White House meeting shortly after the inauguration, when Secretary of State Haig presented a draft directive proposing an established structure in which the State Department would control most of the foreign and national security policy-making machinery. In his memoirs, Haig explains why he believed such a document was necessary.

> The President had to decide, and put in writing, who was going to do what. Without such a charter, the foreign policy machinery cannot function in an orderly way. The alternative is dispute over territory, rivalry over precedence, loss of decorum, and a policy that lacks coherence and consistency.[5]

However well meaning Haig's draft directive might have been, it apparently did not set well with some members of the White House staff. White House Counselor Edwin Meese III, in the presence of Chief of Staff James Baker, Deputy Chief of Staff Michael Deaver, National

Security Advisor Richard Allen, and CIA Director William Casey, began what Haig describes as a point-by-point "critique" of the paper. In the process, Haig reveals,

> my earlier understandings with the President—and Weinberger's too—were disappearing in a haze of nitpicking. At length, Meese tucked the directive into his briefcase. I would like to be able to say that something in his manner warned me that the document would stay there, unsigned for well over a year. But the truth is, I never dreamed that he would not hand it over to the President at the start of the next day.[6]

Meese and White House Chief of Staff James Baker reportedly viewed Haig's draft directive as a "power play."[7] Accordingly, they sought to moderate the Secretary of State's influence by circulating the directive among other officials with the expectation that the plan would be watered down. In the meantime, Haig suggests,

> there was no description of duty, no rules, no expression of the essential authority of the President to guide his subordinates in their task. This failure arose from ignorance: Reagan's assistants saw a routine act of government as a novel attempt to pre-empt power. In fact, it was a plan to share and coordinate those duties in foreign policy that express the President's powers under the Constitution. I left the White House that day with the feeling that Ed Meese and his colleagues perceived their rank in the administration as being superior to that of any member of the Cabinet.[8]

Meese, in his role as Counselor to the President, had indeed been given unprecedented authority for a member of the White House staff, including the privilege of Cabinet rank. He occupied the West Wing office once used by National Security Advisor Henry Kissinger and later by Zbigniew Brzezinski.[9] In another departure from established custom, National Security Advisor Richard Allen reported to Meese rather than to the President. Thus, Meese had wide authority over domestic and national security matters.

In his role as conduit to the President on national security matters, Meese became the focal point of controversy in August 1981, when he decided not to awaken the President to inform him that two Navy jets had been fired on over the Gulf of Sidra and had retaliated by shooting down the two attacking Libyan aircraft.[10] The decision to allow the President to sleep in the aftermath of an event that easily could have triggered a crisis was questioned widely in the press. Given Meese's broad authority, it is not surprising that he was able to curtail for some

time the Secretary of State's attempts to spell out more clearly the
process by which foreign policy would be made.

Former National Security Advisor Robert McFarlane testified before
the House and Senate committees investigating the Iran-Contra affair
that efforts by the White House staff to bottle up Haig's proposals for
a "comprehensive foreign policy decision-making system" created a
"policy vacuum" in the administration.[11] "The administration's first steps
towards pursuing a covert policy in Nicaragua" came about, according
to McFarlane, because of this policy vacuum.

The system advocated by Haig, McFarlane noted, "was designed to
generate alternative approaches to achieving basic aims, consider the
options that emerged, make the decisions among them and implement
the chosen policies. The process provided for consultation with Congress
and with experts in the political and career bureaucracies."[12] It was the
absence of such a system, McFarlane asserts, that led the Central
Intelligence Agency and, later, the staff of the National Security Council
to develop programs of covert aid to the Contras in the absence of
"thorough and concerted governmentwide analysis."[13] According to
McFarlane,

> In December 1981, when the CIA presented a proposal for initiating covert
> action in Nicaragua, there was no framework within which to analyze it.
> . . . It is immensely important to recognize just how crucial the absence
> of such a framework proved to be. . . . For if we had such a large strategic
> stake, it was clearly unwise to rely on covert activity as the core of our
> policy. . . .
> [You] must have the American people and the U.S. Congress solidly
> behind you. Yet it is virtually impossible . . . to rally the public behind
> a policy you cannot even talk about. . . .
> People [in the Reagan administration] turned to covert action because
> they thought they could not get Congressional support for overt activities.
> But they were not forced to think systematically about the fatal risks they
> were running.[14]

That Haig's early proposals for a clearly structured process of decision-
making put the Secretary of State in the center of foreign policy-making
seems less significant, in retrospect, than the clear need for a comprehensive approach to foreign policy. Yet the White House staff seemed
intent on preventing the Secretary of State and, with him, the entire
foreign policy bureaucracy from having the influence that his proposals
would engender. Indeed, Haig's frustration over the lack of a systematic
organization for the conduct of foreign policy turned to despair with
the announcement in late March 1981 that Vice President George Bush
would be in charge of crisis management in the administration. The

Secretary of State publicly denounced Bush's appointment, stating that preparations for emergencies required long-term planning that had to be integrated into the regular conduct of foreign policy by the State Department.[15] Haig reveals in his memoirs that he considered resigning over the issue—which he viewed as a departure from protocol and sound management. After the President explained the arrangement as a mere "housekeeping detail" and publicly affirmed that the Secretary of State was the "chief formulator and spokesman for foreign policy for this administration,"[16] Haig decided to stay in the Cabinet.

In the meantime, tensions between Haig and National Security Advisor Richard Allen had also become evident. Despite the President's commitment to the standard of a low-profile National Security Advisor, Allen had become quite assertive in his position. One of the National Security Advisor's clashes with Haig stemmed from a speech in which Allen chided the United States' allies in Europe for their pacifism. A similar rift developed when Allen's deputy, Richard Pipes, declared publicly that détente with the Soviet Union was dead.[17] Haig spent much of his time as a fire-fighter trying to limit the damage from remarks made by Allen and others on the NSC staff. In one such instance, Haig apologized to West German Foreign Minister Hans-Dietrich Genscher after an NSC staffer suggested that Genscher could be influenced by Moscow.[18]

Haig's problems as Secretary of State only worsened with time. In January 1982, Richard Allen resigned his post as National Security Advisor after becoming embroiled in controversy for accepting custody of a check for $1,000 from Japanese journalists, who through Allen's arrangements had interviewed Nancy Reagan. Allen's successor, William P. Clark, had served as Haig's deputy at the State Department and as Chief of Staff during Reagan's tenure as Governor of California. Although Clark had embarrassingly little knowledge of foreign affairs,[19] Haig wanted him as a deputy because he was a trusted confidant of the President and interacted well with Reagan's top White House aides. Haig and Clark enjoyed a good working relationship at the State Department, but matters changed soon after Clark moved to the White House.

In a sharp break with the pattern of White House supervision established during Allen's tenure as National Security Advisor, the White House announced that Clark would be given central responsibility in the national security field. Unlike Allen, who reported to White House Counselor Edwin Meese, Clark was given direct daily access to the President and dealt personally with Cabinet officials.[20] The expansion of Clark's authority as National Security Advisor planted the seeds for more expansive bureaucratic infighting between the White House and the State Department.

The Israeli invasion of Lebanon in June 1982 precipitated one of the major confrontations of the administration's first term over control of policy-making. The formulation of an American response to the Israeli action would, by Haig's account, engender conflicts "over votes in the United Nations, differences over communications to heads of state," and "mixed signals to the combatants in Lebanon."[21]

From the start, Haig suggests, the handling of the Lebanon matter "was complicated by the fact that William Clark, as National Security Advisor, seemed to be conducting a second foreign policy, using separate channels of communication."[22] As if anticipating the Iran-Contra debacle of Reagan's second term, Haig set forth a trenchant assessment of policy development in the period following the Israeli invasion. "My thoughts," Haig recalled, "were deeply disturbed by the dangerous implications of a situation in which a Presidential assistant, especially one of limited experience and limited understanding of the volatile nature of an international conflict, should assume the powers of the Presidency."[23]

The Secretary of State was particularly dismayed that he had not been consulted regarding a United Nations resolution against Israel that UN Ambassador Jeane Kirkpatrick had been instructed to support.

> In my conversation with the President it seemed clear that he had been under the impression that this recommendation reflected the unanimous judgment of his advisors. After telling him that his Secretary of State had not been consulted, I advised him that the U.S. must veto the resolution. Reagan, listening intently, agreed.
>
> Yet confusion persisted. The State Department [while Haig and Clark were in Europe with the President] was still getting conflicting instructions from the NSC. . . . I telephoned Kirkpatrick and instructed her to veto the resolution, regardless of any other instructions she may have received.[24]

On June 14, 1982, six days after the veto of the UN resolution, the Secretary of State told the President of his dissatisfaction with the policy-making processes in the administration. Ten days later, Haig met with the President again. At this meeting, the Secretary of State brought with him a "bill of particulars, listing the occasions on which the cacophony of voices from the administration and the seeming incoherence of American foreign policy had created dangerous uncertainties."[25] In his account of the meeting, Haig reveals that he told the President that if matters could not be straightened out, "then surely you would be better served by another Secretary of State."[26]

The next day, after an NSC working lunch, Haig was asked to step into the Oval Office to see the President. At this meeting, Haig recalls, "the President handed me an unsealed envelope. I opened it and read the single typed page it contained. 'Dear Al,' it began, 'It is with the most profound regret that I accept your letter of resignation.' The President was accepting a letter of resignation that I had not submitted."[27]

THE ARMS TRANSFERS TO IRAN

With Robert McFarlane as National Security Advisor and George Shultz as Secretary of State, the second term of the Reagan Presidency began on a more harmonious note than had existed during Haig's stormy tenure as Secretary of State. Despite important changes in personnel, however, problems of process and policy persisted. Public revelations in the aftermath of the Iran-Contra affair raised some of the most important questions of Reagan's Presidency concerning the coherence and consistency of American foreign policy and of the process of decision-making within the administration.

After a comprehensive inquiry, the President's Special Review Board, known as the Tower Commission, summarized the problems of policy and process that the Iran initiative encompassed.

> The Iran initiative ran directly counter to the Administration's own policies on terrorism, the Iran/Iraq war, and military support to Iran. This inconsistency was never resolved, nor were the consequences of this inconsistency fully considered and provided for. The result taken as a whole was a U.S. policy that worked against itself.
>
> The Board believes that failure to deal adequately with these contradictions resulted in large part from the flaws in the manner in which decisions were made. Established procedures for making national security decisions were ignored. Reviews of the initiative by all the NSC principals were too infrequent. The initiatives were not adequately vetted below the Cabinet level. . . . The whole matter was handled too informally, without adequate written records of what had been considered, discussed, and decided.[28]

This trenchant summary provides a sobering backdrop for discussion of the Iran initiative. By placing the policy of arms transfers to Iran within the context of national security decision-making processes, the Tower Board provides an eloquent case in support of sound organization and procedures as a requisite to informed policy-making, and of the need for disciplined adherence to established processes once they are in place. With this theme in mind, we will now turn to the development of the decision to sell arms to Iran.

The roots of the Iran initiative can be traced back at least as far as August 31, 1984, when the President's National Security Advisor, Robert McFarlane, requested an interagency study on U.S. relations with Iran. The objective of the study was to address the question of what the United States could do to make inroads with political factions in Iran in the event of the Ayatollah Khomeini's death. As the Tower Commission notes, the United States

> had a latent and unresolved interest in establishing ties to Iran. Few in the U.S. government doubted Iran's strategic importance or the risk of Soviet meddling in the succession crisis that might follow the death of Khomeini. For this reason, some in the U.S. government were convinced that efforts should be made to open potential channels to Iran.[29]

The interagency study initiated by McFarlane concluded that the United States had "no influential contacts" within the Iranian government or Iranian political groups, and that little could be done to establish such contacts.[30] The prospect of establishing meaningful contacts with Iran was dampened by the fact that seven American citizens had been abducted in Beirut, Lebanon, between March 7, 1984, and June 9, 1985. Intelligence strongly suggested that the abductions were sponsored by a fundamentalist Shiite terrorist group that had direct ties with the Khomeini regime.[31] As early as July 1982, the United States had obtained evidence suggesting that Iran was supporting terrorist groups, including those engaged in hostage-taking. By January 1984, Iran's sponsorship of international terrorism and its continuation of war with Iraq led the United States to actively pressure its allies not to ship arms to Iran.

By early 1985, some members of the National Security Council staff began to question the American policy of prohibiting arms sales to Iran. New intelligence suggested that factional fighting could break out in Iran even before the death of Khomeini. A "Special National Intelligence Estimate" of May 20, 1985, added that the Soviet Union was well positioned to take advantage of the potential chaos in Iran. In light of this information, two NSC staff members, Howard Teicher and Donald Fortier, believed that the United States' European allies should be allowed to "fill a military gap for Iran" and thus "blunt Soviet influence" in Iran.[32] Acting on this belief, Teicher and Fortier submitted to McFarlane a draft "National Security Decision Directive," which stated that the United States should "encourage Western allies and friends to help Iran meet its import requirements . . . including provision of selected military equipment."[33]

Because of "the political and bureaucratic sensitivities" involved, the National Security Advisor limited transmission of the draft directive to

Secretary of State Shultz, Secretary of Defense Weinberger, and the Director of the Central Intelligence Agency, William Casey. In letters to McFarlane dated June 29, 1985, and July 16, 1985, respectively, Shultz and Weinberger "objected sharply to the suggestion that the United States should permit or encourage transfers of Western arms to Iran."[34] In contrast, Director Casey "strongly endorsed" the thrust of the draft directive. Despite Casey's support, the strong objections of Shultz and Weinberger "vetoed" the draft and it was not submitted to the President for his signature.

At about the same time that the NSC staff was advocating allowing European allies to sell arms to Iran, the government of Israel was aggressively courting American support for its own proposal to sell arms to Iran. As the report of the Tower Commission notes:

> Iran desperately wanted U.S.-origin TOW and HAWK missiles, in order to counter Iraq's chief areas of superiority—armor and air forces. Since Israel had these weapons in its inventory, it was an alternative source of supply. Israel was more than willing to provide these weapons to Iran, but only if the United States approved the transfer and would agree to replace the weapons.[35]

Iranian businessman Manucher Ghorbanifar, who was known to the CIA as a person of questionable veracity,[36] had taken on the role of intermediary between Iranian factions and the Israelis. It was through this rather dubious source that the Israelis learned of Iran's purported interest in establishing "more extensive" relations with the United States. The Iranians had supposedly stated that release of the seven American hostages held in Lebanon could be achieved in exchange for 100 TOW missiles from Israel. "This was to be a part of a 'larger purpose' of opening a 'private dialogue' on U.S./Iranian relations."[37]

On July 14, 1985, McFarlane recommended to the Secretary of State that the United States indicate interest in a dialogue with Iran, but with no commitment to the proposed arms exchange. According to Chief of Staff Donald Regan, the proposal to open a dialogue with Iran was discussed by McFarlane and the President on the previous day, July 13, in the hospital where Reagan was recovering from cancer surgery. Regan recalled the President saying, "Yes, go ahead. Open it up." However, on February 11, 1987, the President told the Tower Commission that he had no recollection of such a meeting, and no notes that would indicate that the meeting had taken place.[38]

In any case, the Director General of the Israeli Foreign Ministry, David Kimche, met with McFarlane on August 2, 1985, to find out whether the United States would replenish Israeli supplies of HAWKS or TOWS if Israel sold such weapons to Iran. Four days later, on August 6, the Secretary of State met with the President to discuss "a proposal for the transfer of 100 TOW missiles from Israel" to Iran. "The Iranians were for their part to produce the release of four or more hostages." Shultz informed the President of his opposition to the arms sales. Secretary of Defense Weinberger, recalling a separate meeting with the President, says that he too "argued forcefully against arms transfers to Iran."[39] Despite this advice, the President, in his initial account to the Tower Commission, acknowledged that he approved the shipment of arms by Israel to Iran sometime in August 1985. However, it was unclear to the President whether he had approved the transaction before or after the fact.

prag provides no coh.

Given the piecemeal decision-making process in which the President met with his top advisors individually rather than holding a formal meeting of the National Security Council to debate the matter, it is not surprising that the record is "murky" with regard to what took place in August. As the Tower Commission observes: "No analytical paper was prepared for the August discussions and no formal minutes of any of the discussions were made."[40] Nonetheless, the Tower Commission concluded on the basis of the available evidence that the President "most likely" provided his approval "prior to the first shipment by Israel."[41]

On August 30, 1985, the Israelis delivered 100 TOWs to Iran, followed by a shipment of 408 additional TOWs on September 14, 1985. On September 15, 1985, one of the seven American hostages held in Lebanon, Reverend Benjamin Weir, was released by his captors. Although some have inferred that Weir's release resulted from the initial Israeli arms sales to Iran, the record remains unclear as to whether this was the reason that Weir was allowed his freedom.

In November 1985, the staff of the National Security Council became directly involved in the shipment of weapons to Iran. Plans for the third Israeli shipment in November called for the sale of 80 HAWK missiles to Iran in exchange for the release of five American hostages. Forty additional HAWKs were to be delivered at a later time. Lieutenant Colonel Oliver North, a Marine officer detailed to the NSC staff, had taken an active role in all previous discussions with Israel and assured the Israelis that the United States would replace the 120 HAWKs necessary to carry out the operation.

In mid-November, Israel's Defense Minister, Yitzhak Rabin, informed National Security Advisor Robert McFarlane of certain problems that would hamper Israel's ability to carry through with the planned transaction. On McFarlane's instruction, Oliver North became directly involved in the operations of the November shipment of HAWKs to Iran. He enlisted the support of retired U.S. Air Force General Richard Secord to assist in delivering the HAWKs to Iran. Further problems necessitated assistance from the Central Intelligence Agency as well. Ultimately, only 18 HAWKs were delivered to Iran in the improvised operation. Iran later returned all but one of these missiles to Israel, stating that they did not meet Iranian military requirements.

On December 5, 1985, President Reagan signed a retroactive Covert Action Finding to provide after-the-fact authorization for CIA participation in the November arms shipment to Iran. In testimony before Congress on July 15, 1987, Rear Admiral John Poindexter characterized the finding signed by the President as a clear "arms-for-hostage deal."[42]

On November 30, 1985, just a few days before the President signed the retroactive Covert Action Finding, Robert McFarlane resigned his position as National Security Advisor. On December 4, Admiral Poindexter, who had served on the NSC staff for more than five years, was named to succeed McFarlane as the President's National Security Advisor. In the midst of these events, Oliver North was busy formulating yet another arms-for-hostages proposal.[43] The new proposal called for the transfer of 3,300 TOW missiles and 50 Israeli HAWKs in exchange for the release of all the hostages.

North's proposal was discussed with the President on December 7 at a meeting that included Shultz, Weinberger, Regan, Poindexter, former Advisor McFarlane, and John McMahon of the CIA. The Secretary of State and the Secretary of Defense reportedly voiced "strong vociferous objections" to the plan, including a discussion of whether the transaction would be a violation of the Arms Export Control Act. When Weinberger raised the question of legality, the President is said to have responded, "Well, the American people will never forgive me if I fail to get these hostages out over this legal question."[44]

At the end of the meeting on December 7, the President asked Robert McFarlane to fly to London that day to meet with Manucher Ghorbanifar. McFarlane told Ghorbanifar that the United States wanted the American hostages released, and that it would be interested in better relations with Iran but would not send arms to Iran. Ghorbanifar refused to transmit this message, claiming that it would endanger the lives of the hostages. Upon returning from Europe, McFarlane told the President that he had no confidence in Ghorbanifar as an intermediary.

Shultz and Weinberger left the meeting of December 7 satisfied that McFarlane's message to Ghorbanifar would break the arms-for-hostages link. Without their knowledge, however, Lieutenant Colonel Oliver North was working behind the scenes to revive precisely such an initiative. In a memorandum to National Security Advisor Poindexter on December 9, one day before McFarlane was to brief the President on his meeting with Ghorbanifar, North proposed "direct U.S. deliveries of arms to Iran in exchange for release of the hostages."[45]

Because North had accompanied McFarlane to the London meeting, the Tower Commission raised the question of whether the Lieutenant Colonel "had fully supported the thrust of McFarlane's instructions in his own conversations with Mr. Ghorbanifar and others."[46] Indeed, it appears that North became the major catalyst in keeping the arms initiative alive. Making full use of his access to the National Security Advisor, he showed unrelenting perseverance in his efforts to sustain the Iran operation. North's efforts appear to have reinforced the President's preoccupation with finding a solution to the hostage impasse at the very time that an intense and critical review of the Iran situation may well have brought the arms-for-hostages approach into disrepute.

One month later, on January 7, 1986, the President met with Weinberger, Shultz, Casey, Regan, Poindexter, and Vice President George Bush to discuss the latest in a seemingly endless series of arms-for-hostages proposals presented by the Israelis. The proposal under consideration called for shipment of 3,000 Israeli TOWs and an exchange of certain Hizballah prisoners held by Israeli-supported Lebanese Christian forces. At this informal meeting in the Oval Office, Weinberger and Shultz again expressed strong opposition to the proposal, with most of those present favoring it. Unknown to Shultz, Weinberger, and others at the meeting, the President had already signed a draft Covert Action Finding on January 6, approving the arms initiative.

Ten days later, on January 17, 1986, the President signed a finalized version of the Covert Action Finding. This time, however, there was a dramatic change in the language of the Finding that had not been addressed at the meeting on January 7. Rather than using the arrangement suggested by the Israelis, the cover memorandum for the January 17 Covert Finding "proposed that the CIA purchase 4,000 TOWs from the [Department of Defense] and, after receiving payment, transfer them directly to Iran."[47]

The President was briefed on this important change by Admiral Poindexter in the presence of Regan, the Vice President, and Donald Fortier of the NSC staff. Conspicuously absent from the meeting were the Secretary of State and the Secretary of Defense, who, given their opposition to the earlier plan, likely would have expressed even stronger disapproval of the revised plan. The President clearly knew that with the signing of the January 17 Finding, the United States became a direct supplier of arms to Iran. In his diary that day, the President wrote: "I agreed to sell TOWs to Iran."[48] Shultz and Weinberger were not informed of the signed Covert Finding until the story began to unfold publicly in November 1986.

From the President's signing of the January 17 Finding onward, implementation of the Iran initiative took on a distinctively American tone, with the staff of the National Security Council assuming direct operational control. The Tower Commission notes that even though the initiative fell within the traditional jurisdictions of the Department of State, the Department of Defense, and the CIA, these agencies were for the most part ignored. Instead, the President's Review Board states,

> [g]reat reliance was placed on a network of private operators and inter-mediaries. How the initiative was to be carried out never received adequate attention from the NSC principals or a tough working-level review. No periodic evaluation of the progress of the initiative was ever conducted. The result was an unprofessional and, in substantial part, unsatisfactory operation.
>
> In all of this process, Congress was never notified.[49]

Instead of a well thought out plan and methodical implementation, the National Security Council aggressively pursued an improvisatorial approach to the Iran initiative. As the Tower Commission report suggests, "Lt. Col. North, with the knowledge of Vice Admiral Poindexter and the support of selected individuals at CIA, directly managed a network of private individuals in carrying out these plans. None of the plans, however, achieved their common objective—the release of all the hostages."[50] Indeed, although the January 17 Finding signed by the President indicated that arms transfers would cease if all of the American hostages were not released after delivery of the first 1,000 TOWs, the United States continued to pursue the initiative and arranged for another delivery of arms.[51]

A bad policy was made worse by inexperience and naive persistence in negotiating with a nation overtly hostile to the interests of the United States. As the President's Review Board states:

> The U.S. hand was repeatedly tipped and unskillfully played. The arrangements failed to guarantee that the U.S. obtained its hostages in exchange for the arms. Repeatedly, Lt. Colonel North permitted arms to be delivered without the release of a single captive. . . .
>
> Lt. Colonel North and his operation functioned largely outside the orbit of the U.S. government. Their activities were not subject to reviews of any kind. . . .
>
> It was the responsibility of the National Security Advisor and the responsible officers on the NSC staff to call for such a review. But they were too involved in the initiative both as advocates and as implementors.[52]

In testimony before the House and Senate select committees investigating the Iran-Contra affair, Secretary of State George Shultz minced
no words in describing his feelings about the failed initiative. "It galls
me," Shultz said. "Our guys . . . got taken to the cleaners. You look
at the structure of this deal—it's pathetic that anybody would agree to
anything like that. It's so lopsided. It's crazy."[53]

Ultimately, two American hostages, Father Lawrence Jenco and David
Jacobsen, were released by Iran, thus bringing to three the number of
hostages released in the lengthy period of the arms transactions. In the
interim, however, three new American hostages had been taken. Indeed,
as Secretary of State Shultz stated at the Iran-Contra hearings, the U.S.
arms sales to Iran had not, in his view, reduced Iran's terrorist actions
against Americans.

The gains from the Iran initiative were negligible, but the losses in
stature and credibility to American foreign policy were great. For, as
the Tower Commission suggests, the policy contained glaring and damaging inconsistencies.

> Whatever the intent, almost from the beginning the initiative became in
> fact a series of arms-for-hostages deals. . . .
> While the United States was seeking the release of the hostages . . .
> in this way, it was vigorously pursuing policies that were dramatically
> opposed to such efforts. . . . The administration continued to pressure
> U.S. allies not to sell arms to Iran and not to make concessions to terrorists.
> The Board believes that a strategic opening to Iran may have been in
> the national interest but that the United States never should have been
> a party to the arms transfers. As arms-for-hostages trades, they could not
> help but create an incentive for further hostage-taking. As a violation of
> the U.S. arms embargo, they could only remove inhibitions on other
> nations from selling arms to Iran. This threatened to upset the military
> balance between Iran and Iraq, with consequent jeopardy to the Gulf
> States and the interests of the West in that region. The arms-for-hostages
> trades rewarded a regime that clearly supported terrorism and hostage-
> taking.[54]

POLICY-MAKING BY CLIQUE:
THE OBSESSION WITH SECRECY

One of the glaring weaknesses of the Iran initiative, and of the later
diversion of funds to the Contras of Nicaragua, was the excessive concern
for secrecy among the small group of White House aides who directed
the initiatives. The Tower Commission report makes note of the det-
rimental effects of the obsession with secrecy and of the compartmen-
talization of policy.

The concern for preserving the secrecy of the initiative provided an excuse for abandoning sound process. . . .

Because so few people from the departments and agencies were told of the initiative, Lt. Colonel North cut himself off from resources and expertise from within the government. He relied instead on a number of private intermediaries, businessmen and other financial brokers, private operators, and Iranians hostile to the United States. Some of these were individuals with questionable credentials and potentially large personal financial interests in the transactions. This made the transactions unnecessarily complicated and invited kick-backs and payoffs.[55]

The advocates of the Iran and Contra initiatives used secrecy and deception, not just to keep Congress and the press from learning of the initiatives but also to silence critics within the administration. Information was withheld from the Secretary of State and the Secretary of Defense, for example, concerning the three Covert Action Findings signed by the President authorizing the arms transactions with Iran. After Shultz was alerted by the U.S. Ambassador to England about an arms deal involving middleman Adnan Khashoggi, National Security Advisor Poindexter told the Secretary of State, falsely, "that's not our deal."[56]

Because of his opposition to the policies advocated by the NSC staff, Shultz, by mid-1986, could not even get White House staff approval for a plane to take him on scheduled foreign visits. After one such incident in August 1986, Shultz submitted a letter of resignation to the President, but the President would not accept it.[57] "I felt a sense of estrangement," Shultz said. "I knew the White House was very uncomfortable with me. I was very uncomfortable with what I was getting from the intelligence community, and I knew that they were uncomfortable with me. . . . I had a terrible time."[58]

In November 1986, Shultz refused to endorse a draft of a White House news release, which stated that there was "unanimous support for the President's decisions" in the Iran initiative. National Security Advisor Poindexter told the Secretary of State that his decision in the matter was "very unfortunate."[59]

In his testimony before the Iran-Contra investigating committees, Shultz noted that even before the U.S. sales of arms to Iran had begun, "I had come to have grave concerns about the objectivity and reliability of some of the intelligence I was getting."[60] By mid-November 1986, the Secretary of State was convinced that "the President was not being given accurate information."[61] "The people who were giving [the President] information had a conflict of interest."[62] The CIA, Shultz suggested, had become so involved as a policy advocate in the Iran affair that it had distorted information to fit with its policy objectives. "It's too tempting," he added, "to have your analysis and . . . the selection of information that's presented favor the policy that you're advocating."[63]

Shultz was particularly critical of CIA and National Security Council staff analyses in 1985 that suggested Iran was unstable and that the Soviets were poised to increase their influence there.[64] Two high-level CIA analysts involved in the 1985 estimates have since stated that they were wrong.[65]

Shultz also took exception with CIA Director William Casey's assessment that Iran had not been involved in terrorism during the period in which the arms sales had taken place. In apparent confirmation of Shultz's suspicions, the Iran-Contra investigating committees revealed that a CIA report on Iran's continued use of terrorism had in fact been suppressed.

Perhaps the most damaging case of distorted intelligence involved the ready acceptance by CIA Director Casey and National Security Advisor Poindexter of an Israeli assessment which asserted that Iran's military strength was rapidly deteriorating in its war with Iraq. The Israeli assessment was included in a cover memorandum to the President in an apparent effort to bolster the argument that shipping arms to Iran would not contravene official U.S. neutrality in the war or upset the military balance of power in the region. The cover memorandum accompanied the Intelligence Finding of January 17, 1986, authorizing the covert arms transactions approved by the President.

Secretary of Defense Caspar Weinberger, who was not aware of the January intelligence assessment, later testified that the Department of Defense believed at the time that Iraq, not Iran, was at a long-term military disadvantage in the war. Nonetheless, the Israeli assessment of the military balance, as endorsed by Casey and Poindexter, clearly influenced the President's thinking on the arms sales. Chief of Staff Donald Regan's notes on a White House meeting on November 10, 1986, record the President as saying, "[The] side with military superiority will win. This [the arms sales] helps Iran, which was weaker."[66] Senator Sam Nunn of Georgia, a member of the Senate Select Committee investigating the Iran-Contra affair, was dismayed by the import of Regan's notes on the meeting of November 10:

> Here you had the President of the United States giving what is essentially erroneous policy. . . . It wasn't a small detail. It was a question of who our government believed was winning the war . . . and we have classified reports from the whole community, including intelligence, including Defense, including State, saying exactly the opposite of this.[67]

By mid-November 1986, the Secretary of State had become so alarmed by the whole Iran operation that he attempted, unsuccessfully, to wrestle control of Iran policy away from the staff of the National Security Council and William Casey at CIA. Shultz described the battle for control of policy-making as "guerrilla warfare."[68]

As in the case of the Secretary of State, Secretary of Defense Weinberger was systematically shut out from the decision-making during much of the Iran-Contra affair. Like Shultz, Weinberger was outspoken in his early opposition to the Iran initiative. When the Secretary of Defense first reviewed a proposal to sell arms to Iran in mid-1985, he wrote on the document that the plan was "almost too absurd to comment on. . . . It's like asking [Libyan leader Muammar] Qadhafi to Washington for a cozy chat."[69] The Secretary of Defense strongly disagreed with two key assumptions in the document—that Iran was about to fall, and that the United States could open up ties to so-called moderate factions in Iran. In testimony before the Iran-Contra committees, Weinberger said: "I didn't think there were any moderates still alive in Iran . . . and I still think that's true."[70]

Weinberger joined Shultz in voicing strong opposition to the arms sales initiative in the White House meeting of December 7, 1985. And like Shultz, he was gradually phased out of the decision-making process. It was not until January 1986 that National Security Advisor Poindexter informed the Secretary of Defense that the President had decided to proceed with the U.S. arms shipments to Iran. Poindexter told Weinberger that "there's no more room for argument."[71]

As the arms initiative progressed in 1986, the staff of the National Security Council went to great lengths to keep Weinberger in the dark concerning the initiative. Their efforts included the issuance of a directive ordering the Department of Defense Intelligence unit to keep the Secretary of Defense off the distribution list for an intelligence report on the arms deal. Ultimately, Weinberger inadvertently found out about the report through another intelligence source. The screening of intelligence information was part of what Weinberger had characterized as a deliberate effort to keep opposing views from reaching the President. The Iran initiative was, in Weinberger's words, the work of "people with their own agenda who thought this opening was a good thing, who knew that I opposed it, that George Shultz opposed it, [and] did not want the President to hear [opposing] arguments after the decision had been made."[72]

THE DIVERSION OF FUNDS TO THE CONTRAS

Attorney General Edwin Meese told the Tower Commission that during his investigation of the Iran initiative in November 1986, Lieutenant Colonel Oliver North reported that $3 to $4 million of profits from the February 1986 shipments of TOW missiles to Iran had been diverted to the administration-backed rebel forces in Nicaragua known as Contras. Other funds were apparently diverted to the Contras from the shipment of HAWK parts to Iran in May 1986. As the Tower Commission's findings indicate, this information not only enlarged the controversy surrounding the Iran initiative but also raised questions of propriety and of law.[73] In addition, the Tower Commission uncovered evidence of "substantial NSC staff involvement" in promoting "private support for the Contras during the period that support from the U.S. government was either banned or restricted by Congress."[74]

There are important similarities, the President's Review Board noted, between the Iran initiative and the Contra diversion.

> In both, Lt. Colonel North, with the acquiescence of the National Security Advisor, was deeply involved in the operational details of a covert program. He relied heavily on private U.S. citizens and foreigners to carry out key operational tasks. Some of the same individuals were involved in both. When Israeli plans for the November Hawk shipment began to unravel, Lt. Colonel North turned to the private network that was already in place to run the Contra support operation. This network, under the direction of Mr. Secord, undertook increasing responsibility for the Iran initiative. Neither program was subjected to rigorous and periodic inter-agency overview. In neither case was Congress informed. In the case of Contra support, Congress may have been actively misled.[75]

Unlike the Iran initiative, however, the Tower Commission concluded that "the President may never have authorized or, indeed, even been apprised of what the NSC staff was doing. The President never issued a Covert Action Finding or any other formal decision authorizing NSC staff activities in support of the Contras."[76]

Admiral John Poindexter's testimony before the Iran-Contra Investigating Committees in July 1987 was consistent with the Tower Commission's general conclusion with regard to the diversion of funds. Specifically, Poindexter stated that the diversion of funds to the Contras was a mere detail of implementation consistent with the President's well known policy objective to sustain the Contra effort. Poindexter further stated that he wanted to give the President "deniability" by not informing him of the diversion. The former National Security Advisor expressed confidence that the President would have approved of the diversion of funds had he known of it.

Poindexter's testimony was greeted with skepticism in some quarters. The notion that the Contra diversion was carried out in its entirety without the knowledge of the President was accepted by many, but not by all of the members of the congressional investigating committees. In his career as a naval officer, Poindexter's fitness reports portrayed him as "a meticulous staff officer trained to follow the chain of command."[77] Yet the former National Security Advisor testified that he had not informed even the President of the existence of the diversion program. Poindexter was known to have an "almost photographic memory."[78] But the Admiral suffered from an inordinate number of memory lapses during the Iran-Contra hearings. The House and Senate Committees revealed that Poindexter responded 184 times to questions by saying "I can't recall" and "I don't recall."[79]

If, as Poindexter suggested, he and Oliver North were the only officials in government who knew of the Contra diversion,[80] the implications with regard to the breakdown of accountable decision-making processes are perhaps worse than if the President had known all along. For as Senate Select Committee Vice Chairman Warren Rudman states: "With the exception of Admiral Poindexter, every high-level U.S. official who testified stated that Admiral Poindexter did not have the authority to approve the diversion, that the diversion was improper and possibly illegal and that the President would not have approved of the diversion had he been consulted."[81]

Congressman Lee Hamilton, Chairman of the House Iran-Contra investigating committee, was disturbed by the general import of Poindexter's testimony. Addressing his remarks directly to the Admiral, Representative Hamilton said:

> You have testified that you intentionally withheld information from the President that denied him the opportunity to make probably the most fateful decision of his Presidency: whether to divert the funds from the Iranian arms sales to aid the Contras. You said your objective was to withhold information from the Congress, apparently . . . without direction or authority to do so. . . .
>
> Now all of us recognize the need for secrecy in the conduct of government. This member has been privileged to receive, I believe, the highest secrets of our government. And I am quite sympathetic to your pleas that secrecy is often needed and too often violated.
>
> Even so, I believe that, in this instance, we have had testimony about excessive secrecy that has had serious consequences for the decision-making processes of our government. . . .
>
> Instead of bringing each agency dealing with foreign policy into the process, you've cut those agencies out of the process. You told the committees, "I firmly believe in very tight compartmentation."
>
> You compartmentalized not only the President's senior advisors, but in effect, you locked the President himself out of the process.[82]

Representative Hamilton then shifted his focus to the questions of accountability and responsibility raised by Poindexter's testimony. Hamilton once again directed his comments to the former National Security Advisor:

> You told the committees, "The buck stops here with me." That is not where the buck is supposed to stop. You wanted to deflect blame from the President, but that is another way of saying that that is a way to deflect responsibility from the President. And that should not be done in our system of government.
>
> You testified that diverting funds to the Contras was a detail, a matter of implementation of the President's policies. And you felt that you had the authority to approve it. Yet, this was a major foreign policy initiative, as subsequent events have shown, with very far-reaching ramifications. And this member, at least, wonders what else could be done in the President's name if this is mere implementation of policy.[83]

Congressman Hamilton then returned to the theme of secrecy, suggesting that the obsession with secrecy itself had "contributed to disarray in the Oval Office." "The President apparently did not know," Hamilton told Poindexter,

> that you were making some of the most important foreign policy decisions of his Presidency.
>
> You have testified, "I was convinced that the President would, in the end, think the diversion was a good idea." Yet the President has stated that he would not have approved the diversion.
>
> Excessive secrecy placed the President in an untenable position and caused him to make false and contradictory public statements.[84]

As with the Iran initiative, the Secretary of State and the Secretary of Defense were not informed about NSC activities in support of the Contras. Shultz testified that National Security Advisor Robert McFarlane misled him in June 1984 about the solicitation of funds for the Contras. McFarlane's successor, Admiral Poindexter, wrote in a White House note that he did not want Shultz informed of the contributions of Saudi Arabia and other nations to the Contras.

Shultz said that he was shocked that Admiral Poindexter had unilaterally assumed the authority to channel profits from the Iran arms sales to the Contras. "How is it that that decision was solely in his hands?" Shultz queried. "I think that shows what was wrong. It's the President that got elected, and so he's the guy that has the right to make decisions."[85]

In clear disdain for the Contra initiative, the Secretary of State said, "It [was] totally outside of the system of government that we live by and must live by."[86] The Secretary of State added,

> You cannot spend funds that the Congress doesn't either authorize you to obtain or appropriate. That is what the Constitution says, and we have to stick to it. . . . We have this very difficult task of having a separation of powers that means we have to share power. Sharing power is harder, and we need to work at it harder than we do. But that's the only way. And this is not sharing power. This is not in line with what was agreed to in Philadelphia [200 years ago].[87]

DELEGATION REVISITED

Unlike Eisenhower, who clearly proscribed White House or National Security Council staff involvement in policy-making, Ronald Reagan's wide-open style of delegation appears to be responsible, at least in part, for precipitating the Iran-Contra affair.[88] As Congressman Lee Hamilton suggests, the President himself "created the environment" in which Poindexter and North operated.[89] Although Reagan clearly understood the basic outlines of the arms-for-hostages transactions and gave explicit approval for them, questions have been raised about the President's comprehension of the consequences of his actions and of the methods of the operation. The Tower Commission suggests, for example, that the President's overall understanding of the initiative may have been quite superficial.

> In his obvious commitment [to secure release of the hostages], the President appears to have proceeded with a concept of the initiatives that was not accurately reflected in the reality of the operation. The President did not seem to be aware of the way in which the operation was implemented and the full consequences of U.S. participation.[90]

Secretary of State George Shultz's testimony in the Iran-Contra hearings reinforced the notion that the President lacked a sophisticated appreciation for key aspects of the Iran initiative. After the President's press conference of November 19, 1986, for example, Shultz told the President that many of his statements were "wrong or misleading." He also told the President that he was being "deceived and lied to" by members of the administration.[91] According to Shultz, the President responded, "You're telling me things that I don't know, that are news to me." In particular, the President claimed not to be aware of part of a "nine-point" plan drawn up by private middleman Albert Hakim calling for the release of seventeen terrorists held in Kuwaiti jails for attacking the American and French embassies in that country. The proposal clearly violated U.S. policy, and the State Department vetoed the idea. But according to Shultz, the President "reacted like he had been kicked in the belly" when he learned of it.[92]

The Tower Commission concluded that White House Chief of Staff Donald Regan must share responsibility for the Iran debacle, particularly for the disarray after the initial disclosure of the initiative. "More than almost any Chief of Staff of recent memory," the Tower Commission noted, Regan

> asserted personal control over the White House staff and sought to extend this control to the National Security Advisor. He was personally active in national security affairs and attended almost all of the relevant meetings regarding the Iran initiative. He, as much as anyone, should have insisted that an orderly process be observed. In addition, he especially should have ensured that plans were made for handling any public disclosure of the initiative. He must bear primary responsibility for the chaos that descended upon the White House when such disclosure did occur.[93]

White House correspondents Ellen Hume and Jane Mayer have suggested that even if Regan knew little or nothing of the Iran-Contra policies, as he claims, "his operating style, which stifled debate in the name of order," was at least partly to blame for the debacle.[94]

> All his life [Regan] has been a success at accumulating power. In business, he thrived by neutralizing rivals, centralizing command, and taking credit whenever possible. He demanded strict loyalty from a narrow cadre of aides, and he valued order over debate. . . .
> At Merrill Lynch his ability to diminish rival influences cemented his command. But in the White House critics believe the absence of open argument among strong-minded, seasoned players weakened policy and left both the Chief of Staff and the President dangerously isolated.[95]

Unlike his predecessor, James Baker, or his successor, Howard Baker, Regan did not bring to the Chief of Staff position the type of informed political judgment that may have helped the President avert the pitfalls of the Iran-Contra initiatives. Regan once acknowledged his own lack of political adeptness, stating:

> I'm not as smooth as [James] Baker. I don't operate in the same style. He's less abrasive, not always getting into trouble, with the press and with Congress for some remark or some insensitivity to some particular issue.[96]

Early assessments of Donald Regan's role in the Iran-Contra affair run the risk of attributing too much influence and of lapsing into the same mistaken judgments that were rendered in Eisenhower's time with regard to Sherman Adams' authority. Already, several members of the Iran-Contra investigating committees have embraced the view that Regan was left as much in the dark as Shultz and Weinberger had been regarding important aspects of the Iran initiative and most or all elements of the Contra initiative.

Whether Regan could have dug more deeply into matters involving the NSC staff or brought more order to the chaotic state of affairs surrounding disclosure of the initiatives we cannot know with certainty. Although he may well have contributed to the climate of secrecy and isolation in the White House, there are certainly others who must shoulder far more blame for the Iran-Contra debacle. National Security Advisor John Poindexter and his aide, Lieutenant Colonel Oliver North, come immediately to mind.

And, of course, the President himself cannot escape responsibility for his actions or for the actions of his subordinates. Indeed, one of the central lessons drawn by many from the Iran-Contra affair is that the President would be well served by adopting a hands-on approach to the management of advisory and decision-making processes in the final months of his administration. As long-time presidential associate Senator Paul Laxalt put it, "The days of hands-off policy, in connection with serious policy matters, are over for Ronald Reagan."[97]

CONCLUSION:
THE BREAKDOWN OF ORGANIZATION

Behind many of the great foreign policy fiascos of the post–World War II era can be found faulty decision-making processes. The Iran-Contra affair is no exception. Indeed, the Iran and Contra initiatives in many ways present case studies in how *not* to make major foreign policy decisions. The breakdown of organization and the lack of sound decision-making processes made possible the climate of secrecy and deception that surrounded the Iran-Contra affair. The Tower Commission provides an incisive summary of the flaws in decision-making processes that characterized the arms transactions with Iran.

> The Iran initiative was handled almost casually and through informal channels, always apparently with an expectation that the process would end with the next arms-for-hostages exchange. . . .
>   Two or three Cabinet level reviews in a period of 17 months was not enough. . . .

At each significant step in the Iran initiative, deliberations among the NSC principals in the presence of the President should have been virtually automatic. . . . The meetings should have been preceded by consideration by the NSC principals of staff papers. . . . These should have reviewed the history of the initiative, analyzed the issues then presented, developed a range of realistic options, presented the odds of success and the costs of failure, and addressed questions of implementation and execution.[98]

The Tower Commission report underscores the difficulties presented by the informal nature of decision-making processes throughout the Iran-Contra affair. The contrast with decision-making processes during the Eisenhower era is striking. Instead of frequent meetings of NSC principals with formal written agendas and careful consideration of a full range of options, Reagan's top advisors met infrequently and informally, with no agenda, no carefully drafted working papers listing options or splits of opinion, and no written record of what had transpired at the meetings. In contrast to the weekly Record of Action statements of the Eisenhower years, which communicated the President's decisions to all NSC principals, the Iran initiative left even the Secretary of State and the Secretary of Defense unaware of what the President had decided. "The effect of this informality," the Tower Commission notes, "was that the initiative lacked a formal institutional record. This precluded the participants from undertaking the more informed analysis and reflection that is afforded by a written record, as opposed to mere recollection."[99]

Much has been made of the point that the Reagan administration *did have* formal advisory machinery in place throughout the Iran-Contra affair, but that the formal organization, including four Senior Interagency Groups of the National Security Council, *was simply not used.* Yet, one of the key lessons from the Eisenhower years is that advisory institutions and processes, to be effective, must be used routinely and frequently. To allow an advisory and administrative apparatus to fall into disuse, or infrequent use, defeats the purpose of organization. Under Eisenhower, the Planning Board of the NSC met twice a week on average. The National Security Council, Operations Coordinating Board, and Cabinet met about once a week, with the President personally chairing the vast majority of Cabinet and NSC meetings. These forums gave the administration a coherence and a consistency in policy-making that is seldom seen today in the Presidency. The experience of the Reagan administration throughout the Iran-Contra affair would suggest that a White House arrangement that lacks routine, discipline, and systematic review of major policy decisions scarcely deserves to be called an organization at all.

NOTES

1. Reagan, quoted in Hedrick Smith, "Foreign Policy: Costly Feud," *New York Times,* March 26, 1981, p. 1.

2. "An Interview With Ronald Reagan," *Time,* November 17, 1980, p. 37.

3. Ibid.

4. Alexander Haig, Excerpts (Part 1) from *Caveat: Realism, Reagan and Foreign Policy,* reprinted in *Time,* April 2, 1984, p. 44.

5. Ibid.

6. Ibid., p. 50.

7. Hedrick Smith, "Haig, Quick to Leap," *New York Times,* February 8, 1981, p. E-3.

8. Haig, Excerpts (Part 1), *Time,* April 2, 1984, p. 50.

9. Ronald Brownstein and Nina Easton, *Reagan's Ruling Class* (New York: Pantheon Books, 1982), p. 664.

10. Ibid.

11. Quoted from Robert McFarlane's opening statement before the Iran-Contra Investigating Committees of the House and Senate, testimony of May 11, 1987, reprinted in the *Washington Post,* May 12, 1987, p. A-14.

12. Ibid.

13. Ibid.

14. Ibid.

15. Smith, "Foreign Policy: Costly Feud," p. 8.

16. Ibid.

17. "Haig Versus the White House," *Newsweek,* April 6, 1981, pp. 27, 29.

18. Ibid.

19. At the time of his nomination, Clark reportedly told Haig, "I don't know a thing about foreign policy." During confirmation hearings, several Senators were surprised when Clark admitted that he did not know the names of the leaders of South Africa and Zimbabwe, and had no opinion on other major foreign policy issues.

20. *New York Times,* January 5, 1982, p. 1.

21. Haig, Excerpts (Part 2) from *Caveat: Realism, Reagan and Foreign Policy,* reprinted in *Time,* April 9, 1984, p. 63.

22. Ibid.

23. Ibid., p. 66.

24. Ibid., p. 65.

25. Ibid., p. 66.

26. Ibid.

27. Ibid., pp. 66–67.

28. *Report of the President's Special Review Board,* John Tower, Chairman, with Edmund Muskie and Brent Scowcroft (Washington, D.C.: U.S. Government Printing Office, February 26, 1987), p. IV-1. Hereinafter cited as the *Tower Commission Report.*

29. Ibid., p. III-2.

30. Ibid., p. III-3.

31. Ibid., p. III-2.

32. Ibid., p. III-4.

33. Ibid.

34. Ibid.

35. Ibid., pp. III-4, III-5. The acronym TOW stands for tube-launched, optically tracked, wire-guided missile. It is a man-operated, portable anti-tank missile. A HAWK is a type of ground-launched, anti-aircraft missile.

36. Ibid., p. III-5.

37. Ibid., p. III-6.

38. Ibid.

39. Ibid.

40. Ibid.

41. Ibid., p. III-8.

42. Testimony of Rear Admiral John Poindexter before the Iran-Contra Investigating Committees of the House and Senate, July 15, 1987, quoted in the *Washington Post,* July 16, 1987, p. A-16.

43. *Tower Commission Report,* p. III-10.

44. Testimony of Secretary of State George Shultz before the Iran-Contra Investigating Committees, July 23, 1987, quoted in the *Washington Post,* July 24, 1987, p. A-1.

45. *Tower Commission Report,* p. III-11.

46. Ibid.

47. Ibid., p. III-12.

48. Ibid.

49. Ibid., p. IV-1.

50. Ibid., p. III-13.

51. Ibid., p. III-14.

52. Ibid., p. IV-7.

53. Testimony of George Shultz before the Iran-Contra Investigating Committees, July 23, 1987; notes transcribed from television broadcast.

54. *Tower Commission Report,* pp. IV-2 to IV-3.

55. Ibid., pp. IV-5 and IV-6.

56. Testimony of George Shultz before the Iran-Contra Investigating Committees, July 23, 1987, quoted in the *Baltimore Sun,* July 24, 1987, p. 18-A.

57. Ibid.

58. Ibid.

59. Testimony of George Shultz before the Iran-Contra Investigating Committees, July 23, 1987; notes transcribed from television broadcast.

60. Charles Babcock, "Shultz Sees Lesson in Casey's Dual Roles," *Washington Post,* July 26, 1987, p. A-16.

61. Testimony of George Shultz before the Iran-Contra Investigating Committees, July 23, 1987, quoted in the *Washington Post,* July 24, 1987, p. A-8.

62. Ibid.

63. Shultz, quoted in the *Baltimore Sun,* July 24, 1987, p. 18-A.

64. Babcock, "Shultz Sees Lesson in Casey's Dual Roles," p. A-16.

65. Ibid.

66. Regan's notes, quoted in the *Washington Post,* August 1, 1987, p. A-10.

67. Ibid.

68. Testimony of George Shultz before the Iran-Contra Investigating Committees, quoted in the *Washington Post,* July 24, 1987, p. A-8.

69. Weinberger, quoted in the *Baltimore Sun,* August 1, 1987, p. A-3.

70. Ibid.

71. Ibid.

72. Testimony of Secretary of Defense Caspar Weinberger before the Iran-Contra Investigating Committees, July 31, 1987, quoted in the *Washington Post,* August 1, 1987, p. A-11.

73. *Tower Commission Report,* pp. I-1, III-20.

74. Ibid., p. III-21.

75. Ibid.

76. Ibid., p. III-22.

77. *Washington Post,* August 4, 1987, p. A-7.

78. Ibid.

79. Ibid.

80. Lieutenant Colonel North's Deputy, Colonel Robert Earl, apparently knew of the diversion as well. The late Director of the CIA, William Casey, also may have known.

81. Rudman, quoted in the *Washington Post,* August 4, 1987, p. A-6.

82. Excerpts from the prepared statement of Congressman Lee Hamilton, Chairman of the House Iran-Contra Investigating Committee, printed in the *Washington Post,* July 22, 1987, p. A-8.

83. Ibid.

84. Ibid.

85. Shultz, quoted in the *Baltimore Sun,* July 26, 1987, p. 2-A.

86. Shultz, quoted in Haynes Johnson, "Shultz's Story of Humiliation and Betrayal," *Washington Post,* July 24, 1987, p. A-6.

87. Ibid.

88. Ellen Hume and Jane Mayer, White House correspondents for the *Wall Street Journal,* are among those who have written about the excesses of Reagan's style of delegation in "The Rise and Fall of Don Regan," *Regardie's,* January 1987, pp. 96–105.

89. Excerpts from Congressman Lee Hamilton's statement, *Washington Post,* July 22, 1987, p. A-8.

90. *Tower Commission Report,* p. IV-10.

91. Shultz, quoted in the *Baltimore Sun,* July 24, 1987, p. 18-A.

92. Ibid.

93. *Tower Commission Report,* p. IV-11.

94. Hume and Mayer, "The Rise and Fall of Don Regan," p. 98.

95. Ibid., pp. 96, 98.

96. Ibid., p. 102.

97. Laxalt, quoted in *USA Today,* March 2, 1987, p. 5-A.

98. *Tower Commission Report,* pp. IV-3, IV-4.

99. Ibid.

8

Organizing the Presidency for Effective Leadership

LESSONS FROM THE EISENHOWER YEARS

In 1976, Stephen Hess, a Brookings Institution scholar and student of executive branch organization, wrote that "our Presidents, more often than not, have been atrocious administrators. They often come from an occupation (legislator) and a profession (law) that ill prepares them for management."[1] In the modern era, the importance of bringing effective organization and management to the White House grows with each new President. Yet, few Presidents since Eisenhower have shown an appreciation for the importance of organization in enhancing the Chief Executive's capacity to lead.

At a minimum, our assessment of the record of management of Eisenhower's successors in the Oval Office reinforces the National Academy of Public Administration's recent recommendation that White House organization should not be "so flexible as to subordinate the central machinery of government to personal whim."[2] Short-term political considerations and "immediate crises" must not, the Academy cautioned, outweigh the President's "responsibility for promoting orderly, ongoing processes of government management." The Iran-Contra debacle of Ronald Reagan's Presidency underscores the wisdom of the Academy's findings. Indeed, recent experience offers a compelling case for a return to the practices and principles of sound management that characterized Eisenhower's Presidency.

There is at least as much need today as there was in Eisenhower's era for the positions of Chief of Staff and Staff Secretary. These positions should be instituted, with only minor variation in format, by all presidential transition teams. The staff secretariat and the White House Chief of Staff, when used in the Eisenhower mold of neutral coordinators and facilitators of advice and information, can serve as a valuable clearing-house and as a bulwark against chaos and confusion. The utility of the Chief of Staff position is perhaps best illustrated by the management problems that arose in the absence of such a position early in the Ford and Carter administrations.

Ideally, a White House Chief of Staff should be a person of broad experience in government. Eisenhower's choice of a former governor, and later an army officer with years of experience in working directly with Congress, comported closely with the political and organizational complexities faced by the staff director. The Nixon and Carter experiences, on the other hand, suggest that the choice of a good campaign organizer may not by itself be a good indicator of potential for dealing effectively with the diverse demands of the Chief of Staff position. Likewise, the experience of the Reagan administration during Donald Regan's tenure as Chief of Staff underscores the need for a politically adept staff director.

Of course, a Chief of Staff is of little use if the President is reluctant to delegate authority. But unchecked delegation of the type that came to light in the Iran-Contra affair is even less desirable. Jimmy Carter, without a formally designated Chief of Staff, immersed himself in so much detail that the broader implications of policy decisions were sometimes obscured from view. Ronald Reagan appears to have had an equally troubling tendency, at least during the Iran-Contra episode, to delegate authority too broadly. Eisenhower's carefully managed style of delegation rested squarely in between the Carter and Reagan extremes. While Eisenhower delegated authority for routine matters through an administratively competent and politically astute Chief of Staff, all major policy decisions came under the direct scrutiny of the President himself, in close consultation with his top advisors.

Another Eisenhower era concept that deserves repetition in future administrations is the commitment to teamwork, fostered by the President, between department heads and the White House staff. As Richard Immerman suggests, Eisenhower not only recognized the need for systematically staffed administration but was also quite adept at evaluating personalities and molding individuals into an effective team. "Many have remarked," writes Immerman,

> that much of Eisenhower's reputation prior to World War II resulted from his successes as a football coach. But as hackneyed as it may sound, his contact with football prepared him well for his more important assignments. His emphasis was always on coordinated effort as opposed to individual performances, and he preached that victory was the collective responsibility of all the participants. The analogy between football and life has certainly been overstated, but in this case parallels are often appropriate.[3]

Eisenhower's emphasis on teamwork played an important role in keeping conflicts over policy from boiling over in public. In a sense, the British doctrine of Cabinet responsibility was played out in the American setting. As early as 1956, Robert Donovan perceptively noted that

> [a] Cabinet member may be opposed to a certain course of action, but as a general rule Eisenhower wants such opposition argued before the Cabinet and not before him personally. He has conducted the Cabinet on the principle that since all are free to participate, the ultimate decision is binding upon all. And under these terms it would be bad medicine for one Cabinet member to go off and start feuding with another over a policy that had been settled upon in the Cabinet. One of the conspicuous traits of the Eisenhower administration, especially in contrast with the two preceding administrations, has been the lack of public vendettas among its high officials.[4]

This is not to say that the Eisenhower administration was devoid of clashes based on personality and on policy. As former White House staffer William Ewald notes, the Eisenhower organization "did not always exude sweet harmony."[5] Nelson Rockefeller was known to simmer behind the scenes over policy differences with Under Secretary of State Herbert Hoover, Jr. Similarly, Arthur Burns, Chairman of the Council of Economic Advisors, found himself, more than once, on the receiving end of Treasury Secretary George Humphrey's acerbic criticism.[6] But as Ewald suggests, the policy differences between Burns and Humphrey were aired openly at Cabinet meetings and then put to rest. After the President had made up his mind, members of the administration were expected to close ranks behind him—and with few exceptions, they did.

Granted, frequent meetings and open debate among top advisors of the type relished by Eisenhower are difficult to sustain under a President who is less extroverted and less enthusiastic about facing candid exchanges. Richard Cheney, who served in the Nixon administration prior to his appointment as Chief of Staff in the Ford White House, offered an insightful comparison of the operational styles of the two Presidents.

> Nixon was not one who liked extensive policy debates with large numbers of people. He liked to work off paper. He liked to consult with one or two individuals but never with a group. Most of the group meetings in which I participated with Nixon, like a Cabinet or Cost of Living Council session, were almost like a public meeting. It was not a place where you'd seriously discuss policy. Under President Ford, it is a very different situation. When there is a major decision to make, he likes to get everyone in the room so you may end up with 15 or 20 people sitting around the Cabinet table.[7]

Jimmy Carter apparently shared with Nixon a preference for isolation in his decision-making. John Kessel provides us with an illuminating example of Carter's approach to decision-making.

> When he [Carter] was making his decision about whether to produce the B-1 aircraft in 1977, he went over all of the review memoranda from State, Defense, NSC, and so on, and extracted 47 arguments which he listed on a yellow legal pad. Next President Carter assigned numerical values to each argument, two points or five points depending on the force of the argument. Finally, he added up the totals, and since there were more negative points than positive, the decision went against building the B-1.[8]

The B-1 bomber decision provides a good example of "orderly, inductive reasoning," but it does not reveal a decision-making process conducive to exploiting the strengths and weaknesses of arguments.

Eisenhower's commitment to making decisions in a group setting, with the active participation of all principal advisors at meetings of the Cabinet and the National Security Council, certainly offered advantages over the isolated approach to decision-making used by some of his successors. The critical caveat about group decision-making is that efforts must be made to avoid conformity. For as Irving Janis has cogently demonstrated, the President's most intimate advisors may, at times, exhibit a natural tendency toward conformity.[9] Janis illustrates this point in his discussion of the Kennedy administration's decision-making process during the Bay of Pigs fiasco. Parallels can be drawn to the Carter administration's planning for the hostage rescue attempt in Iran, and to the arms-for-hostages initiative with Iran during Reagan's Presidency. In each of these cases, those individuals who objected to White House plans were generally shut out of the inner group's decision-making processes. Pressures to conform were accompanied by a strong sense of cohesion among the relatively small number of presidential aides who seized the initiative.

The combination of Planning Board papers and weekly meetings of all members of the National Security Council helped Eisenhower avoid such pitfalls. The frequent splits written into Planning Board papers and the lively debate evidenced in the minutes of Eisenhower's formal NSC meetings reflect a conscientious effort to foster a type of genuine "multiple advocacy." Furthermore, the President was careful to avoid offsetting the advantages of open debate by tipping his hand too forcefully or too early. Whatever flaws the Eisenhower NSC system may have had, the dangers of too much consensus from within the President's group of top advisors was not one of them.

Even if there had been a problem of excessive cohesion among the President's top advisors, which emphatically there was not, Eisenhower, as noted, was not solely dependent on his White House staff and advisory bodies for advice and information. In addition to his frequent use of outside consultants and other informal channels of information gathering, Eisenhower, contrary to popular myth, was a voracious reader of newspapers and books. His private correspondence is replete with references to contemporary journalism and to more sophisticated theoretical works in the realm of politics and history. During debate over the proposed Bricker amendment, for example, the President consulted relevant portions of the *Federalist Papers* for guidance. His diary entry of July 2, 1953, contains extensive remarks on Lenin's work on the "contradictions" inherent in a capitalist system. A letter to General Bradford Chynoweth of July 20, 1954, finds Eisenhower discussing Rousseau's essay on the "Origin of Inequality Among Men" and the books of *The Social Contract*. In a White House memorandum to the Acting Secretary of State dated July 31, 1957, Eisenhower enthusiastically discussed his latest reading of a political science work that he thought had important theoretical insights. As Eisenhower put it:

A man named Henry A. Kissinger has just written a very provocative book entitled "Nuclear Weapons and Foreign Policy." The book was brought to my notice by Cabot Lodge, who spoke of it in terms of great admiration.

I have not read the complete book, but I am sending you herewith a copy of a fairly extensive brief made by General Goodpaster of my office. This at least I think you will want to read, and I believe that when Foster returns he will have some interest in it also.

I do not mean that you will agree with everything the man says. I think there are flaws in his arguments and, at the very least, if we were to organize and maintain military forces along the lines he suggests, we would have what George Humphrey always calls "both the old and the new." This would undoubtedly be a more expensive operation than we are carrying on at this time.

However, the author directs his arguments to some general or popular conceptions and misconceptions, and, as I say, I think you will find interesting and worth reading at least this much of the book.[10]

Clearly, Eisenhower's reading habits were not limited to the one-page cover memorandums that accompanied many White House documents. Indeed, Ann Whitman's diary entry of March 15, 1958, indicates that the President could be a meticulous reader of important documents:

The President read the "Estimate of the World Situation" dated February 26, 1958, as prepared by CIA. Despite Bobby Cutler's comment that it was a very superior piece of work, the President does not appear to think so. He said, for example, that page five could have been written by a high school student.[11]

Although Eisenhower liked to read, he did not like to make decisions solely on the basis of memorandums. He was not, in modern parlance, a "paper" President. As in the realm of national security policy, Eisenhower's appreciation for the virtues of group decision-making carried over into domestic policy-making as well. Eisenhower knew that Cabinet members are, to paraphrase Stephen Hess, by far the best resource for extending the reach and effectiveness of presidential leadership.[12]

Future Presidents would be well advised to follow Eisenhower's lead in appointing a Cabinet Secretary to assist the President in formulating the agenda for meetings and in invigorating the role of the Cabinet in policy development. A Cabinet secretariat staffed by a small group of individuals who subscribe to the canons of "neutral competence"[13] can push issues to the top, prepare meaningful agendas, and ride herd over the departments in the implementation of policy.

One operations change that might offer an improvement over the Eisenhower system would entail giving the Cabinet Secretary direct access to the President in shaping the agenda. Such access would undoubtedly reduce the opportunities in which a Cabinet member could keep an item off the Cabinet's agenda when the item warrants full debate in the Cabinet setting.

In restoring the Eisenhower era primacy of the Cabinet as an advisory body, it would seem prudent, in line with the recommendations of the National Academy of Public Administration, to reverse the trend toward enlargement of the immediate White House staff.[14] The larger the White House staff, the greater the temptation for members of the staff to speak on behalf of the President. Furthermore, the greater the number of individuals serving the President, "the more likely they are to duplicate the expertise of executive agencies, to develop their own biases, [to] intervene where they should not, and in short to create unnecessary work."[15]

As Stephen Hess has forcefully argued, trends aimed at putting greater operational responsibilities in the White House have been counterproductive.[16] The White House staff has become so large that it, too, has become a burden on the President. A large staff increases the chances that the President's wishes will be distorted or delayed because of an extended chain of command. Ironically, centralization of responsibility in the White House has impeded rather than enhanced the President's ability to carry out the duties of the office.[17] Presidential transition teams would do well to take note of the Eisenhower era experience in which Cabinet members were given greater responsibility and White House staff members were given less.

To prevent White House dominance of policy processes in the realm of foreign affairs and defense policy, Presidents would be well advised to follow Eisenhower's example of placing strict limits on the role of the person serving in the position of Assistant to the President for National Security Affairs. The notion that a highly outspoken "National Security Advisor" can better serve the President than his Secretary of State in formulating and articulating the nation's foreign policy is sharply at odds with the role envisioned by Eisenhower when he created the Special Assistant's position. Eisenhower made it very clear that the person holding this position was to serve as a neutral facilitator and coordinator of advice and information—not as a policy advocate or visionary strategist.

Whatever weaknesses the State Department may have as a center for the formulation of foreign policy, a President can be far better served by a competent and compatible Secretary of State who utilizes the collective wisdom and professional competence of the State Department than by turning to a highly visible National Security Advisor as his principal policy-maker. The latter only serves to blur the lines of authority and detract from the Secretary of State's time-honored role as the President's principal spokesman in foreign affairs. What should not be repeated is the arrangement that President Carter gave us for a time— two principal spokesmen in foreign affairs who held very different perspectives with regard to the scope and direction of American foreign policy.

Interestingly, the most visible of all Special Assistants for National Security Affairs, Henry Kissinger, conceded in his memoirs that "a President should make the Secretary of State his principal advisor and use the National Security Advisor primarily as a senior administrator and coordinator to make certain that each significant point of view is heard."[18] Kissinger's prescription seems quite appropriate—particularly in light of the relative success of this formula during Eisenhower's Presidency.

The Reagan administration's arms-for-hostages initiative with Iran clearly demonstrates the perils of a situation in which the staff of the National Security Council takes on a direct role in operations. Eisenhower was so emphatic in his belief that the NSC staff should not take on operational responsibilities that no one ever questioned this basic rule. Future Presidents can be just as forceful in delimiting the authority of the White House staff and in drawing a clear line of distinction between Cabinet officers and staff.

The Iran-Contra affair has brought to light several additional reform proposals relevant to our discussion. First, as Secretary of State George Shultz has suggested, the "function of gathering and analyzing intelligence" should, in the future, be separated "from the function of developing and carrying out policy."[19] Relatedly, it would seem prudent, in line with recent experience, not to repeat the Reagan administration's precedent of granting Cabinet status to the Director of the CIA. William Casey's standing as a member of the Cabinet undoubtedly created a climate in which he would inevitably become a policy advocate in the Iran affair and in other matters. This type of advocacy should be avoided in future administrations.

Another idea deserving careful study in the aftermath of the Iran-Contra affair is the proposal for creation of a small, permanent staff secretariat for the National Security Council that would serve as the custodian of "institutional memory" for each new administration. This proposal has been advocated by Gordon Hoxie, the Director of the Center for the Study of the Presidency, and by the Tower Commission.[20] Such an organization would be expected to subscribe to the canon of neutral competence, faithfully serving each new President but tempering a President's decision-making with historical perspective and detached professionalism.

In the realm of foreign policy recent history confirms William Bundy's observation that "Presidents should be graded heavily as administrators."[21] Our Chief Executives must learn to adapt to the role of manager— even if that means subordinating their own stylistic preferences to meet the demands of leadership. As Bundy puts it:

> If a worldwide foreign policy is to be conducted today with all the resources in (and sometimes out of) government, any style must ensure proper inputs from the departments and agencies that embody experience and expertise. There is little likelihood that American foreign policy will ever be taken over by the professionals; the opposite danger, of their neglect, is more serious. White House coordination is essential, and with it constant prodding and gingering of the line departments, but the great White House operators—Harry Hopkins comes at once to mind—have been those who worked with rather than against senior appointed officials and strengthened, rather than weakened, their ties of trust and confidence to the President.[22]

Eisenhower sought to institutionalize departmental participation in the making of foreign policy through such formal mechanisms as the Planning Board and the Operations Coordinating Board. Similar coordinating bodies would likely be as valuable today as they were in the Eisenhower era. A mechanism comparable to the Planning Board would be especially useful in the initial stages of an administration in defining the broad outlines of American foreign and national security policy. A reduction in the size of the staff of the National Security Council would further enhance the role of the departments by reducing the temptation for Presidents to run foreign policy from the White House.

This is not to say that emulation of Eisenhower's administrative system will provide an ideal framework for policy-making by all future Presidents under all circumstances. Nor do we wish to suggest that Eisenhower's policy-making apparatus was infallible. The administration's confusing response when an American U-2 reconnaissance plane was shot down over the Soviet Union on May 1, 1960, does not evidence the type of decisive planning or careful deliberation that had generally characterized the Eisenhower system. In this case, at least, the President was caught off guard and was slow to respond. Nor was the American response to the events leading to the Soviet invasion of Hungary in 1956 a model of prescient foreign policy.

Yet, on balance, the Eisenhower system was both disciplined and foresighted. It generally provided the type of cogent analysis, reasoned advice, and broad options to which all Presidents are entitled but which few Presidents have demanded with the same exacting standard set by Eisenhower. Eisenhower's administrative system unquestionably provided him with the breadth of expertise and administrative backup that is necessary in the coordination of foreign policy in the modern era.

Not surprisingly, suggests historian Stephen Ambrose, "Eisenhower's greatest successes came in foreign policy, and the related area of national defense spending."[23] In support of this claim, Ambrose writes:

> By making peace in Korea, and avoiding war thereafter for the next seven and one-half years, and by holding down, almost single-handedly, the pace of the arms race, he achieved his major accomplishments. . . . He made peace, and he kept peace. Whether any other man could have led the country through the decade without going to war cannot be known. What we do know is that Eisenhower did it.[24]

Eisenhower's strongest suit, Ambrose suggests, was "managing crises."[25] Whether it was the crisis over Dien Bien Phu in 1954, or the Quemoy and Matsu crisis of 1955, the Suez crisis of 1956, or the Berlin crisis of 1959, "Eisenhower managed each one without overreacting, without going to war, without increasing defense spending. . . . He downplayed each one, insisted that a solution could be found, and then found one." It was, writes Ambrose, "a magnificent performance."[26]

Eisenhower's domestic policy accomplishments are often overshadowed by his illustrious foreign policy record, but a good many of his successors would likely have been happy to seek reelection on the basis of Eisenhower's domestic policy record alone. Although he faced a Congress that for six years was controlled by the opposition party, Eisenhower was notably successful in addressing the issues that concerned him most. When it came to balancing the federal budget, checking inflation, or fine-tuning the economy, Eisenhower was indeed a skilled leader. Unquestionably, the President's policies were instrumental in shaping the economic prosperity of the 1950s. It is not an accident that Eisenhower holds the record for the largest budget surplus in American history— $4 billion in 1956.

In appraising Eisenhower's domestic accomplishments, Stephen Ambrose writes:

> First and foremost, he presided over eight years of prosperity, marred only by two minor recessions. By later standards, it was a decade of nearly full employment and no inflation.
>
> Indeed by almost every standard—GNP, personal income and savings, home buying, auto purchases, capital investment, highway construction, and so forth—it was the best decade of the century.[27]

Given this record of accomplishment, it is no wonder that Eisenhower left office more popular than he had been upon entering. His tremendous popularity with the public was an asset that Eisenhower labored carefully to sustain. Even so harsh an early critic as political scientist Richard Neustadt now finds merit in Eisenhower's contributions to the enhancement of the dignity of the Presidency. In the William Cook lectures on American Institutions delivered at the University of Michigan in 1976, Neustadt said:

> Prestige seems to have been always on the mind of at least one modern President, Eisenhower. In light of subsequent events, this is an aspect of his Presidency which I, among others, find more attractive now than I did then. As a national hero from the Second World War, he lent the office his own aura, and was conscious that he did so.[28]

As we review Eisenhower's accomplishments for the historical record, we would do well to keep in mind that Eisenhower extended the scope of the Presidency beyond any one man. For his greatest legacy may well rest with his ability to shape the presidential office into a vital extension of the President's reach.

If, as William Bundy suggests, we grade our Presidents heavily as administrators, Eisenhower will unquestionably be at the top of the list. His innovations in organizing the White House were the most impressive of this century, and his philosophy of leadership was among the most enlightened. Future Presidents will be well served by taking note of Eisenhower's important contributions to executive branch management and his rich legacy for the office of the Presidency.

NOTES

1. Stephen Hess, *Organizing the Presidency* (Washington, D.C.: Brookings Institution, 1976), p. 146.

2. A panel of the National Academy of Public Administration, headed by Donald K. Price, articulates this idea in its monograph *A Presidency for the 1980s* (Washington, D.C.: National Academy of Public Administration, 1980), p. 15.

3. Richard H. Immerman, "Eisenhower and Dulles: Who Made the Decisions?" *Political Psychology*, vol. 1, no. 2, Autumn 1979, p. 29.

4. Robert Donovan, *Eisenhower: The Inside Story* (New York: Harper, 1956), p. 67.

5. William Bragg Ewald, Jr., *Eisenhower the President: Crucial Days, 1951–1960* (Englewood Cliffs, N.J.: Prentice-Hall, 1981), p. 67.

6. Ibid., pp. 67–68.

7. Cheney, quoted in R. Gordon Hoxie, "Staffing the Ford and Carter Presidencies," in Bradley D. Nash et al., *Organizing and Staffing the Presidency* (New York: Center for the Study of the Presidency, 1980), p. 53.

8. John Kessel, *Presidential Parties* (Homewood, Ill.: Dorsey Press, 1984), p. 162.

9. Irving L. Janis, *Victims of Group Think*, 2nd ed. (Boston: Houghton Mifflin, 1982). Alexander George outlines a strategy for avoiding the malfunctions of presidential advisory systems in "The Case for Multiple Advocacy in Making Foreign Policy," *American Political Science Review*, vol. 66, no. 3, 1972, pp. 751–785.

10. Memorandum from Dwight D. Eisenhower to the Acting Secretary of State, Folder: "July '57 Dictation," Ann Whitman File, DDE Diaries Series, Box 25, Eisenhower Library.

11. Diary entry of March 13, 1958, Folder: ACW Diary March 1958 (1), Ann Whitman Diary Series, Box 9, Eisenhower Library.

12. Hess, *Organizing the Presidency*, p. 154.

13. For a discussion of the concept of "neutral competence," see Hugh Heclo, "OMB and the Presidency—The Problem of Neutral Competence," *The Public Interest*, Winter 1975, pp. 80–98.

14. National Academy of Public Administration, *A Presidency for the 1980s*, p. 17.

15. Ibid.

16. Hess, *Organizing the Presidency*, p. 147.

17. Ibid.

18. Henry Kissinger, *White House Years* (Boston: Little, Brown, 1979), p. 30.

19. George Shultz, testimony before the Iran-Contra Select Committees of the House and Senate, July 23, 1987, quoted in the *Washington Post*, July 24, 1987, p. A-6.

20. See R. Gordon Hoxie, "Considerations on Decision-Making and the Iran Ordeal," *Presidential Studies Quarterly*, vol. 18, Winter 1987, p. 15. See also *Tower Commission Report*, p. V-4.

21. William P. Bundy, "The National Security Process," *International Security*, vol. 7, Winter 1982-1983, p. 108.

22. Ibid.

23. Ambrose, *Eisenhower the President*, p. 626.

24. Ibid., pp. 625–626.

25. Ibid., p. 626.

26. Ibid.

27. Ibid., p. 627.

28. Richard Neustadt, *Presidential Power: The Politics of Leadership* (New York: John Wiley and Sons, 1976 edition), p. 10.

Appendix 1

ATTENDANCE AT NSC MEETINGS
AS OF JANUARY 1957

A. SEATED AT TABLE

Statutory Participants

1. The President
2. The Vice President
3. Secretary of State
4. Secretary of Defense
5. Director of ODM

General Standing Request

6. Secretary of Treasury
7. Director of Budget
8. Special Assistant for Disarmament

Ad Hoc Standing Request

9. Attorney General
10. Chairman of AEC
11. Director of FCDA

Nonstatutory Participants and Observers

12. Chairman, Joint Chiefs of Staff
13. Director of Central Intelligence

General Standing Request

14. Special Assistant for Operations Coordinating Board
15. Director, USIA
16. Director, ICA

Staff

17. Special Assistant for National Security Affairs
18. Executive Secretary, NSC
19. Deputy Executive Secretary, NSC

B. NOT SEATED AT TABLE

Occasional

20. Assistant to President
21. White House Staff Secretary
22. Chairman, Council Foreign Economic Policy

Less Frequent Ad Hoc

23. Secretary of Army
24. Secretary of Navy
25. Secretary of Air Force
26. Chief of Staff—Army
27. Chief, Naval Operations
28. Chief, Air Staff
29. Commandant, Marine Corps

Source: White House Office, Office of the Special Assistant for National Security Affairs, NSC Series, Administrative Subseries, Folder: NSC Organization and Functions (11), Eisenhower Library.

Appendix 2

MEETINGS WITH PRESIDENT
DURING MAY AND JUNE
OF THE SPECIAL ASSISTANT
FOR NATIONAL SECURITY AFFAIRS

Monday, May 4 - 11:15–11:40 — President's Office

Tuesday, May 5 - 8:30–9:30 — Meeting with President (Herter, Quarles, Dulles, Killian, McCone)

Monday, May 11 - 10:15–11:30 — President's Office

Friday, May 15 - 10:45 — Meeting with President (Dillon, Murphy, McElroy, Taylor, Dulles, Goodpaster) - *Berlin/Germany*

Monday, May 18 - 9:00–9:40 — President's Office

Monday, May 25 - 10:50 — President's Office

Tuesday, May 26 - 11:45–12:20 — Meeting with President - *Defense Construction*

Monday, June 1 - 10:00–10:30 — President's Office

Monday, June 1 - 2:15–3:00 — President's Office

Monday, June 8 - 9:30–10:30 — Meeting with President - *Test Suspension*

Monday, June 8 - 11:45 — President's Office

Tuesday, June 9 - 3:00–4:15 — Meeting with President (Vice President, McElroy, Dillon, Gates, Holaday, Lemnitzer, Burke, White, Killian) - *Air Defense*

Friday, June 12 - 9:00 — President's Office

Wednesday, June 17 - 9:00–9:30 — Meeting with President (Dillon, McElroy) - *IRBMs to Greece*

Thursday, June 18 - 10:30 — Meeting with President (Dr. Killian and Dr. Brooks) - a.s.w.

Monday, June 22 - 10:00 — President's Office

Monday, June 22 - 10:30 — Meeting with President (Consultants)

Tuesday, June 23 - 11:40 — Meeting with President - *Nuclear-Powered Aircraft*

Wednesday, June 24 - 9:00–10:00 — Meeting with President (McElroy, Pugh, Loper, Sides, Boyd, McCone, Stewart, Dunning, Killian, Goodpaster) - *Immediate Long-Range Effects of a Massive Nuclear Exchange*

Wednesday, June 24 - 5:15–6:45 — President's Study - *Jackson Committee Report*

Thursday, June 25 - After NSC — Meeting with President - *Intelligence Activities in Berlin*

Source: White House Office, Office of the Special Assistant for National Security Affairs. Presidential Subseries, Box 4, Meetings with the President 1959 (1), Eisenhower Library.

Appendix 3

THE PRESIDENT'S SCHEDULE FOR
THE WEEK OF MARCH 19, 1956

THE PRESIDENT'S APPOINTMENTS:
Monday, March 19, 1956

9:05 A.M.	The President, accompanied by General Alfred Gruenther, Mr. William Robinson, and Mr. George Allen, departed the Farm and motored to the White House.
11:32 A.M.	Arrived at the White House and went to the office
11:34–11:37 A.M.	Colonel Robert L. Schulz
11:40–11:47 A.M.	Hon. Howard Pyle
12:02 P.M.	The President departed the office and went to swimming pool.
12:07 P.M.	The President went to the Mansion.
1:00 P.M.	LUNCH
1:55 P.M.	The President returned to the office.
2:00 P.M.–2:20 P.M.	Hon. James Hagerty
2:30–3:03 P.M.	Hon. Herbert Hoover, Jr.
3:04–3:47 P.M.	General John S. Bragdon Hon. Gabriel Hauge
3:50–4:12 P.M.	Hon. Sherman Adams Hon. Gerald Morgan
4:14–4:34 P.M.	Hon. Gabriel Hauge
4:35–4:43 P.M.	Colonel Andrew J. Goodpaster
5:08 P.M.	The President departed the office and went to the swimming pool.
5:50 P.M.	Returned to the office
6:15 P.M.	The President went to the Mansion.

Tuesday, March 20, 1956

8:22 A.M.	The President arrived at the office.
8:23–8:26 A.M.	Mr. William J. Hopkins

8:28–8:42 A.M.	Mrs. Ann Whitman in for dictation
8:43–9:00 A.M.	Hon. Wilton B. Persons
	Hon. Bryce Harlow
	Hon. I. Jack Martin
9:00–10:00 A.M.	LEGISLATIVE LEADERS MEETING
	The Vice President
	Senator Styles Bridges
	Senator William F. Knowland
	Senator Leverett Saltonstall
	Senator George D. Aiken
	Representative Joseph W. Martin, Jr.
	Representative Charles A. Halleck
	Representative Leslie C. Arends
	Hon. Rowland Hughes
	Hon. Ezra Taft Benson
	Mr. Jack Anderson
	Hon. Sherman Adams
	Hon. Wilton B. Persons
	Hon. Bernard M. Shanley
	Hon. Gerald Morgan
	Hon. James Hagerty
	Hon. Howard Pyle
	Hon. Gabriel Hauge
	Hon. Bryce Harlow
	Hon. I. Jack Martin
	Hon. Earle D. Chesney
	Hon. Homer Gruenther
	Colonel Andrew J. Goodpaster
10:22–10:37 A.M.	Hon. Richard T. Nixon
10:38–10:55 A.M.	Hon. Meyer Kestnbaum
	Hon. Sherman Adams
10:50–11:08 A.M.	(Hon. James Hagerty) OFF THE RECORD
11:10–11:55 A.M.	Reverend Billy Graham
12:00 noon	The President departed the office and went to the swimming pool.
12:18 P.M.	The President departed the pool and went to the Mansion.
1:00–2:15 P.M.	Hon. Herbert Hoover, Jr.
	Hon. John McCloy (Had luncheon with the President)
2:25 P.M.	The President returned to the office.
2:35–3:11 P.M.	Mr. James Bishop
	Hon. James Hagerty
3:12–3:20 P.M.	Hon. Rowland Hughes
	Hon. Percival Brundage
3:35–3:50 P.M.	Colonel Andrew J. Goodpaster
3:50–4:12 P.M.	Hon. Herbert Brownell
	Hon. Sherman Adams

4:13–4:35 P.M.	The President went to the South Grounds to hit golf balls.
4:40 P.M.	The President returned to the office.
4:45–5:00 P.M.	Mrs. Ann Whitman in for dictation
5:00 P.M.	The President departed the office and went to the Mansion.

Wednesday, March 21, 1956

8:12 A.M.	The President arrived in the office.
8:13–8:16 A.M.	Mr. William J. Hopkins
8:14–8:28 A.M.	Hon. Wilton B. Persons
	Colonel Andrew J. Goodpaster
9:00–9:50 A.M.	Hon. Lewis Strauss
	Hon. William H. Jackson
	Hon. Herbert Hoover, Jr.
	Colonel Andrew J. Goodpaster
10:00–10:30 A.M.	Hon. Sherman Adams
	Hon. James Hagerty
	Hon. Fred Seaton
	Hon. Gabriel Hauge
	Hon. Gerald Morgan
	Hon. I. Jack Martin
	Hon. Murray Snyder
	Colonel Andrew J. Goodpaster (Pre-Press Conference Briefing)
10:30–11:05 A.M.	PRESS CONFERENCE
11:06 A.M.	The President returned to the office.
11:10–11:15 A.M.	(The following attended the swearing-in of Mr. Peter Grimm as Director, United States Operations Mission to Italy, which was held in the President's office): OFF THE RECORD
	Mrs. Peter Grimm
	Mr. and Mrs. Joseph Binns
	Hon. and Mrs. Percival Brundage
	Countess Casagrande
	Mr. and Mrs. William J. Demarest
	Dr. D. A. Fitzgerald
	Mr. and Mrs. John W. Harris
	Mrs. John B. Hollister
	Major B. C. Ormerod
	Colonel and Mrs. Harold Reigelman
	Mr. Howard Sloane
	Mr. and Mrs. Arthur Snadbeck
	Mr. and Mrs. James P. Sutton
	Mr. and Mrs. Conrad Thibault

11:15–11:30 A.M.	Hon. Sherman Adams
	Hon. James Hagerty
11:30–11:32 A.M.	Hon. Sherman Adams
11:38–11:42 A.M.	Hon. James Hagerty
11:45 A.M.	The President went to the swimming pool.
1:00 P.M.	LUNCH
2:45 P.M.	The President, accompanied by Mr. Barry Leithead and son, returned to the office.
3:10–3:20 P.M.	Hon. I. Jack Martin
3:20–3:30 P.M.	Mr. James Durfee, Madison
	Hon. Sherman Adams
3:30–3:38 P.M.	Colonel Andrew J. Goodpaster
4:00–4:07 P.M.	Hon. Bernard M. Shanley
4:18–4:25 P.M.	Colonel Andrew J. Goodpaster
4:28 P.M.	The President went out on the South Grounds to hit golf balls.
5:05 P.M.	The President returned to the office.
5:10 P.M.	The President walked over to the Mansion.
5:30 P.M.	Hon. John Foster Dulles
	Hon. Herbert Hoover (Met with the President in the Mansion)

Thursday, March 22, 1956

7:52 A.M.	The President arrived at the office.
8:24–8:28 A.M.	Hon. Wilton B. Persons
8:28–8:30 A.M.	Hon. John Foster Dulles
	Hon. Bernard M. Shanley
8:30–9:50 A.M.	BIPARTISAN LEGISLATIVE MEETING
	The President
	Senator Styles Bridges
	Senator Walter F. George
	Senator Theodore F. Green
	Senator Carl Hayden
	Senator Lyndon Johnson
	Senator William F. Knowland
	Senator Richard B. Russell
	Senator Leverett Saltonstall
	Senator H. Alexander Smith
	Senator Alexander Wiley
	Representative Carl Albert
	Representative Leo E. Allen
	Representative Leslie C. Arends
	Representative Charles A. Halleck
	Representative John W. McCormack
	Representative Joseph W. Martin, Jr.
	Representative Sam Rayburn
	Representative James R. Richards

Representative Dewey Short
Representative John Taber
Representative Carl Vinson
Representative John M. Vorys
Hon. John Foster Dulles
Hon. Herbert Hoover, Jr.
Hon. Douglas MacArthur II
Hon. Sherman Adams
Hon. Bernard M. Shanley
Hon. Gerald Morgan
Hon. Howard Pyle
Hon. Murray Snyder
Hon. I. Jack Martin
Hon. James Hagerty
Hon. Homer Gruenther
Hon. Bryce Harlow
Colonel Andrew J. Goodpaster

9:50–10:00 A.M.

Hon. John Foster Dulles
Hon. James Lay

10:00–12:17 P.M.

NATIONAL SECURITY COUNCIL
The President
Hon. John Foster Dulles, Secretary of State
Hon. Charles E. Wilson, Secretary of Defense
Hon. Reuben Robertson, Deputy Secretary of Defense
Hon. Arthur Flemming, Director, ODM
Hon. George M. Humphrey, Secretary of the Treasury
Hon. Herbert Brownell, Jr., the Attorney General
Hon. Amos J. Peaslee, for the Special Assistant to the
    President for Disarmament
Hon. Rowland Hughes, Director, Bureau of the Budget
Hon. Lewis L. Strauss, Special Assistant to the Pres-
    ident for Atomic Energy
Hon. Abbott Washburn, Acting Director, USIA
Hon. Percival Brundage, Deputy Director, Bureau of
    the Budget
Hon. Arthur W. Radford, Chairman, Joint Chiefs of
    Staff
Hon. Allen W. Dulles, Director of Central Intelligence
Hon. Sherman Adams
Hon. Wilton B. Persons
Hon. Herbert Hoover, Jr.
Hon. Robert Bowie, Assistant Secretary of State
Hon. John B. Hollister, Director, ICA
Hon. William H. Jackson, Special Assistant to the
    President
Hon. James S. Lay, Jr.
Hon. S. Everett Gleason
Colonel Andrew J. Goodpaster

12:17–12:24 P.M.	Colonel Andrew J. Goodpaster
	Mrs. Ann Whitman
12:25 P.M.	The President departed the office and went to the swimming pool.
12:57 P.M.	The President went to the Mansion.
1:00 P.M.	LUNCH
2:16 P.M.	The President returned to the office.
2:20–3:00 P.M.	Hon. Sherman Adams
2:30–3:00 P.M.	Hon. Herbert Hoover, Jr.
	Mr. Dana Latham, Los Angeles, California
	Hon. Sherman Adams
3:30–3:40 P.M.	Hon. Bernard M. Shanley
3:40 P.M.	The President went to the South Grounds to hit golf balls.
4:45 P.M.	The President returned to the office.
4:55 P.M.	The President went to the Mansion.
5:30–7:00 P.M.	(OFF-THE-RECORD MEETING AT THE MANSION)
	(Hon. George M. Humphrey)
	(Hon. James P. Mitchell)
	(Mr. David McDonald)

Friday, March 23, 1956

8:13 A.M.	The President arrived at the office.
8:15–8:17 A.M.	Mr. William J. Hopkins
8:17–9:28 A.M.	Hon. Bernard M. Shanley
8:32–8:35 A.M.	Colonel Andrew J. Goodpaster
8:33–8:34 A.M.	Hon. Sherman Adams
8:45–8:50 A.M.	Hon. Sinclair Weeks
	Hon. James Hagerty
9:00–11:00 A.M.	CABINET MEETING
	The President
	Hon. John Foster Dulles
	Hon. Herbert Hoover, Jr.
	Hon. David W. Kendall (for Secretary Humphrey)
	Hon. Charles E. Wilson
	Hon. Herbert Brownell
	Hon. Arthur Summerfield
	Hon. Fred G. Aandahl, Assistant Secretary of Interior
	Hon. Ezra Taft Benson
	Hon. Sinclair Weeks
	Hon. James P. Mitchell
	Hon. Marion B. Folsom
	Hon. Rowland Hughes
	Hon. Percival Brundage
	Hon. Arthur Flemming
	Hon. Philip Young

	Hon. Arthur Burns
	Hon. Henry Cabot Lodge
	Hon. Sherman Adams
	Hon. Wilton B. Persons
	Hon. Bernard M. Shanley
	Hon. Fred Seaton
	Hon. Howard Pyle
	Hon. Gerald Morgan
	Hon. I. Jack Martin
	Colonel Andrew J. Goodpaster
	Hon. Bryce Harlow
	Hon. William Jackson
	Hon. Charles Masterson
	Hon. James Hagerty
	Hon. Gabriel Hauge
	Hon. Murray Snyder
	Hon. Maxwell Rabb
	Hon. Bradley Patterson
	Hon. Arthur Minnich
	Hon. Edward McCabe
11:00–11:10 A.M.	General J. Lawton Collins
11:10–11:37 A.M.	The President returned to Cabinet Meeting.
11:37–11:55 A.M.	Hon. Val Peterson
	Hon. James Lay
	Mr. Ralph Spear
12:00 noon	The President departed the office and went to the swimming pool.
12:45 P.M.	The President departed the pool and went to the Mansion.
1:00 P.M.	LUNCH
2:12 P.M.	The President departed the White House and motored to Burning Tree Country Club.
2:37 P.M.	Arrived at Burning Tree
2:55 P.M.	The President teed off from the 10th tee, playing from the 10th hole to the 18th with Mr. John McClure.
4:20 P.M.	The President, accompanied by Mr. John McClure, departed Burning Tree and motored to the White House.
4:46 P.M.	Arrived at the White House and went to the office
4:47–5:00 P.M.	Colonel Andrew J. Goodpaster
5:00–5:15 P.M.	Hon. Herbert Brownell
	Hon. Sherman Adams
	Hon. Gerald Morgan
	Hon. Maxwell Rabb
5:15–5:20 P.M.	The President departed the office and went to the Mansion.

5:30 P.M.   Senator Walter F. George (Saw the President at the
                                 Mansion)

Saturday, March 24, 1956

8:17 A.M.   The President arrived at the office.
8:21–8:55 A.M.   Hon. Wilton B. Persons
8:55–8:57 A.M.   Hon. I. Jack Martin
8:57–9:07 A.M.   Hon. Herbert Hoover, Jr.
                                 Hon. Sherman Adams
9:00–10:17 A.M.   Hon. Charles E. Wilson
                                 Hon. Herbert Hoover, Jr.
                                 Hon. Allen Dulles
                                 Hon. Donald Quarles
                                 Hon. Arthur Radford
                                 Hon. Nathan Twining
                                 Colonel Andrew J. Goodpaster
10:17–10:20 A.M.   Hon. Charles E. Wilson
                                 Hon. Arthur Radford
                                 Hon. Herbert Hoover, Jr.
                                 Colonel Andrew J. Goodpaster
10:20–10:46 A.M.   Hon. Herbert Brownell, Jr.
10:47–11:06 A.M.   Hon. James Hagerty
11:35–11:42 A.M.   Hon. Gerald Morgan
                                 Colonel Andrew J. Goodpaster
11:42–11:54 A.M.   Colonel Andrew J. Goodpaster
12:20 P.M.   The President departed the office and went to the
                                 swimming pool.

Source: President's Appointments, Folder: March 1956, Miscellaneous (1), Papers
of Dwight D. Eisenhower as President of the United States, Ann C. Whitman
File, Dwight D. Eisenhower Diary Series, Box 14, Eisenhower Library.

Bibliography

PRIMARY SOURCES

All manuscripts cited in this book are housed in the Eisenhower Library in Abilene, Kansas.

—Dwight D. Eisenhower, Papers as President of the United States, 1953–61, Ann Whitman File (divided into the following series):
  Administration Series
  Ann Whitman Diary Series
  Cabinet Series
  DDE Diaries Series
  International Series
  Legislative Meetings Series
  Letter Series
  NSC Series
  Presidential Transition Series
  Press Conference Series
  Speech Series

—Dwight D. Eisenhower, Records as President, White House Central Files, 1953–61.

—Staff Files:
  Jack Z. Anderson, Records, 1956–61
  James Hagerty Diary
  Bryce Harlow Records, 1953–61
  Wilton B. Persons, Records, 1953–61

—U.S. President's Advisory Committee on Government Organization (Rockefeller Committee).

—White House Office, Cabinet Secretariat: Records, 1953–60.

—White House Office, Executive Branch Liaison Office: Records, 1953–58.

—White House Office, Staff Research Group (Albert Toner and Christopher H. Russell): Records, 1956–61.

—White House Office, Office of the Special Assistant for National Security Affairs (Robert Cutler, Dillon Anderson, and Gordon Gray): Records, 1952–61 (divided into the following series):
    NSC Series, Administrative Subseries
    OCB Series, Administrative Subseries
    Presidential Subseries
    Special Assistants Series, Chronological Subseries

—White House Office, Office of the Staff Secretary: Records of Paul T. Carroll, Andrew J. Goodpaster, L. Arthur Minnich, and Christopher H. Russell, 1952–61 (divided into the following series):
    Arthur Minnich Series
    Subject Series, Alphabetical Subseries
    White House Subseries

INTERVIEWS

All of the interviews listed below, with the exception of the author's, are available at the Eisenhower Library.

—By Author:
    Andrew J. Goodpaster
    Bradley H. Patterson, Jr.

—By Columbia Oral History Project:
    Sherman Adams
    Dillon Anderson
    Robert R. Bowie
    Herbert Brownell
    Percival Brundage
    Earl L. Butz
    Dwight D. Eisenhower
    Andrew J. Goodpaster
    Stephen Hess
    Edward McCabe
    L. Arthur Minnich
    Bradley H. Patterson, Jr.
    Wilton B. Persons
    Maxwell Rabb
    Ralph Reid
    Stanley Rumbough
    Raymond J. Saulnier
    Murray Snyder

—By Eisenhower Library:
    Jack Z. Anderson
    Herbert Brownell
    Dwight D. Eisenhower
    Andrew J. Goodpaster
    Gordon Gray
    L. Arthur Minnich
    Bernard Shanley

—By Hoover Library:
    Dwight D. Eisenhower

—By Princeton University:
    Dwight D. Eisenhower

REFERENCES

Adams, Sherman. *Firsthand Report: The Story of the Eisenhower Administration.* Harper and Bros., 1961.

Ambrose, Stephen E. "The Ike Age." *New Republic,* May 9, 1981, pp. 26–34.

───── . *Eisenhower: The President.* New York: Simon and Schuster, 1984.

Anderson, Dillon. "The President and National Security." *Atlantic* 197 (January 1956): 41–46.

Bailey, Thomas A. *Presidential Greatness.* New York: Appleton-Century-Crofts, 1966.

Barber, James David. *The Presidential Character: Predicting Performance in the White House,* 1st and 2nd editions. Englewood Cliffs, N.J.: Prentice-Hall, 1972 and 1977.

Benson, Ezra Taft. *Cross Fire: The Eight Years with Eisenhower.* Garden City, N.Y.: Doubleday and Company, 1962.

Binkley, Wilfred E. "West Pointers in the White House," *New Republic,* March 9, 1953, pp. 15–17.

Bonafede, Dom. "The Collapse of Cabinet Government?" *National Journal,* April 22, 1978, p. 641.

Brownlow, Louis. *A Passion for Anonymity: The Autobiography of Louis Brownlow.* Chicago: University of Chicago Press, 1958.

Brownlow, Louis; Merriam, Charles E.; and Gulick, Luther. *Report of the President's Committee on Administrative Management.* Washington, D.C.: Government Printing Office, 1937.

Bundy, William P. "The National Security Process." *International Security* 7, no. 3 (Winter 1982-1983): 94–109.

Burke, John P. "Political Context and Presidential Influence: A Case Study." *Presidential Studies Quarterly* 15, no. 2 (Spring 1985): 301–319.

Cameron, Juan. "The Management Problem in Ford's White House." *Fortune,* July 1975, pp. 74–81.

Childs, Marquis. *Eisenhower: Captive Hero.* New York: Harcourt, Brace and Company, 1958.

Clark, Keith C., and Legere, Laurence J., eds. *The President and the Management of National Security.* New York: Praeger Publishers, 1969.

Cook, Blanche W. *The Declassified Eisenhower.* New York: Doubleday and Company, 1981.

Cronin, Thomas. "The Textbook Presidency and Political Science." In *Perspectives on the Presidency* (pp. 54–74), edited by Stanley Bach and George T. Sulzner. Lexington, Mass.: D. C. Heath and Company, 1974.

Cutler, Robert. "The Development of the National Security Council." *Foreign Affairs* 34 (1956): 441–458.

───── . *No Time for Rest.* Boston: Little, Brown, 1966.

Dangerfield, George. "Eisenhower: The Image Fades." *Nation* 187 (September 20, 1958): 155–156.

De Santis, Vincent. "Eisenhower Revisionism." *Review of Politics* 38 (April 1976): 190–207.

Destler, I. M. *Presidents, Bureaucrats, and Foreign Policy: The Politics of Organizational Reform.* Princeton, N.J.: Princeton University Press, paperback edition, 1974.

Donovan, Robert. *Eisenhower: The Inside Story.* New York: Harper, 1956.

Drummond, Roscoe, and Coblentz, Gaston. *Duel at the Brink.* Garden City, N.Y.: Doubleday and Company, 1960.

Edwards, David. *The American Political Experience.* Englewood Cliffs, N.J.: Prentice-Hall, 1982.

Eisenhower, Dwight D. *The White House Years: Mandate for Change.* Garden City, N.Y.: Doubleday and Company, 1963.

———. *Waging Peace, 1956–1961.* Garden City, N.Y.: Doubleday and Company, 1965.

———. *At Ease: Stories I Tell to Friends.* Garden City, N.Y.: Doubleday and Company, 1967.

———. "Some Thoughts on the Presidency." *Reader's Digest* 93 (November 1968): 49–55.

Eisenhower, Milton. *The President Is Calling.* Garden City, N.Y.: Doubleday and Company, 1974.

Ewald, William Bragg, Jr. *Eisenhower the President: Crucial Days, 1951–1960.* Englewood Cliffs, N.J.: Prentice-Hall, 1981.

Falk, Stanley L. "The National Security Council Under Truman, Eisenhower and Kennedy." *Political Science Quarterly* 79, no. 3 (September 1964): 403–434.

Fallows, James. "The Passionless Presidency: The Trouble with Jimmy Carter's Administration." *Atlantic,* May 1979, pp. 33–48.

Fenno, Richard F., Jr. *The President's Cabinet.* New York: Vintage Books, paperback edition, 1959.

Ferrell, Robert H., ed. *The Eisenhower Diaries.* New York: W. W. Norton, 1981.

George, Alexander L. "American Policy-Making and the North Korean Aggression." *World Politics* 7 (1955): 209–232.

———. "The Case for Multiple Advocacy in Making Foreign Policy." *American Political Science Review* 66, no. 3 (1972): 751–785.

———. *Presidential Decisionmaking in Foreign Policy: The Effective Use of Information and Advice.* Boulder, Colo.: Westview Press, 1980.

George, Alexander L., and Smoke, Richard. *Deterrence in American Foreign Policy: Theory and Practice.* New York: Columbia University Press, 1974.

Gray, Robert K. *Eighteen Acres Under Glass.* Garden City, N.Y.: Doubleday and Company, 1962.

Greenstein, Fred I. "Eisenhower as an Activist President: A Look at New Evidence." *Political Science Quarterly* 94 (Winter 1979-1980): 575–599.

———. *The Hidden-Hand Presidency: Eisenhower as Leader.* New York: Basic Books, 1982.

Greenstein, Fred I., and Wright, Robert. "Reagan . . . Another Ike?" *Public Opinion,* December-January 1981, pp. 51–55.

Halperin, Morton H. *Bureaucratic Politics and Foreign Policy.* Washington, D.C.: Brookings Institution, 1974.

Hammond, Paul Y. "The National Security Council: An Interpretation and Appraisal," *American Political Science Review* 54 (December 1960): 899–910.

Hargrove, Erwin C. *Presidential Leadership: Personality and Political Style.* New York: Macmillan, 1966.

Hess, Stephen. *Organizing the Presidency.* Washington, D.C.: Brookings Institution, 1976.

Hobbs, Edward H. "An Historical Review of Plans for Presidential Staffing." *Law and Contemporary Problems* 21 (Autumn 1956): 663–709.

_____ . "The President and Administration—Eisenhower." *Public Administration Review* 18 (1958): 306–313.

Hoxie, R. Gordon. *Command Decision and the Presidency: A Study of National Security Policy and Organization.* New York: Reader's Digest Press, 1977.

_____ . "Staffing the Ford and Carter Presidencies." In *Organizing and Staffing the Presidency* (pp. 44–85), by Bradley D. Nash et al. New York: Center for the Study of the Presidency, 1980.

_____ . "The National Security Council." *Presidential Studies Quarterly* 12 (Winter 1982): 108–113.

_____ . "Eisenhower and Presidential Leadership." *Presidential Studies Quarterly* 13, no. 4 (Fall 1983): 589–612.

Hoxie, R. Gordon, ed. *The White House: Organization and Operations.* New York: Center for the Study of the Presidency, 1971.

Hughes, Emmet John. *The Ordeal of Power: A Political Memoir of the Eisenhower Years.* New York: Atheneum, 1963.

Hyman, Sidney. Review of *The Ordeal of Power: A Political Memoir of the Eisenhower Years,* by Emmet John Hughes. *New York Times Book Review,* April 7, 1963, pp. 3–4.

Immerman, Richard H. "Eisenhower and Dulles: Who Made the Decisions?" *Political Psychology* 1, no. 2 (Autumn 1979): 21–38.

Jackson, Henry M., ed. *The National Security Council.* New York: Praeger Publishers, 1965.

Janis, Irving L. *Victims of Group Think,* 2nd edition. Boston: Houghton Mifflin, 1982.

Johnson, Richard Tanner. *Managing the White House.* New York: Harper and Row, 1974.

Kegley, Charles W., Jr., and Wittkopf, Eugene R. *American Foreign Policy: Pattern and Process.* New York: St. Martin's Press, 1979.

Kempton, Murray. "The Underestimation of Dwight D. Eisenhower." *Esquire,* September 1967, pp. 108–109, 156.

Kessel, John. *Presidential Parties.* Homewood, Ill.: Dorsey Press, 1984.

Killian, James R., Jr. *Sputnik, Scientists, and Eisenhower.* Cambridge: MIT Press, 1977.

Kinnard, Douglas. *President Eisenhower and Strategy Management: A Study in Defense Politics.* Lexington: University Press of Kentucky, 1977.

Kirschten, Dick. "Beyond the Vance-Brzezinski Clash Lurks an NSC Under Fire." *National Journal,* May 17, 1980, pp. 814–818.

Kissinger, Henry. *White House Years.* Boston: Little, Brown, 1979.

Kistiakowsky, G. B. *A Scientist at the White House: The Private Diary of President Eisenhower's Special Assistant for Science and Technology.* Cambridge: Harvard University Press, 1976.

Koenig, Louis W. *The Invisible Presidency.* New York: Rinehart and Company, 1960.

————. *The Chief Executive,* 2nd edition. New York: Harcourt, Brace and World, 1968.

Larson, Arthur. *Eisenhower: The President Nobody Knew.* New York: Charles Scribner's, 1968.

Leacacos, John P. "Kissinger's Apparat." *Foreign Policy* 5 (Winter 1971-1972): 3–28.

Lyon, Peter. *Eisenhower: Portrait of the Hero.* Boston: Little, Brown, 1974.

Malek, Frederic V. *Washington's Hidden Tragedy: The Failure to Make Government Work.* New York: Free Press, 1978.

Morrow, Frederic. *Black Man in the White House: A Diary of the Eisenhower Years by the Administrative Officer for Special Projects, The White House, 1955–60.* New York: Coward, McCann, 1963.

Murphy, Charles J. "Eisenhower's White House." *Fortune,* July 1953, pp. 75–77, 176, 178, 180–181.

Nash, Bradley D.; Eisenhower, Milton S.; Hoxie, R. Gordon; and Spragens, William C. *Organizing and Staffing the Presidency.* New York: Center for the Study of the Presidency, 1980.

Nathan, Richard P. *The Plot that Failed: Nixon and the Administrative Presidency.* New York: John Wiley and Sons, 1975.

Neustadt, Richard E. *Presidential Power: The Politics of Leadership.* New York: John Wiley and Sons, 1960 and 1976.

————. "Staffing the Presidency: Premature Notes on the New Administration." *Political Science Quarterly* 93 (Spring 1978): 1–9.

Nixon, Richard M. *Six Crises.* New York: Doubleday and Company, 1962.

Parmet, Herbert S. *Eisenhower and the American Crusades.* New York: Macmillan, 1972.

Patterson, Bradley H., Jr. *The President's Cabinet: Issues and Questions.* Washington, D.C.: American Society for Public Administration, 1976.

————. "An Overview of the White House." In *Portraits of American Presidents Volume III: The Eisenhower Presidency* (pp. 113–141), edited by Kenneth W. Thompson. Lanham, Md.: University Press of America, 1984.

Pinkley, Virgil. *Eisenhower Declassified.* Old Tappan, N.J.: Fleming H. Revell Company, 1979.

Porter, Roger B. *Presidential Decision Making: The Economic Policy Board.* New York: Cambridge University Press, 1980.

A Presidency for the 1980s, A Report on Presidential Management, by a panel of the National Academy of Public Administration. Washington, D.C.: National Academy of Public Administration, 1980.

Pusey, Merlo J. *Eisenhower, the President.* New York: Macmillan, 1956.

Reichard, Gary W. *The Reaffirmation of Republicanism: Eisenhower and the Eighty-Third Congress.* Knoxville: University of Tennessee Press, 1975.

Rossiter, Clinton. "The Constitutional Significance of the Executive Office of the President." *American Political Science Review* 43 (1949): 1206–1217.

Rushkoff, Bennett. "Eisenhower, Dulles, and the Quemoy-Matsu Crisis, 1954–55." *Political Science Quarterly* 96 (1981): 464–480.

Salamon, Lester M. "The President and Policy Making." In *Analyzing the Presidency* (pp. 208–229), edited by Robert E. DiClerico. Guilford, Conn.: Dushkin Publishing Group, 1985.

Schlesinger, Arthur M., Jr. *A Thousand Days: John F. Kennedy in the White House.* Greenwich, Conn.: Fawcett Publications, paperback edition, 1965.

———. "Roosevelt as Chief Administrator." In *Public Administration: Concepts and Cases* (pp. 266–273), edited by Richard J. Stillman. Boston: Houghton Mifflin, 1980.

Seidman, Harold. *Politics, Position, and Power: The Dynamics of Federal Organization,* 3rd edition. New York: Oxford University Press, 1980.

Seligman, Lester G. "Developments in the Presidency and the Conception of Political Leadership." *American Sociological Review* 20 (1955): 706–712.

Shannon, William V. "Eisenhower as President." *Commentary* 26 (November 1958): 390–398.

Sidey, Hugh. "Assessing a Presidency." *Time,* August 18, 1960, pp. 10–15.

Sorensen, Theodore. *Kennedy.* New York: Harper and Row, 1965.

Strauss, Lewis. *Men and Decisions.* Garden City, N.Y.: Doubleday and Company, 1962.

Strout, Richard. Review of *Eisenhower: Captive Hero,* by Marquis Childs. *New Republic,* September 5, 1958, pp. 20–21.

Thompson, Kenneth W. Review of *Power and Principle,* by Zbigniew Brzezinski. *Presidential Studies Quarterly* 13 (Fall 1983): 666–668.

U.S. Congress. "Report on the General Management of the Executive Branch." *Commission on the Organization of the Executive Branch of the Government.* 83rd Congress, 1st Session, 1949.

Watson, Richard A., and Thomas, Norman C. *The Politics of the Presidency.* New York: John Wiley and Sons, 1983.

Wayne, Steven. *The Legislative Presidency.* New York: Harper and Row, 1978.

Wellford, Harrison. "Staffing the Presidency: An Insider's Comments." *Political Science Quarterly* 93 (Spring 1978): 10–25.

Wills, Garry. "The Kennedy Imprisonment, Part I." *Atlantic Monthly,* January 1982, pp. 27–40.

———. "The Kennedy Imprisonment, Part II." *Atlantic Monthly,* February 1982, pp. 52–66.

Index

Fallows, James, 33, 34, 140
Farm Program, 43
Farrell, F. W., 104
Federalist Papers, 179
Fenno, Richard F., Jr., 50, 51
Firestone, Leonard, 49
Flemming, Arthur, 56, 58, 72, 98, 110
Ford, Gerald R., 15, 35, 50, 138
  as administrator, 15, 34
  and Cabinet, 61
  and Chief of Staff position, 34. *See also* Cheney, Richard
  and NSC, 81, 138
Foreign policy, 134, 139–140, 181, 182, 183
  advisory process, 1, 2, 17, 147
  control over, 69, 100, 142, 152, 163, 181
  decision-making, 1, 2, 30–31, 100–101, 105, 114, 116, 139, 147, 148, 150–151, 165, 166, 169, 170, 178, 183
Foreign Policy, 137
Formosa, 105, 106, 107, 109, 110, 111, 112, 113, 114
Formosa Resolution (1955), 100
Formosa Strait crisis, 7. *See also* Quemoy-Matsu crisis
Forrestal, James, 71
Fortier, Donald, 154, 158
Fortune, 17
Foster, William C., 117
France, 21, 97

Gaither, H. Rowan, Jr., 117
Gaither Committee (1957–1958), 117, 118
Gallup poll, 5
Gardner, John, 49
Gates, Thomas, 49
Geneva summit (1955), 31, 118
Genscher, Hans-Dietrich, 151
George, Alexander L., 100
George, Walter F., 50
Ghorbanifar, Manucher, 155, 157, 158
Gifford, Walter, 29, 30
Glad, Betty, 62
Gleason, S. Everett, 75, 77, 78
Goldman, Eric, 6
Goodpaster, Andrew J., 18, 22, 26, 28, 115–116, 179
Grant, Ulysses S., 6
Gray, Gordon, 88, 89, 115, 116, 124, 128, 129
Great Britain, 19, 29–30, 47, 97
Greenstein, Fred I., 8–9, 10, 25, 30, 112
Gruenther, Alfred, 17, 112, 114

Hagerty, James C., 7, 8, 22, 29, 31
Haig, Alexander, 64, 69, 148, 149, 150, 151, 152, 153
Hakim, Albert, 167
Haldeman, H. R., 34
Halleck, Charlie, 43
Halperin, Morton H., 117
Hamilton, Lee, 165–166, 167
Hammond, Paul Y., 78
Harlow, Bryce, 27, 28, 46, 48
Harriman, Averell, 49
Harrison, Benjamin, 5
Hartmann, Robert, 34
Harvard Graduate's Magazine, 18
HAWK missiles, 155, 156, 157, 164, 172(n35)
Health, Education, and Welfare, Secretary of. *See* Califano, Joseph; Flemming, Arthur
Heckt, Oswald, 23
Hell's Canyon controversy, 22
Herter, Christian, 89
Hess, Stephen, 63, 175, 180
Hickel, Walter, 61
"Hidden-hand leadership," 30

Hill, Bill, 43
Hizballah prisoners, 158
Hobbs, Edward H., 16
Hofstra University, 5
Holaday, William H., 101, 102
Holman, Eugene, 122(n94)
Hoopes, Townsend, 132
Hoover, Herbert, 5, 17
Hoover, Herbert, Jr., 177
Hoover Commission, 17, 26
Hopkins, Harry, 182
House International Relations Committee, 139
Housing and Urban Development, Secretary of, 62. *See also* Romney, George
"How Shall We Forge a Strategy for Survival?" (Jackson), 124
Hoxie, R. Gordon, 61, 63, 74, 142, 182
Hughes, Emmet John, 25, 41, 44, 45, 49, 55
Hume, Ellen, 168
Humphrey, George M., 48, 55, 96, 109, 110, 114, 177, 179
Hungary, 183
Hyman, Sidney, 24

ICBM. *See* Intercontinental ballistic missile
Ichiang Island, 108
Ickes, Harold L., 22
Immerman, Richard H., 176
India-Pakistan crisis (1971), 137
Inflation, 102, 184
Institutionalization, 14, 15, 142, 182
Institutional Presidency, 3, 128
Intercontinental ballistic missile (ICBM), 125
Interior, Secretary of the. *See* Hickel, Walter; Ickes, Harold L.; McKay, Douglas
Intermediate-Range Ballistic Missiles (IRBMs), 102, 103
Iran-Contra affair, 1, 2, 147, 150, 153–170, 175, 176, 182
  congressional investigation hearings, 160, 161, 162, 164–165, 167
  Special Review Board. *See* Tower Commission
Iranian hostage crisis (1979), 141, 178
Iran-Iraq war, 162
Iraq, 160, 162
IRBMs. *See* Intermediate-Range Ballistic Missiles
Israel, 152, 155–156, 157, 158, 162, 164

Jackson, Henry M. ("Scoop"), 123, 124–125
Jackson, William, 88
Jackson Committee (1959), 116
Jackson Subcommittee reports (1960, 1961), 123, 124, 125–126, 127, 128, 129, 133
Jacobsen, David, 160
Janis, Irving L., 178
Japan, 76
Japanese journalists, 151
Javits, Jacob, 22–23
Jenco, Lawrence, 160
Jewish community, 28
Johnson, Andrew, 5
Johnson, Lyndon B., 28, 48, 50, 100, 141
  and Cabinet, 59–60
  and NSC, 119, 132, 136, 137
  Press Secretary. *See* Reedy, George, Jr.
Johnson, Richard Tanner, 31, 60, 70, 71
Johnston, Eric, 48
Joint Chiefs of Staff (JCS), 82, 83, 84, 97, 98, 99, 100, 101, 104, 107, 112, 115
Jordan, Hamilton, 34
JSC. *See* Joint Chiefs of Staff
JUPITER missiles, 102